Stone Villages
of England

Millstone Grit: Bonsall, Derbyshire.

Stone Villages of England

by

BRIAN BAILEY

ROBERT HALE · LONDON

© *Brian Bailey 1982*
First published in Great Britain 1982

ISBN 0 7090 0540 7

Robert Hale Limited
Clerkenwell House
Clerkenwell Green
London, EC1

Photoset by Rowland Phototypesetting Ltd
Printed in Great Britain by
St Edmundsbury Press, Bury St Edmunds, Suffolk
Bound by Woolnough Bookbinding Ltd

Contents

To
KENNETH SCOWEN
who explores England with
rare vision and exposes it
with uncommon artistry

Illustrations

CREDITS

Permission to reproduce illustrations has been granted by the following: The author, 5, 7, 8, 10–12, 15, 16, 20, 21, 23, 26, 32, 33, 36, 42, 43, 45, 56–60, 64–6, 68, 69, 72, 78, 79, 81, 85, 91, 93–102, 106; Kenneth Scowen, 1–4, 6, 9, 13, 14, 17, 19, 22, 24, 25, 28–31, 37, 39–41, 44, 46–51, 53, 55, 61–3, 67, 70, 71, 73, 75, 77, 80, 82–4, 86–8, 104, 107; Tony Craddock, 18;

A. F. Kersting, 34, 35; Frank Rodgers, 74; V. K. Guy, 89, 92; *Architects' Journal*, 27; Leeds Art Galleries, 38; Cambridge University Collection, 52; National Monuments Record, 54, 76; Cumbria County Library, Kendal, 90; Building Research Establishment, Crown Copyright, 103; Birmingham Museums and Art Gallery, 105.

Acknowledgements

I am most grateful to Mr Peter Medwell of Clipsham Quarry, Leicestershire, and to Mr A. S. Ireson, Secretary of 'Men of the Stones', for the trouble they took to answer my questions on matters of quarrying and masonry.

Several friends and relations have provided hospitality during my researches, and without their kindness I would have found it very difficult to do as much travelling as has been necessary in a relatively short time.

My thanks are also due to Laurie Lee and the Hogarth Press Ltd for kind permission to quote from *Cider with Rosie*.

My wife, having given me the idea for the book, has had to work very hard at it herself. She has driven me about the country, without a word of complaint, from the Tamar to the Tweed, from Mousehole to Robin Hood's Bay.

We are both grateful to those unsung heroes of travellers' Britain, the Ordnance Survey, without whose maps the job would have been a great deal harder, if not impossible.

Preface

There is a story – probably apocryphal – of a young man who wrote to a publisher offering him a novel of so many thousand words. The publisher's reply was brief: "Which words, and in what order?" In the present book, the choice and order of words are the medium, but the *matter* is the choice and order of stones. Throughout history men have dug stones from beneath their feet and turned them, by careful selection and arrangement, into villages.

It was my wife who suggested that I ought to write a book about England's villages of stone. I assumed for a while that someone must have done it, but as I came to realize that no one had, I dropped the idea into conversation with one or two friends, each of whom assumed that I was referring to the Cotswolds.

This determined me to venture, with some trepidation, into what was, in literary terms at any rate, relatively unexplored territory. I have come to think of it as a petrified odyssey.

Trees, clouds and rivers are enjoyable even by the careless; but the stone under his foot has for carelessness nothing in it but stumbling: no pleasure is languidly to be had out of it, nor food, nor good of any kind; nothing but symbolism of the hard heart and the unfatherly gift. And yet, do but give it some reverence and watchfulness, and there is bread of thought in it, more than in any other lowly feature of all the landscape.

John Ruskin
Modern Painters
Volume IV

CHAPTER 1

The Hard Rock

Most books about the villages of England are impartial as to location, seeking only the ideal, exploited so much on calendars and chocolate boxes, of a few thatched cottages grouped cosily round a sunny green, where bees grow drowsy on the nectar of roses and honeysuckle at the cottage doors, and the dazzling aerobatics of the summer swallows round the church tower are matched only by the dragonflies swooping over the village pond.

This book is a little more specialized. It is about those villages which are built of natural stone. When I first started to plan it, I had in mind a qualification – a touchstone if you like – for any village which was to find a place in the volume. It would be that sort of village which had not only its whole nucleus built of stone, but the stone was to be clearly visible and distinguishable in its natural colour. It would be the sort of village where, ideally, all the walls and many of the roofs are of stone, the windows often stone mullioned, and where you might suppose that the only important structure not of stone was the sight-screen on the village cricket green.

I soon had to revise this intention rather drastically, for I found many villages which did not fit this image at all, though they were unquestionably built of stone. So I proceeded with a more open mind. But the basic requirement remains valid – that we should be able to see the colour and texture of the stone that went into the making of these villages of England.

Immediately we are creating – or at least distinguishing – a boundary. Draw a straight line on a map of England from Weymouth to the Wash. Almost without exception, our stone villages will be found to the north and west of that line, which I propose to call the Jurassic Boundary. It is, I think, a more meaningful and significant division of the country than that rather vague and redundant horizontal, somewhere between Watford and Birmingham, which has often been supposed to separate the south from t'north.

Beyond this boundary, there are scarcely half a dozen quarries working today. On our side of it, there are at least a hundred. The line follows the course of a belt of rock known as Jurassic limestone, formed

Walls of slate in the village of Delabole, Cornwall.

more than 150 million years ago. Upon this rock, so to speak, I will build my thesis. To the north and west of it, the rock is older and progressively harder; to the south and east, younger and softer. In very rough and ready terms, the Jurassic Boundary separates the highest and wettest ground from the drier lowlands; the heavy industrial areas from the mainly agricultural; the pasture land from the predominantly arable; the Celtic retreats from the region completely dominated by later immigrants; and the areas of longest-lasting pagan influence from the strongholds of the established Church. It is tempting to suggest that it separates Tory from Socialist England, but the contradictions make one tread warily. It is sufficient to say, perhaps, that it distinguishes the broadest dialects from the more or less standard English of London, Oxford and Cambridge.

It is worth bearing in mind at this point that the word 'pagan' comes from the Latin for 'peasant' or 'villager'. It took on its meaning of 'non-Christian', presumably, because the message was slower reaching the villages of the hills than the towns of the plains. Successive waves of invaders drove the existing settlers in England to our side of the Jurassic Boundary and ensured the survival of ancient influences there. The south-east is the land of diplomats and the civilizing arts. Our side is the country of heroes and heretics – King Arthur and Robin Hood, Wycliff and George Fox, Hardy and the Brontës.

It is more than a coincidence that most of the noted non-fiction writers about rural England have been natives of the lowlands. William Cobbett and George Sturt were Surrey men; George Borrow and Rider Haggard were East Anglians; Gilbert White and Mary Russell Mitford belonged to Hampshire; Edward Thomas and H. J. Massingham were Londoners. W. H. Hudson was born abroad, but he, too, was essentially a man of the south-east.

Generally speaking, all these writers were conservative (though not necessarily in the political sense) and conventionally religious, and they wrote about contemporary rural matters with a kind of fixed image of what the countryside had been like once, so that they railed against what they saw as change-for-the-worse. It is from the south-east that the myth of the idyllic life of the countryman – as opposed to the increasing madness of urban living – has spread.

It is not in the thoughtful, sometimes angry, frequently downright sentimental reflections of these country-lovers that we shall find the true spirit of the stone regions of England, for the people are not given to that kind of contemplation which almost seems to substitute literature for real life. Villagers whose homes are built out of the hard rock are too busy living their lives to construct political theories around them, much less to romanticize their common lot. The colder climate urges them to greater physical concern with life. Some of those southern writers spent too much time professing to remember an England that never was, in which lads and girls with rosy cheeks and flaxen hair spent eternally happy summers in fields of ripe corn whilst the old sat in contentment at their cottage doors.

The true images of the country above the "soft underbelly", to borrow a phrase of Churchill's, come from the poets and novelists who faced the harsh realities of life carried on in subjection to nature, where fields and farms on rock or infertile soil were christened with despairing names like Labour in Vain, Knackers Hole and Starveacre. Hardy in Wessex, George Eliot, John Clare and D. H. Lawrence in the Midlands, Mary Webb in the Welsh borderland, the Brontës and Wordsworth in the north – these are the writers who reflect the brooding and generally pessimistic outlook of the rigorous and restless people of the stone country. Poets are born in the hills; politicians are made in the plains.

The geographical distinctions I have made are far from being precise ones, of course. It is easy enough to point out a host of exceptions to such a rule of thumb. But there is a real and demonstrable sense in which the region of England north and west of that boundary line has an underlying unity, dictated by the rock of which it is made. Nature has made the land, as well as the men who have settled upon it, harder and tougher than the rest. The stone is an ever-present feature of the scene. Men earn their livelihoods from it, as well as building their homes with it. It is the foundation of their existence, and no pun is intended. The very words that come most readily to mind in thinking of stone and its working are as characteristically hard and blunt as the regions where the stone occurs – rock, split, flint, crag, cold, sharp, grit.

The rock is what makes the people of the Midlands and the north generally more hospitable than those of the south. They are more united by their common cause – winning a living in the face of hostile forces. Witness the crowd gathering at the pithead after a mine disaster, or men in the street doffing their cloth caps as a funeral passes by. They are all brothers and sisters in sympathy with a member of the family who has lost the battle for survival.

It is only recently that we have begun to interpret as picturesque and exciting those elements of the landscape that once seemed barren and forbidding, especially to those from the 'soft' side of the line: "You travel for twenty or five-and-twenty miles over one of the most unfortunate desolate counties under heaven, divided by stone walls, and abandoned to the screaming kites and larcenous crows; after travelling really twenty and to appearance ninety miles over this region of stone and sorrow, life begins to be a burden, and you wish to perish." Thus Sydney Smith on the Cotswolds, and here is Daniel Defoe on the Lake District: "Here we entered Westmoreland, a country

eminent only for being the wildest, most barren and frightful of any
that I have passed over in England, or even in Wales it self. . . ."

Since the Industrial Revolution, we have come to appreciate nature a
little more, and the special quality of a stone village – unlike a brick or
timber one – is that it looks as if it has grown up out of the soil with the
trees. Reaction to the industrialization of England, however, has led us
to the opposite extreme from Smith's and Defoe's gloomy views. We
now invest our country villages with an imaginary wholesomeness
they never actually possessed, and one result of this romantic delusion
is that any estate agent worth his salt is liable to go into raptures of
superlative lyricism over some dank hovel in a muddy field, surviving
miraculously from the seventeenth or eighteenth century. It might
have a leaking roof, crumbling walls and no mains water, drainage or
electricity, but commercial imagination will transform it into a 'picturesque olde worlde cottage of charm and character in lovely unspoilt
rural setting'. I hope to steer a more realistic course between these two
extremes.

The Jurassic limestone is the predominant geological feature in
England, from the point of view of our subject. Surfacing at Portland
Bill and sweeping in a great ogee curve from the coast of Dorset up to
Yorkshire, it consists, broadly speaking, of two parallel bands. One is
the fine-grained Oolitic limestone, whence comes the finest building
material, commonly called Cotswold stone although it runs almost
through the whole length of the belt. Along its north-western edge is a
band of Liassic limestone, providing building material which, though
less serviceable, is sometimes exceptionally attractive. The oolite and
the lias between them produce stones of warm colour varying from
cream and buff to rich brown and even pink. This belt is more than
three hundred miles in length and provides the link between the
south-western and north-eastern extremities of the England we are to
explore.

The limestone has provided, on the whole, the most famous and
picturesque of all our building stones, and the quarries dotted along it –
some of them long abandoned, some still working on a reduced scale –
are the most important ingredients in the story of our stone villages,
and we shall take due notice of them as we proceed,

> . . . then shall their names,
> Familiar in our mouths as household words, –
> Portland the king, Ketton and Clipsham,
> Doulting and Purbeck, Taynton and Ancaster,
> Be in their glowing colours freshly remember'd.

In the south-west corner of the country, various types of stone have
been used for building, but many of them are rendered and

whitewashed, and our chief interest in this region will be in granite, which also occurs, along with slate, in Leicestershire and Cumbria. The main area left to us then will be the complicated geological region stretching north up the Pennines into Northumberland, rich in various limestones and sandstones. Thus it is a convenient approximation to say that, as we travel westward from the Jurassic Boundary, we cross limestone country first, sandstone country next and granite country last, moving towards older and harder stone all the time. (Of course, geology is never really that simple. Sometimes it is very difficult to tell limestone from sandstone, and the two may even occur in the same quarry.)

These, at any rate, are the areas where we shall find most of our stone villages, for although vernacular building has been done with stone elsewhere on our side of the line – notably in the counties bordering Wales – complete villages of stone are few and far between there. South Shropshire, in particular, has a good deal of building in the local sandstone of venerable antiquity and variable colour, but the haphazard presence of timber and brick, as well as much rendering of rubble walls, denies the area any right to a leading place in this book.

The vast majority of stone-built houses in England are of either limestone or sandstone. The limestone is almost a million times older than the houses built of it. Both limestone and sandstone are sedimentary rocks. That is, they were laid down in layers, or strata, over immense periods of time, and the stone in some layers is more suitable for building purposes than that in others; just as, if you make a chocolate sandwich cake with icing on top, you may say the icing is the sweetest part, and the cake the lightest, but if you want sweetness, flavour and colour, then the chocolate in the middle will be the best bit, even though it is only thin.

Most of the building sandstones are older than the limestones and may be more than twice their age, being formed in some cases more than 400 million years ago. If these figures make the mind boggle, there is little point in discussing the age of the granite, which is an igneous rock formed by volcanic action, far earlier.

When our distant ancestors came down from the trees and dispersed to the uttermost parts of the earth, they showed great ingenuity in adapting whatever natural materials they could lay hands on locally for providing roofs over their heads to protect them from wind and rain – the skins of animals, the leaves of the tropical forests, timber, blocks of ice and the stone beneath their feet. It took men a long time to become wise to all the possibilities of building houses of stone, but the story of our stone villages goes back a very long way.

Landscape history is a fashionable study nowadays. There is much discussion and a great deal of rapidly accumulated literature about how man has affected nature. But we do not hear so much about how nature has affected man. We are reluctant to surrender one iota of what we fondly imagine to be our free will. But evolution is a window, not a mirror, and the limits of ecology ought not to be defined by our self-exaltation. As man shaped the rock, so the rock shaped man.

The soil on the oldest and hardest acid rock is generally less fertile than on the clay beyond the Jurassic Boundary. Hence it came into use primarily as pasture land. You will find far more sheep and cattle grazing to the north and west of the boundary than on the lowlands beyond it. At the same time, the rock provided the foundations of industry. Early men used stone to make tools and weapons, until they discovered that they could make better ones with metals and that the best metals were under the ground. Mining and quarrying are the keys to the kind of men who colonized the inhospitable stone areas of Britain. They were primarily Celtic – dark men of small stature – and they were the first specialists.

Just as the men who farmed the Cumbrian fells in the wildest and wettest part of England were a different breed from the Anglo-Saxons who took over the southern lowlands, so, when the Industrial Revolution came, the men needed in Burnley and Bolton, Doncaster and Sheffield as miners and ironfounders were there ready-made, among the descendants of the powerful and independent Brigantes, who had resisted the Roman military machine longer than anyone else. They were used to fiercer climates and tougher conditions and had gone deep into the earth to extract the treasures – salt and lead and iron ore – before the Romans came. The men who tamed and plundered the most inhospitable parts of England, from Dartmoor and Bodmin to Cumbria and the North Yorkshire Moors, used the rock for building and created a tradition of industry which is more evident than the baseless popular division of sophisticated south and unrefined north. It is sometimes called 'the Protestant work ethic', but this is misleading. The Jurassic Boundary forms a kind of frontier for Roman Catholicism and the Church of England against Nonconformism, which goes hand in hand with the influence of the rock. (The high density of Catholics in certain urban areas of the north-west is due to Irish immigration.) I think that both the tradition of labour and the tradition of dissent arose more from the culture of the stone country than from any absorption of Calvinist philosophy.

Ironically, the earliest evidence of stone in the walls of houses in England occurs in Devon and Cornwall, where the material is granite, the hardest of rocks and that which resisted, longer than any other, man's efforts to work it. It was only in the fourteenth century that stonemasons began to master the craft of working granite, and only

Stonehenge, Wiltshire. Stone selected for the purpose was transported from distant sites.

after the Industrial Revolution that the material could be used on a wide scale, but north of Penzance men built a village with houses of moorland granite about two hundred years before the birth of Christ. It was one of the first stone villages in England.

What is undoubtedly the country's most famous stone structure represents one of the features of raising important buildings in stone which has remained with us, and for good reason. Stonehenge virtually sits astride the Jurassic Boundary, but the stone used to build it came from our side of it. The choice of site was important, for the builders had to bring stone to the spot, rather than put the building up where the stone was. They brought colossal bluestones from the Prescelly Mountains in South Wales, perhaps floating them on rafts round the coast and up the Bristol Channel. At a later period an extension was built with huge sandstone boulders, called sarsens, hauled from the Marlborough Downs, several miles to the north.

This early practice of transporting stone to where the building was required set a pattern which has lasted to this day. The Romans used Purbeck marble in the building of Viroconium in Shropshire, 150 miles away. In medieval times, stone was carried sixty miles on horse-drawn wagons from the famous quarries at Taynton, in Oxfordshire, to Windsor. During the great period of church rebuilding in the thirteenth and fourteenth centuries, colossal amounts of stone were moved about the country. River barges carried stone for Beverley Minster along the Ouse and Humber from quarries near Tadcaster. Lincoln Cathedral contains 'marble' from Purbeck in Dorset. Limestone from the Isle of Wight was shipped across the Solent to build Beaulieu Abbey. Exeter Cathedral is built of stone from France as well as from Portland. The accounts for building the Cistercian Vale Royal Abbey in Cheshire include payment for more than forty thousand cartloads of stone. Sometimes monasteries owned the quarries which provided their materials – Peterborough owned those at Barnack; Exeter owned one at Beer; Quarr Abbey owned some of those on the Isle of Wight; Dunstable Priory owned the quarry at Totternhoe.

London itself, standing in a basin of clay, is entirely without stone, so every famous building of stone in the capital is of imported material, from Kent and Dorset, Devon and Somerset, Northamptonshire and Yorkshire. Sir Christopher Wren used fifty thousand tons of Portland stone to rebuild St Paul's Cathedral after the Great Fire.

More recently, sandstone from Yorkshire was transported by sea to King's Lynn and then overland by teams of horses to build Houghton Hall for Sir Robert Walpole. Granite from Dartmoor was carried by sea to London to build the British Museum. During the great period of canal transport, the carriage of roadstone and building stone was the chief source of revenue for the operating companies, next to coal. Stone from Portland was used to face the new Waterloo Bridge, and stone was brought from Rutland to rebuild the bombed House of Commons after the Second World War.

Thus the superiority of stone for buildings of importance has been taken for granted ever since men have been capable of using it, and it has been aptly called 'the aristocrat of building materials'. For the residence of a VIP, it is arguable that the material used has been regarded as of greater importance than the size of the house. Queen Elizabeth's scornful observation to Sir Nicholas Bacon when she saw Gorhambury for the first time ("My Lord, what a little house you have gotten!") was as nothing compared with George III's withering contempt on seeing Morton Pitt's house at Kingston Maurward: "Brick, Mr Pitt, brick!" Mr Pitt lost no time in facing the house with Portland stone.

Transporting stone was, however – and still is – a very expensive business. Old accounts often show the cost of transportation to have been greater than the cost of the stone. So whilst buildings of stone are found all over England, they are nearly always, when outside the stone areas, country houses built by wealthy landowners, civic buildings or

West Dean, Sussex. Flint is the only stone widely used in vernacular building beyond the Jurassic Boundary.

churches in towns and villages where the houses themselves are built of brick or timber. Vernacular building in stone occurs only where the material is readily available on the spot, and that is – with minor exceptions – to the north and west of the Jurassic Boundary. Besides, stone taken out of its natural environment, for vernacular building purposes, can look very odd and almost artificial.

The fact that most rock can be used for construction of some sort provides the exceptions. On the chalk downs of southern England, and in East Anglia, the churches are built of the readily available flint, and walls, farm buildings and even castles of flint are relatively common. But flint is a shapeless and difficult material, and when brick became available, it quickly replaced flint as the cheapest and best local material for building houses and cottages. So although there are a great many buildings of flint to be seen in this part of England, there are no flint villages.

The chalk itself has also been used for building, but it is soft and does not weather well, and although some important buildings of chalk survive, there are no chalk villages. The spectacular Ashridge House in Hertfordshire is a good example of both the possibilities and the

Ashridge House, Hertfordshire, built of chalk from quarries at Totternhoe, Bedfordshire.

limitations of building with chalk. Built by Wyatt for the Earl of Bridgewater early in the nineteenth century on the site of a monastery, the exterior walls are already in worse condition than the interior walls of the surviving crypt, built of the same Totternhoe chalk more than five hundred years earlier. This material – also called 'clunch' in its harder form – is fine for interior use, however, and it can be seen in Westminster Abbey and in the Lady Chapel of Ely Cathedral. Clunch was quarried extensively in Cambridgeshire at one time.

A belt of stone in Kent, Surrey and Sussex has provided building materials in the past such as Greensand, Wealden sandstone and Kentish ragstone, but the first is of doubtful durability, rarely seen without brick as well; the second is a good stone of which Bodiam Castle is built, but not used extensively in vernacular work; and the third was used mainly for rubble walling faced with something else, as it was very hard to work. So there are no stone villages in these materials.

Thus nature has dictated that to the south and east of the Jurassic Boundary men must use materials other than natural stone for their dwellings – timber, mud, clay, brick. It is no coincidence that the world's largest brickworks lie in this region.

Geology specifies not only the colour and quality of the stone used in building but also to a large extent the architecture and style of the villages in each region. You can build a house of flint, but not with mullions in the windows. You can build a church of granite, but not with finely carved statuary in the walls. Thus we find plainer churches in Cornwall than in the Cotswolds, and ruder dwellings in the Pennines than in Dorset.

The hard rock dictates other things, too. The Oolitic limestone of the south of England lies in thin beds, so when the carvers of stone effigies for the early tombs in village churches set about their work, they were preconditioned into producing flat figures, lying full length with their heads perhaps supported by cushions, but not with legs bent or reclining on one elbow, or head raised above the level of the body. Where freestone could be obtained in thicker blocks, as on the Magnesian limestone of the north, it gave more freedom to the sculptor, but as the taste for Italian marble grew, native stones became less popular for monumental work anyway, although alabaster and Purbeck limestone continued to be used.

The first signs of one's approach into a stone-building area are very often the dry-stone walls which take over from hedges and fences to enclose the fields of the upland pastures. The art of building these walls is an ancient one. Most of those that exist today were originally built in the eighteenth century, but dry-stone walling goes back to the pyramids of Egypt. The method of construction makes the field walls resistant to frost action and able to withstand the elements for a very long time. Walls in different parts of the country are as distinctive locally as the men who build them, called 'wallers' in some parts and 'dykers' in others. But the men are all alike in being patient country craftsmen, working with little more equipment than a pick and a heavy hammer to construct perhaps fifteen feet of wall a day. The appearance of their walls is not only dictated by the type of stone they use. The docile sheep of the Cotswolds do not need such high walls to confine them as the more robust and agile animals of the Pennines and Cumbria.

In walls built of rubble, as opposed to those built of stones which have been dressed to more or less regular shape, the large flat stones used as foundations are usually called 'grounders', and large boulders crossing one or more courses of average stones are called 'jumpers' – a name applied to large stones in house walls as well as field walls. Dry-stone field walls of rubble usually have courses of 'throughs' built into them – long stones laid *across* the wall and sometimes projecting on either side – to give the wall extra stability.

The men who built these walls were often incapable of writing their own names, but they made their marks across the upland landscape of

A waller at work in the Lake District.

Contrasts in dry-stone walls: a typical wall of granite, Dartmoor.

Near Bainbridge, North Yorkshire, showing courses of 'through' stones.

A stone coffin in the churchyard
at Crantock, Cornwall.

A rain-filled quarry pit in Swithland Wood,
Leicestershire.

England – in Cotswold meadows, in Pennine dales and on the Cumbrian fells – as enduring as the works of all the scholars of Oxford and Cambridge. The men whose walls have clung, without aid of cement, to the mountain-sides of the Lake District for two hundred years without tumbling into heaps of stones, had a sort of genius, surely.

A large part of the aesthetic appeal of stone villages lies in their apparent great age and naturalness, being built haphazardly and without planning. In actual fact, the use of stone in cottage building did not begin on a large scale until the seventeenth century, so that most of our stone villages, as we see them today, are less than three hundred years old, although their origins may go back to Saxon or earlier times. The church is usually the oldest building in the village, but the village is nearly always much older than the church.

Before the Conquest, most churches were built with timber – the Normans greatly accelerated the use of stone in churches and castles. When, centuries later, stone began to be widely used in vernacular building, those parts of England where it was readily available – the Cotswolds, for instance – used it not only for the walls, roofs and floors of the cottages but for practically everything in them, including the kitchen sink. Coffins were also carved out of great blocks of stone.

During the course of our explorations, we shall come across the quarries from which the villages' stones were taken. Alas, a great many

Drilling a block of limestone at Clipsham Quarry, Leicestershire.

of them are closed now, enormous holes in the ground, or rain-filled pits, abandoned because building in stone became uneconomical in competition with brick and hideous concrete. Disused quarry pits have melancholy associations – they are scenes of suicide and accidental death. I had a childhood friend who was drowned in one. And they make their appearances in both fact and fiction as ideal dumping places for murderers' victims.

There are many quarries still at work, producing roadstone, cement and other materials, but relatively few produce building stone today, although there have been some signs of a revival of interest in stone building. They are operated now by few men and much machinery – giant crushers, walking draglines and circular saws with diamond cutting edges which can go through granite as if it were cottage cheese. But when our stone villages were built, each quarry might be peopled with a hundred or more craftsmen and their apprentices, spending their working lives blasting, splitting and shaping the rock they knew as intimately as the carpenter knows his timber. (We ought to note, in passing, that in some places stone has been mined, rather than quarried, and we shall come across examples in subsequent chapters.)

While it was still attached to its mother earth, the material was the geologist's 'rock', but as soon as it was disengaged by hammer and chisel, or gunpowder, it became the mason's 'stone'. Old quarrymen and masons spoke of it as if it lived. They called it 'green' when it was freshly quarried and had the 'sap' in it. And it *did* have a character of its own, after all. If you treated it right, it would co-operate. If it was difficult to work, they called it 'stubborn'. An academic expert might call such stone 'hard and intractable'; a practical expert would have other words to describe it: "You works away at it for hours and suddenly the bugger splits right down the middle, so you've to start all over agen. Unreliable, see?"

Quarrymen and masons, like most tradesmen, had their own vocabularies – their 'rag' and 'feathers', their 'scabbers' and 'puncheons', their 'grounders' and 'jumpers', their 'cock-ups' and 'presents', and 'hawks' and 'snail-creep'. An experienced quarryman could split a stone the size of a piano, with a chisel and a twenty-eight-pound hammer, and cut and dress it into blocks suitable for the builder's purpose with great skill.

Before the introduction of power saws, the time-honoured method of splitting a huge block was with 'plugs' and 'feathers'. The method is still in use. The quarryman drills a series of holes along the line of the required split. Into each hole he inserts a pair of feathers – curved metal pieces which form a slot for the plug, or wedge. When the row of plugs is loosely in position, he hammers them in, causing outward pressure on the feathers, which splits the stone.

What vernacular building really means in our context is that, unlike the master masons who were employed by kings and noblemen to supervise every stage of growth of their great houses and palaces, the masons who built our stone villages were local craftsmen who worked without benefit of architects, surveyors, slide-rules, laboratory information on stresses, or academic theories of aesthetics. That their houses and cottages still stand, and look a great deal better in their environment than most of the building that has succeeded them, is a testament to their makers' knowledge and love of the stone, which they passed on to their sons and apprentices.

What makes a house, a wall or a barn of stone so superior aesthetically to anything build of brick or concrete is not only the stone's intrinsic qualities of texture and colour but the fact that – unlike conveyor-belt bricks or the regurgitations of a concrete mixer – every stone in the wall has passed through the hands of quarryman and mason and been specially chosen for its purpose. Each separate stone bears the metaphorical fingerprints, and often the visible chisel marks, of a village craftsman, who selected this piece, with his long experience and knowledge, to serve this particular end. It is this individual workmanship which makes village architecture so attractive and fascinating, for there is nothing standardized or perfect in it, and as Ruskin said: "The demand for perfection is always a misunderstanding of the ends of art . . . to banish imperfection is to destroy expression, to check exertion, to paralyse vitality."

The village builder in stone continued to exercise his individuality long after the monumental mason ceased to. After the Black Death, when village masons and carvers, like other tradesmen, were reduced in number, the rise of the workshop and the trade guild put an end to exuberant self-expression such as we shall see on churches of the Norman period, and a degree of uniformity, at least in regional terms, came into the carving of church ornament. But the house builder was under no such restraint. He remained what he had always been – a purely local craftsman working in his own and neighbouring villages.

These country craftsmen had little to do with the combined talents – as architects, estimators, site foremen and so on – of the urban master masons, and even less with the mysteries and ritual of Freemasonry, which likes to trace its origins to the Tower of Babel, or Solomon's Temple, or the Great Pyramid of Gizeh, when Christians are not looking, but really evolved from the medieval trade guilds to which master masons belonged. The masonic guilds were breaking up in the seventeenth century and were only kept alive by the activities of men like Elias Ashmole, who helped to turn them from practical trade unions into speculative secret societies. Ashmole wore three spiders about his person as a protection against the ague.

Freemasons were originally craftsmen who were skilled in carving fine-grained stone, which is sometimes called freestone. The men who prepared rougher and less co-operative material were called hewers.

The skills of the old country craftsman, the master mason and the modern building contractor coincide, however, in the more or less unchanged methods of building a wall of stone, whether it be the wall of a humble country cottage or that of a stately home. The method depends on the type of stone being used and falls broadly into one of three classes – rubble, coursed blocks or ashlar.

Rubble walling is built of stone varying in size and shape, usually stone which is too hard to be dressed into regular shape for laying in courses. It can be set dry – that is, as dry-stone walling – or in mortar. The more evenly shaped rubble can be laid in courses, but 'random' rubble walling can include stones of enormous variety as regards both shape and size. Flint, though of irregular shape, is laid in courses by the device of thick beds of mortar. Coursed blocks are larger stones which have been dressed to fairly regular shapes and sizes with squared faces, so that they can be laid and well jointed like bricks.

Ashlar is stone which can be dressed to a smooth and even surface. Portland stone is the outstanding example of this, but we shall scarcely see it in our stone villages, since it is expensive and of monumental

Random rubble walling of sandstone in a cottage in Shropshire.

effect, seen to best advantage in great buildings such as St Paul's and the United Nations Building in New York.

The stone is present in the folklore of the country, and in its place-names too, from Stone in Gloucestershire and Stonesfield in Oxfordshire to Stonethwaite in Cumbria and Stonegrave in North Yorkshire. Around the Charnwood Forest area of Leicestershire, where some of the oldest Pre-Cambrian rock in Britain surfaces in scattered outcrops, a whole collection of village names testifies to the hard ground beneath them – Bilstone, Congerstone and Odstone, Ravenstone, Swepstone and Thringstone, among others. These, oddly enough, are not among our stone villages. The hard granite could not be used for building when these communities grew up, and they are nearly all industrial villages of red brick.

Quarrying is one of man's oldest occupations, and it is hardly to be wondered at that stone exercises a powerful influence on his way of life. Rock alone – not trees, nor rivers, nor desert, only the stone beneath our feet – has remained relatively unchanged as silent witness to the whole of human history. Shakespeare put into the mouth of the guilt-stricken Macbeth the thought that the stone was witness to his foul deed:

> Thou sure and firm-set earth,
> Hear not my steps, which way they walk, for fear
> Thy very stones prate of my whereabout.

Sometimes ancient stones make us apprehensive, for their old and naked forms have lingering paganism in them. What has been well called "the secret influence of antiquity in stonework"shows itself not only in our everyday imagery but in witchcraft, paganism, folklore and rural customs. Circles of standing stones and other prehistoric monuments, ill understood for centuries, have assumed magical and fearful properties, and even natural formations of unusual shape are personified and credited with wills of their own. Just as we see the shapes of strange creatures in the clouds, so people have been ready to perceive the petrified forms of sinister or ill-fated persons in the standing stones. Thus we have such as Long Meg and Her Daughters in Cumbria, and the Whispering Knights in Oxford-shire.

Sometimes the grotesque landscapes left by quarrying activity have earned local appellations, like the 'Devil's Chimney' at Leckhampton in Gloucestershire, and the 'Hills and Holes' at Barnack in North-amptonshire. In the chalk areas beyond the Jurassic Boundary, it is often counted lucky by children to find a flint with a hole in it, whilst adult folklore ascribes to such a 'hag-stone' a power against witchcraft or a protection against disease in horses. A holed flint was also representative of the pagan All-Seeing Eye (or the Eye of Horus) which, enclosed in a triangle, was a symbol used by the Freemasons. It derived from Egyptian mythology, in which Horus, son of Osiris and Isis, lost an eye which was restored to him. Horus was sometimes identified with the moon, which could see in the dark.

Ancient stone bridges in various parts of the country are credited to the masonic talents of the Devil, whilst a geological freak such as St Michael's Mount is popularly attributed to a giant and his wife, who had to carry the granite, of which it is unaccountably made, from some distance away. One day when the giant was sleeping, his wife tried to shirk the job by using the handy local greenstone instead, but she was caught out, and her pile of abandoned greenstone can still be seen nearby. It is called Chapel Rock.

Veneration of ancient stones extends to belief in their healing powers and their effectiveness in promoting fertility in women. The so-called 'rattling eagle-stone' (aetites or gagites) was thought particularly effec-tive in this respect at one time. It was a hollow stone with another inside it, which rattled when shaken, and legend had it that it was found in the nests of eagles. The Countess of Newcastle was among the women who wore such a stone during her pregnancy in 1633 in the belief that it would ease her labour pains.

Many groups of stones, or large and prominent single stones, are supposed to move of their own accord at certain times, and it is predicted that when a certain stone near Manchester sinks out of sight

Overleaf. Natural outcrops and dry-stone walls of Carboniferous limestone in Ribblesdale, Yorkshire Dales National Park.

below the ground, as it surely will, then the world will end. Through-out the stone areas of England you can feel the presence of ancient forces which never existed in the south-east. The pagan spirit of Cornwall drove the super-sensitive Walter de la Mare away with a haunted determination never to stay there again.

Thus the stone maintains a strong hold on the imaginations of people whose collective unconscious is associated with the rock over thousands of years. It is not merely a convenient material of civiliza-tion, like bricks or concrete, but one of nature's venerable elements, there long before man arrived on the scene, knowing things unknown to man, and an obvious symbol of indestructibility. That is why we make gravestones of it and why we carve our initials on the defiant walls of ruins and other ancient structures. The stone lends us a little hope of immortality, although it does not last for ever, being subject to natural decay like everything else. As Ruskin put it: "The same processes of time which cause your Oxford oolite to flake away like the leaves of a mouldering book only warm with a glow of perpetually deepening gold the marbles of Athens and Verona; and the same laws of chemical change which reduce the granites of Dartmoor to porcelain clay bind the sand of Coventry into stone which can be built half-way to the sky."

So, armed with a little awareness of the material, we can set out to explore the A to Z of stone villages, from Abbotsbury to Zennor. I have avoided any conservative interpretation of the word 'village', upon which dictionaries are singularly unhelpful. "An accumulation of houses, larger than a hamlet, and smaller than a town" begs more questions than it answers. I have felt free to include hamlets as often as I liked but have avoided any place that seems to me to have the character of a town, although here and there places which make proud claims to be towns must have crept in.

There are many artificial – 'model' or 'estate' – villages throughout England, and those of them which are built of stone have as inalienable a right to be recorded in this book as those of ancient foundation, but they are unquestionably different from, if not necessarily inferior to, the old villages we are mostly concerned with. However attractive they may be (and a few of them are splendid), they invariably appear to be wearing brand-new uniforms, in contrast to the casual dress of their ancient neighbours.

This is, in any case, no book for purists. I have not sought out villages which fit snugly, like pieces of a jigsaw puzzle, into a concept of the English countryside cherished by urban civilization. Nor have I sought those which architectural purists would approve. There are thirteen thousand villages in England (I take the information on trust, not having counted them personally), and only a minute proportion of them are pure stone villages today. The number will continuously decrease.

As an aid to tourists who might wish to see the variety of stone villages for themselves during their travels, I have added an appendix to the book in which a hundred of what are, in my own view, the best or most interesting stone villages in England are listed by county, and these are all included on the map, which could not possibly accommodate all villages mentioned in the text. Anyone who has seen these hundred will have a good grasp of how different rocks have been used to build villages down the centuries and throughout the land.

I have taken care to mention counties in both text and index, so that villages not marked on this book's map can easily be found on the reader's own more detailed maps. The chief purpose of the map in this book is to give an extremely simplified guide to the whereabouts of different building stones, and some of the most famous quarrying villages are also marked.

It is a happy fact that rock which provides building stone also forms much of the best landscape. The journey before us passes through most of England's National Parks and Areas of Outstanding Natural Beauty. The rock also, of course, dictates what kind of vegetation we find in different regions. Along the course of the limestone belt, we should not expect to find azaleas or juniper trees; nor will the fine beeches that shade the Cotswold slopes be familiar companions of moorland villagers, who have to make do with heather and bilberry.

There will be no lack of local specialities to refresh us on our way. They eat hoggan and figgy duff in Cornwall (never too far from Looe) and drink scrumpy along the route to the Cotswolds, where lardy cakes come into their own. Cobs are more to the taste of the East Midlands, whilst in Yorkshire they are so mad about tusky that they grow whole fields of it, and in the north-west clap bread is specially favoured. If any of these goodies should be in short suppy, however, I presume that everyone knows how to make stone soup.

It is a very old recipe, credited to a beggar who asked for bread at a great house but was refused. He asked the servants if they would at least let him have a little warm water to make soup of the stone he held out. Filled with curiosity, they gave him water and a pan to boil it in. Putting in the stone, he stirred and tasted it and begged a little salt and pepper to flavour it, which they provided. Then, tasting it again, he said that it would be improved by any scraps of meat and vegetables they might have left over, and these, too, were added to the pan. The soup thus prepared, the tramp consumed it gratefully and went on his way. Stones, as I said, have great power over the mind.

CHAPTER 2

The South West

The ancient granite which rises from the Atlantic at Land's End, seemingly impregnable as it stands up to the lashing seas and forms mighty cliffs that Cornwall's lovers know so well, provides much of the building material of the south-west peninsula, for it breaks out in great inland plateaus such as Dartmoor and Bodmin Moor, as well as round the coast. But granite is not alone here, and Devon and Cornwall between them show contrasts in building which make this a very interesting area for seeing some of the variety in our stone villages right from the outset.

Most of Cornwall and Devon consists of sandstone of one sort or another, and this produces most of the local building material outside the granite areas, apart from cob. Cottages of cob are a familiar feature of the Devon countryside but are of no interest in our present context, as cob walls are a mixture of clay and earth bound with straw and coated with plaster which is usually painted white. Cob building is found mainly in the central area of Devon formed by Carboniferous sandstone known as Culm Measures. Some Culm stone has been used for building. It is quarried as small, dark pieces of rubble.

Around it, and over most of Cornwall, Old and New Red Sandstone form the rock. Some of this has undergone metamorphosis into slate, which is hard enough to be used for building as well as for roofing. Some of the Old Red Sandstone, nearly 400 million years old, has been used for building purposes, and the New Red Sandstone which produces the richly coloured soil of so much of Devon also makes its appearance in village building.

Despite this apparent wealth of material, however, we shall find it necessary to be very selective in this part of the country. We cannot, as in the Cotswolds, go to almost any village confident of seeing natural stone everywhere. Much of the stone does not weather well enough to be permanently exposed, and not only cob cottages, therefore, are rendered and whitewashed. Sometimes buildings of granite or other stone are given a coat of whitewash without being rendered, as happens particularly in the fishing villages of the Cornish coast. This practice obscures the colour but shows the contours. It seems a bit like

Igneous basalt at Ashprington, Devon.

dressing a Greek god in cotton underpants, but we will take note of one
or two villages where it occurs, for the sake of completeness, although
holiday resorts generally are excluded from our notice because of their
inevitable modern development. Too many bungalows, supermarkets, souvenir shops and double yellow lines have sneaked their way
into these villages to allow the old stone to proclaim the spirit of the
place as it once did. Their narrow, steep and winding streets are among
the most densely packed in England during the summer months, but
from the present point of view they are lost stone villages, as hopeless-
ly irretrievable as those of the lost land of Lyonesse, which according to
legend linked the mainland and the Islands of Scilly before the sea
swept over it and drowned its luxuriant soil for ever. Much of coastal
Cornwall, notwithstanding its romance, has become boring, with
caravan parks here, filling-stations there, and various places tiresome-
ly proclaiming themselves the most southerly this or the most westerly
that. And, if truth be told, much of inland Cornwall is exceptionally
ugly, for it is a landscape of industry and dereliction. But then there is
much in this whole subject that is grim, for the hardness of the stone
country insinuates itself into the character of the people. We must
ignore the songs of the Cornish sirens, perhaps stuffing our ears with
cotton wool and keeping our seat belts fastened in imitation of Odysseus and his companions, if we are to seek the villages of stone and not
succumb to the sea nymphs' temptations.

Nevertheless, the Penwith peninsula, though only the tip of the
legendary land of Cornwall, offers some fascinating contrasts to start
us on our journey. Let us begin at the beginning in more ways than
one. On the higher ground of the peninsula, north of Penzance,
Chysauster lies, a ghost village built of moorland granite, where Celtic
people lived and worked at least a hundred years before the birth of
Christ. It is a most remarkable place, unquestionably a stone village,
though deserted for two thousand years. The lower walls of the houses
can be seen flanking the wide village street. They are built without
mortar and very roughly coursed. They are fifteen feet thick in places
and still stand to a height of six feet here and there. Nearby is a
'fougou', one of those mysterious underground chambers built with
dry-stone walls and roofs of stone slabs and then covered with earth.
No one knows their purpose, though there are plenty of theories about
them. It seems certain that they had some sort of protective function –
artificial caves where people or stores or animals, perhaps, could be
secreted in times of danger.

The settlers of Chysauster had a thriving trade in tin, at any rate, and
built their village of the granite which centuries of more sophisticated
masons considered too hard and unworkable to be used for building
purposes. I wonder if these folk knew the tales of Troy and Odysseus,

Moorland granite in the prehistoric walls of Chysauster, Cornwall.

A characteristic dry-stone wall of slate-stone in North Cornwall.

already ancient when they lived in these 'tin islands' under threat of invasion by the Romans, whom some writers say 'taught the Britons how to build houses'! A more up-to-date use of the local granite in house building can be seen in the nearby village of Newmill.

Zennor, near the north Atlantic coast, lays claim to our attention, since much that is typical of the area is to be found in or near it. The village is built of grey granite in a hollow, half a mile from the sea. Great boulders of granite lie about it, and the dry-stone walls round its fields have been built with them. Its much-restored church has a bench-end carving of a mermaid who is said to have enticed the squire's son into the sea when she heard him singing, for the men of Zennor were famed once for their fine voices. The village inn is called 'The Tinners' Arms', for this is one of the areas where tin mining was a thriving industry until the beginning of this century, when cheap imported tin killed the local mining tradition almost stone dead. The surrounding moorland has engine houses and chimney stacks of granite with brick tops, derelict and ivy-clad, like ruins of medieval castles in a desolate landscape. For two thousand years men have laboured in the bowels of the earth, sometimes beneath the sea, to bring up tin and copper from some of Europe's most valuable deposits, and the district was well populated in prehistoric times on that account.

D. H. Lawrence and his wife stayed at 'The Tinners' Arms' during the First World War whilst looking for a cottage. Lawrence wrote *Women in Love* here. And W. H. Hudson had been here not long before, doing research and sitting near a local quarry to watch birds, and discovering that stone walls are called 'hedges' here (as they are in the hunting country of the Shires). They may be called hedges, and are actually walls, but they often look like banks, for they become so overgrown with grass and weeds that you would never guess there was a stone structure underneath. They are often capped with two rows of thin slabs laid in herring-bone pattern.

Seeing so much granite lying about everywhere recalled to Hudson's mind an old story of a traveller whimsically asking a native "where the people of these parts procure stone with which to build their houses". Hudson could not, however, remember the witty answer and, when he tried the question out on Cornishmen and got only blank looks, took them to task for having no sense of humour! I am not much amused myself by Hudson's starting the joke and then failing to deliver the punch-line.

Zennor Quoit, half a mile from the village, is a megalithic burial chamber unique in England, for its massive stone roof, weighing twelve tons, covered not one sepulchre but two, and a round barrow once enveloped the whole structure. There are many other prehistoric remains in the vicinity, as well as stones and rocks with superstitions attached to them, such as Witches' Rock, which you have to touch nine times at midnight to insure against bad luck or worse.

Legend and superstition are always strongest in the west, feeding the imaginations of men leading hard lives as fishermen, miners or quarrymen whose traditions have grown over many centuries of withstanding, like the hard-living granite beneath them, lashing seas and winds. Many ancient stones stand on the high ground inland, not least among them the stone circle called 'the Merry Maidens', from which T. C. Lethbridge claimed to have received a tingling sensation like an electric shock. Also here is the well known 'Men-an-Tol'. 'Men' or 'maen' is the Celtic word for stone. It is a curiously erotic granite monument, with two phallic symbols flanking a circle, through which children were once passed in symbolic rebirth to cure diseases such as rickets. The stones may have formed part of a burial chamber once, but historic superstition is a more powerful agent than prehistoric probability.

Stones have been found in Cornwall with Celtic mazes and spirals carved on them, and we shall come across other ancient maze patterns in the course of our explorations. They occur almost entirely on this side of the Jurassic Boundary and had magical significance for the Celtic peoples. They are remembered in the children's game of hop-scotch, and in Cornwall a spiral form of this game was known as 'snail creep', which also happens to be the name given by Cornish masons to a type of pointing, used in random rubble walls, in which mortar is pressed into the edges of the stone to define their shape and form a central ridge along the line of mortar. Gulval, just outside Penzance, is one place where much snail-screep pointing can be seen in the walls of the houses.

Garden walls, as well as field walls, are often built with boulders of granite rubble, and in areas where mining and quarrying have occupied men for so many centuries (tin towards Land's End, china clay around St Austell, slate near Bodmin Moor and granite and other stone almost everywhere), workers' cottages crop up in neat stone terraces in otherwise uninteresting villages or in detached isolation near working sites. Near Land's End, the grey villages typical of the region are often enlivened by warm brown and buff tints in the granite.

Mousehole's mis-spelt and consequently mispronounced name is perhaps better known than the village itself, with its little fishing harbour tucked into a tiny bay, and houses of slate and browny-grey granite rising up the slopes from the sea in narrow streets and passages. Curved granite quays form a narrow harbour entrance. In the sixteenth century, when the village was known as Port Enys, four Spanish galleys sailed into it and two hundred Spaniards raided the village, burning it to the ground and raping the women. The only building to survive intact was the manor house in Keigwin Street, named after the squire who was killed defending it. The house has been much restored, after serving as a public house for a long period, but its porch still supports an upper room on granite pillars, as it did in its Elizabethan days. The modern village has inevitably lost some of the character it possessed once, with some rendering on the stone walls and looking a little chic in places, but it is easier here than in many other popular old villages of the Cornish coast to imagine its life before British tourists resumed the invasion begun by Spanish adventurers.

The origin of Mousehole's name is obscure – some say it means 'maiden's brook' from the Cornish *'mouz hel'*, but the pronunciation, in any case, is closer to 'muzzle'. The place was notorious for coarse and lecherous smugglers once, for where houses are of granite, there you will find hard men, and women too. Dolly Pentreath was born and died here. Her grave is in the parish churchyard at Paul, half a mile inland, where a monument erected by Prince Louis Napoleon – God knows why – credits her, incorrectly, with being the last person to speak in the ancient Cornish tongue. *"Gurra perthi de taz ha de mam; mal de Dythiow bethenz hyr war an tyr neb an arleth de Dew ryes dees'* (Exodus XX, 12). Dolly, who died in 1777, would doubtless have approved the commandment, though she was no respecter of persons. She abused with foul language anyone who refused to pay a tanner to hear her talk, and her funeral was interrupted for a whisky break. She must have heard Wesley preach but probably resented him as a rival, whose gift of the gab people flocked to hear free of charge, and him only speaking English, if you please!

Many of Cornwall's coastal villages and hamlets grew up as tiny fishing appendages of inland communities and do not have their own churches (though they often enough have their Methodist chapels). The village possessing the parish church is called 'the church town', and Paul is the church town of Mousehole, where the loss of the crew of the Penlee lifeboat is being mourned as I write these lines.

Penlese Quarry is near the coast road north of Mousehole. Blasting is still done here to free stone from its host rock. It is one of several in the area which supplied great quantities of building stone once, one of their recipients being St Michael's Mount. Insofar as the island settlement can be termed a village at all, it must be counted among the most spectacular in England, and much of its building was done with granite from quarries at Lamorna Cove. It is owned by the National Trust now but still has a small population in addition to the St Aubyn family who have lived in the castle since the seventeenth century. At low tide you can walk to it across a granite causeway.

Inland to the east are St Hilary and Godolphin Cross, the latter built of dark stone around a crossroads and named after the Godolphin family which owned local tin mines and practically everything else in the vicinity. Godolphin's tinners were notorious wreckers, according to report, luring ships on to the rocks and plundering their treasures, but I know of no real evidence for this unsavoury legend. The mansion is Godolphin House, the pub 'Godolphin Arms'; the church down the road at Breage has a Godolphin Chapel, and the Godolphin tin mines were reckoned the world's richest at one time. Yet John Evelyn's friend Margaret Blagge, who was married to Sidney, the first Earl of Godolphin, felt it necessary to beg of her husband by letter that her body might be brought to Cornwall from London, where she was dying, adding pathetically: ". . . if I were carried by Sea, the expence would not be very great. . . ." In fact, a regiment of cavalry accompanied her coffin on the journey by land, which cost Godolphin a thousand pounds. He was a close friend of the Duke of Marlborough and lost his job as Lord Treasurer during Queen Anne's little tiff with Churchill. His descendants became Governors and Lord Protectors of the Islands of Scilly, but the family ran out of male heirs, and the house became a bit of television scenery for the *Poldark* series.

St Hilary is an attractive village which became well known between the two World Wars because of the Popish inclinations of the vicar, the Reverend Bernard Walke. Feelings became so strong in Protestant circles that a gang was employed to smash up the more ritualistic furnishings of the church, and it remains a sort of monument to bigotry beneath its broach spire, rare in these parts.

Cadgwith is an unspoilt and beautiful little coastal village with stone houses below Goonhilly Downs, where the space-age architecture of the satellite tracking station keeps incongruous company with the prehistoric architecture of barrows and hut circles. Sometimes here on the Lizard peninsula one sees a house or church built of Serpentine, a hard stone quarried in small blocks of various colours from green and grey to brown and red, often heavily veined or mottled. It is an igneous rock like granite but liable to flaws which limit its use in building. Houses in Cadgwith and the wharves are built of it, and those who cannot resist the smell of seaweed and the screaming of gulls can get a bit of both worlds here.

The creeks on the north side of the Helford estuary lead to Porth Navas and Constantine, very different from the coastal fishing villages, and this is Daphne du Maurier country, with Frenchman's Creek nearby. Constantine's unknown houses of slate and granite – the bigger ones with mullions in their windows – stand on a hillside with fine views of the Helford river, whilst Porth Navas, tucked into a little heavily wooded inlet, like a native village in a tropical forest, breeds oysters for the Duchy of Cornwall. Beyond these villages, the silent upper reaches of the beautiful river seem a million miles away from

seaside holiday crowds. Constantine is the site of the huge Bosahan quarry, where granite is still being worked for building purposes.

We have to travel some way up the Cornish peninsula, beyond the Falmouth-Newquay stretch, to find more villages where stone is visible in any worthwhile quantity. Luxulyan, beyond St Austell, is a good stopping-place. It is a small village in quiet countryside, which became prosperous through stone quarrying, and the older houses and the church are built of the local grey granite. The church, dedicated to two of those multitudinous Cornish saints – Ciricius and Julitta – has huge blocks of granite in its walls, and colossal boulders of the stuff lie about in the valley. The pink and black mottled porphyritic granite quarried in this area, locally named 'luxulianite', was used for the Duke of Wellington's sarcophagus in the crypt of St Paul's.

Across the Luxulyan Valley is a viaduct, also of granite, built by Joseph Treffry in 1839 to carry his quarry products by rail. It is an aqueduct as well, its canal flowing white with china clay nowadays, whilst the railway is disused. On the other side of the River Fowey, beside a tributary stream, Lerryn is a pretty hamlet with trees shading its stone cottages and a couple of sixteenth-century bridges, while Herodsfoot, farther inland by the stripling West Looe river, has slate cottages on the slopes of a steep valley.

Towards the opposite coastline, St Mawgan and St Breock are interesting villages, both showing slate and granite in their buildings. St Mawgan is properly called Mawgan-in-Pydar to distinguish it from Mawgan-in-Meneage near the Helford river. The church has a set of sixteenth-century brasses to members of the Arundell family, whose old mansion has been a convent since the end of the eighteenth century. In the garden, with an old slate wall behind it, is a Saxon cross of Pentewan stone. This material, once quarried near Mevagissey, is a quartz-porphyry igneous rock called 'elvan' in Cornwall and even harder to work than granite. Fowey's church is built of it. St Mawgan is remarkably peaceful considering its proximity to Newquay Airport, the popular Bedruthan Steps and, perhaps even more ominously, Watergate Bay.

On the coast to the north are the neighbours Port Isaac and Portquin, one discussed in every guidebook and the other scarcely ever mentioned at all. Port Isaac swoops down to a little bay between two protecting cliffs. There is some tourist development here, but cement rendering has not yet conquered the old village where slates hang on the house walls and the houses hang on steep streets and passages whose narrowness is indicated by the name Squeezibelly Alley. Wesley preached his fiery sermons to fishermen and their families in the little harbour where boats still set out for mackerel, and a long warehouse of stone is the shell fishermen's HQ.

Cadgwith – houses built of local Serpentine stone remain visible among rendered and painted properties.

Quarrying residue at Delabole, with abandoned tin mine above.

Portquin is a different kettle of fish altogether. Steeply situated like its neighbour and hardly more than a mile away, it is a half deserted place preserved by the National Trust, with derelict stone cottages, overgrown gardens and a silent, disused quay. Romantics say that all the men in the village lost their lives at sea in a terrible storm. Cynics like me prefer the rumour that they emigrated to Australia at a time of economic decline. Whatever happened to the men, it is easy to see what happened to their cottages.

A little farther north-east, on the western fringes of Bodmin Moor, is Delabole, where anything that is not made of slate is not made here. The famous slate quarry lies east of the long street village beyond the old railway track, where one of the biggest man-made holes in Britain gapes back mockingly at the curious who gawp at it from a visitors' viewing platform. Slate was quarried here at least as far back as Henry VII's time and has continued ever since, though the industry has declined somewhat with the advent of cheaper roofing materials. The slate comes in shades of blue, grey and green and is strong and fine-grained but light in weight. The vast chasm which has for so long put roofs over Cornish heads is a mile and a half round its perimeter and five hundred feet deep. Quarrymen's tools give the local pub its name, 'Bettle and Chisel', and the village buildings have walls of slate-stone, as well as roofs. The place has a profitable sideline in selling to tourists all sorts of things you do not imagine being made of slate.

At the coast nearby, Tintagel is a monument to the fanciful among us through the decades since tourism became such a thriving industry. It is a place on slate though not altogether of it and in fact is a village of no great distinction, its buildings being mostly Victorian. If it qualifies for inclusion in this book, it is because it possesses two of the best-known stone buildings in England, so it is difficult to ignore. Far more difficult is the Arthurian connection. A Celtic monastery stood on the majestic site of the supposed birthplace, on a rocky promontory known as the Island, but the castle ruins are Norman and, thundering waves and Fellowship of the Round Table notwithstanding, I doubt that even Merlin himself could conjure up a convincing vision of Uther Pendragon, Ygraine and their immortal son in this place of coach parties, souvenir shops, car-parks, yellow lines, litter baskets and council estates.

No visitor to Tintagel, however, should miss the Old Post Office, and believe me, no one will. It is preserved by the National Trust now, and you can go inside, but the floorboards shriek for relief from tramping feet, and the interior is no match for the outside walls and roof of this wonderful building. It was built perhaps late in the fourteenth century as a small manor house, entirely of local material, and its survival seems to me the one and only miraculous happening in this repository of British legend.

Tintagel's church (St Merteriana!) stands isolated in bleak surroundings on a cliff top, and slate headstones in the large churchyard are buttressed against gale-force winds which also buffet Trevalga, a couple of miles along the coast and more to the point in our present context. It is an isolated and unspoilt place of slate, and though there is not much of it – church, farms and a few cottages – it has a crazy roof to challenge Tintagel's.

We have now to move inland towards the villages of Bodmin Moor, and Altarnun and Polyphant await us at its north-east side. Polyphant is one of the places here where stone has long been quarried, for the local material was in favour in medieval times as an easily worked stone which weathered well. It has a dark colour, bluish-grey spotted with iron, can be polished like marble and is found in many Cornish

The Old Post Office at Tintagel.

churches. Sculptors are among the customers for this rare stone, which was also used in Truro Cathedral.

Quarrying villages are rarely pretty in themselves but are the cause of prettiness in others, and neighbouring Altarnun has been, and still is, one of the best-kept villages in Cornwall. Its picturesque stone cottages are on a hillside, some of them slate-hung, others painted white. Its large church is reached via a narrow packhorse bridge across the fast-flowing stream, and as the centre of the second largest parish in the county it is known as 'the Cathedral of the Moor'. It has one of Cornwall's highest towers and is dedicated to the mother of St David of Wales, St Nonna. Its collection of bench-end carvings by Robert Daye made in the sixteenth century is especially notable.

Bolventor stands right at the centre of the misty and boggy moor, a tiny hamlet below the slopes of Brown Willy on the only major road to cross this desolate and often forbidding landscape. Daphne du Maurier's 'Jamaica Inn' is here, a stone building with hung slates, looking entirely respectable and quite beyond the rum goings-on in that splendid Cornish tale, as indeed it should be, for it was the Bolventor Temperance Hotel before it acquired its more romantic appellation.

Other, more ancient tales have attached themselves to Dozmary Pool in this parish. No stream flows into it – only rain – and the isolated stretch of water was confidently said to be bottomless until it dried up one summer, but it is still reckoned by some to be the place where Sir Bedivere flung Arthur's sword Excalibur into the water, reluctantly obeying the command of the mortally wounded king. Arthur had acquired the magic sword, you will remember, by withdrawing it from a stone, which no one else could do.

Blisland, at the moor's south-western edge, is unusual among Cornish villages in that it is built round a green, but its cottages of slate and granite are typical enough, as are the rough granite headstones in the churchyard. The village's stately elms have been lost in the great epidemic, and there is nothing to match their upright dignity now – not even the granite columns in the church, which tilt alarmingly out of vertical. A superbly restored rood screen enhances this building, which Sir John Betjeman has called "the most beautiful of all the country churches of the West". It was built of coarse-grained granite from the De Lank quarries, a little to the north, with a floor of local slate.

St Cleer, right across the moor at its south-eastern corner, Menheniot near Liskeard, and Minions, farther north, are also quarrying villages of old, but dark hints of ancient forces gather about them as well as the ghosts of industry. Three stone circles called 'The Hurlers' are reputed to be men turned to stone for hurling on the Sabbath, and the Trevethy Quoit casts its prehistoric spell over the area, while a Holy Well and King Doniert's Stone, standing with the shaft of a Celtic cross at the roadside, add to the mysterious atmosphere of the place, despite the presence of a television transmitter overlooking all. But the most eerie presence of all in this part of the moor is that weird and wonderful granite formation known as the Cheesewring. It is hard to believe that it is natural. Locals say that the topmost of its great pile of flattish boulders turns round three times at cock-crow.

Cheesewring Quarry, no longer in operation, produced granite of pink as well as the more common grey colour. The quarries and local copper mines between them brought an industrial railway line here, long since gone, but it left in its wake hideous un-Cornish names like Railway Terrace. One of the local stonecutters in the eighteenth century was Daniel Gumb, well known here as an eccentric. In truth, he was an early opter-out from the eighteenth-century rat-race, being something of a scholar, who turned to earning a modest living from carving stone. He lived with his family in a home-made rock house near the quarry, on Caradon Hill, sleeping on granite beds and sitting on granite benches at a granite table.

Below Bodmin Moor to the east are Linkinhorne and, farther away,

St Dominick. The churchyard of St Melor at Linkinhorne has some gravestones carved by Daniel Gumb. The parish of St Dominick contains a magnificent mansion of brown granite, Cotehele, the finest Tudor house in Cornwall, now owned by the National Trust, which acquired it in lieu of death duties. It was the home of the Edgecumbe family, one of whose members, having announced his support for Henry Tudor, leapt into the river, or at least pretended he had, to escape from what we should now call a 'hit man' with a 'contract' from Richard III. A chapel on the cliff marks the alleged spot.

Toward the coast again, Landrake and St Germans present a contrast in village styles, though both containing some of the local 'elvan' stone, rust-coloured in parts. Landrake is on a hill top and has narrow streets with a few stone cottages dominated by its church tower, a hundred feet high but swamped by modern development. Snakes with heads at both ends coil round the ancient stone font in the church.

St Germans is also on a hill, overlooking a harbour, but it has an aristocratic look if you ignore the modern development and signs of old quayside industry. Its church was chief in the whole county before the building of Truro Cathedral, having been in Anglo-Saxon days the seat of the Bishops of Cornwall, and its great west doorway is one of Cornwall's best Norman remains, built of blue-green stone from quarries near Landrake. It is time-worn like the font of Purbeck marble inside. The windows include stained glass by Burne-Jones, and its monuments to the Eliot family, Earls of St Germans, include one by Westmacott and a splendid work by Rysbrack to Edward Eliot as a Roman senator, not much helped aesthetically by the iron railings in front of it.

A curious row of seventeenth-century almshouses, recently restored, adds to the interest of St Germans. They are on two floors, with projecting tile-hung gables supported by stone piers and allowing timber balconies to the upper flats, which are reached by outside steps of granite. Kingsand and Cawsand, on the nearby peninsula, also show much granite in their buildings, though there is much rendering and painting too.

Crossing the Tamar into the red sandstone county of Devon, we are still in seafaring country, but softer with it. Drake may have been a pirate, but he was not a hard man like Cornish Bligh of the *Bounty*. He liked music as well as a game of bowls, and you feel in Devon a little less of the paganism that pervades Cornwall. We have not done with granite yet, however, for the villages of Dartmoor beckon us from their misty heights. Most of the stone building is round the moor's north-east fringe, but granite has been quarried at various places on Dart-moor for many centuries and still comes from one or two of them, this being the most extensive outcrop of granite in England. The stone

Almshouses at St Germans.

Decorated window tracery in plain granite walls – Bridford, Devon.

walls here often contain colossál slabs of granite weighing several hundredweight, and so the walls are of an entirely different character from the regular limestone walls of the Cotswolds.

The greatest monuments to Dartmoor granite, which is generally coarser than the Cornish variety, include the British Museum, the National Gallery and Nelson's Column, but we do not have to go all the way to London to see its essential character in large-scale building, for there is nowhere a more daunting example of granite's massive strength and durability than right here in Princetown's vast two-centuries-old prison, with its suspect sentiment carved over the gate, *"Parcere subjectis"* – "Pity the Humbled". The man who suggested building the prison, Sir Thomas Tyrwhitt, was he who owned the local quarries which supplied the stone. The prison held nearly nine thousand Frenchmen during the Napoleonic Wars, and they and later convicts worked as stonebreakers for the roads which were then being made through the wilderness in an abortive effort to reclaim the land for agriculture.

Granite can sometimes seem a grim material, but if one travels to Dartmoor through south Devon and sees so many housing estates in the vicinity of Plymouth with multi-coloured houses like bags of dolly mixtures, the restraint of grey granite is more than welcome by the time one reaches the moorland villages. The road across the moor from Plymouth leads to Moretonhampstead on the other side, and around this market town are gathered the best of Dartmoor's villages. To the north-west Gidleigh, Throwleigh and Drewsteignton are good hill villages with their granite cottages, usually thatched, among fine moorland scenery.

South Tawton lies off the moor on the Carboniferous sandstone, and is a place of superstition. Its abandoned quarries have fathered much dark rumour, and its church contains stone carvings of humans and animals, one of which might be a sheela-na-gig, that grotesque fertility figure which the Christian Church was happy to embrace in its earlier days, though less than twenty examples are now known in England.

Dunsford and Bridford, at the north-eastern fringe of the moor, have some thatched houses of granite, though most are of cob, and even brick occurs here and there. Some of the stone is painted too, so that little is actually visible. But Bridford's granite church is the highlight of this pair, with some good medieval stained glass in the Lady Chapel and, in this county of exquisitely carved rood screens, one of its finest treasures. Its sixteenth-century red, blue and gold paint is still detectable, though faded with age, and its figures in relief are too lively to represent the conventional solemn saints and angels, one of them disporting herself like a modern chorus girl. This fantastic work of art and craftsmanship is matched in the superb pulpit done by the same expert and self-confident hand.

North Bovey and Lustleigh have some cob and colour-washed buildings among their grey moorland granite but cannot be totally disqualified on that account, stone being their primary ingredient. North Bovey is grouped round a green with the ancient village inn called the 'Ring of Bells', and the massive Easdon Tor rises across the river, beyond which is the wilder moor and the Bronze Age settlement of Grimspound, one of the best known and most impressive of Dartmoor's prehistoric remains. 'Grim' was one of the names given to the Norse god Odin by early Christians, who identified him, naturally enough, with the Devil, so the village name means the Devil's livestock enclosure, and indeed its only inhabitants now are the Dartmoor ponies which wander here for the grass around three-thousand year-old stone foundations. The long-deserted village of two dozen living quarters was surrounded by a circular wall ten feet thick, built no doubt to protect the humans and domestic animals inside from the wild beasts which roamed the moor in those times.

The primitive beliefs of those early inhabitants of our island remained with us a long time. In the church at North Bovey, one of the carved bosses on the chancel roof shows what are usually described as three rabbits. The animals are chasing one another with their ears joined to form a triangle, and of course Christians say they are symbols of the Holy Trinity, though why God the Father, God the Son and God the Holy Spirit should be represented by rabbits I cannot quite see. In fact, the animals are not rabbits but hares. They can also be seen in the churches at Spreyton and Widecombe-in-the-Moor, among other places. No animal has more pagan superstition attached to it than the hare. Throughout Europe it is regarded as a symbol of fertility and is a common embodiment of the corn spirit, as Sir James Frazer pointed out: "When the rest of the corn has been reaped, a handful is left standing to form the Hare. It is divided into three parts and plaited, and the ears are tied in a knot. The reapers then retire a few yards and each throws his or her sickle in turn at the Hare to cut it down."

The device of the three hares seems to have been used as an emblem by the tin miners, just as the pagan All-Seeing Eye was adopted by the Freemasons, and this explains its frequent appearance in south-west England. Many local churches were built with the wealth produced by exploitation of the tin deposits.

Widecombe-in-the-Moor and Buckland-in-the-Moor are perhaps Dartmoor's most famous villages, the former known far beyond our native shores on account of Uncle Tom Cobleigh's journey with his companions to Widecombe Fair. But Widecombe was a tin-mining centre of old, eight hundred feet up among bleak-sounding heights like Haytor, Hound Tor, Rippon Tor and Bonehill Down – names which may remind us that Arthur Conan Doyle used the forbidding aspects of the moor to good effect in his most famous Sherlock Holmes story, *The Hound of the Baskervilles*. But truth can be quite as terrifying as fiction, as Widecombe knows only too well. One Sunday in October 1638 an almighty thunderstorm plunged Widecombe into afternoon darkness, and lightning struck the church, killing four people and injuring over sixty others. One ghastly account of the event tells of women with their clothes on fire being burnt through to the bones and of a man whose head was "rent into three pieces". Some put the storm down to the Devil, coming for the soul of one of the villagers. There was no lack of 'evidence' for such beliefs. A Widecombe 'doctor' in the seventeenth century persuaded one of his patients that the ghost of a neighbour who had committed suicide was the cause of his trouble, and organized an elaborate ritual in which a strong man drove a sword through the dead man's grave to pierce his heart, whilst the patient had a mutilated owl bound to his head and had to wear a horseshoe under one armpit and a pincase under the other. In this instance, the treatment failed to effect a cure!

Neither storm nor Devil had been forgotten, but the church had been repaired by the time Tom Pearce's grey mare was commandeered to carry Tom Cobleigh and his neighbours to Widecombe Fair, "all-along,

Overleaf: Looking down from Dartmoor's granite outcrops on Widecombe-in-the-Moor.

Buckland-in-the-Moor, Devon.

down-along, out-along lee'', as West Country folk might still express their journeys through hill and dale. Tom Cobleigh is as world-famous through popular ballad as Cumbria's John Peel, but whereas the latter in his coat of grey is a well-documented hunting man of Caldbeck, the identity of Tom Cobleigh is more obscure. Some say he was the 'gent' who is buried in Spreyton churchyard, but it seems more likely that he was a yeoman farmer of the same parish who lived a couple of generations earlier. At any rate, it was the Reverend Sabine Baring-Gould, author of 'Onward, Christian Soldiers', who re-discovered the ballad and made Tom Cobleigh famous. As for the grey mare which took ill and died, it is supposed to haunt Dartmoor still.

What Buckland-in-the-Moor lacks in such world-wide fame, it makes up for in its quiet beauty. Its thatched cottages of silvery moorland granite snuggle together in a sylvan glade whose stream meanders lazily toward the River Dart. One could perhaps do without the fake sentiment of the words 'My Dear Mother' replacing the figures on the church clock – they do not seem to me to have any more relevance, or reverence, in that context than the average graffiti chalked up in public places – but for all that, Buckland is a delightful example of village building in moorland stone and, on the whole, the brightest jewel in Dartmoor's encircling crown.

The deserted village of Hallsands.

We must now head coastwards again to look at one or two of Devon's English Channel villages which qualify for mention. Holbeton is a little-known place of stone farms and houses with roofs of thatch or slate forming a steep village street, and there is much of interest in the church of All Saints standing above it, not least the monument to the Hele family, piled up in four tiers almost as if they were a medieval circus act, with Sir Richard as the centre of attention.

Just above the craggy Start Point is a tiny place called Hallsands, a fishing village little visited by tourists and scarcely mentioned in guidebooks. It was known as Hall Cellar once, when its population specialized in crab fishing. In the early years of this century, after dredging had removed masses of shingle from the shore, storms lashed the coast and washed away the unprotected cottages, and the place was deserted. Objects met by the irresistible force of the sea are not immovable, even when they are built of stone. Some rebuilding has been done there now, but ruined stone cottages remain on a beach which is still victim to furious and unrelenting seas in bad weather.

Some of the building stone in this corner of Devon is slatey, and basalt rock, quarried at Kingsbridge and Buckfastleigh among other places, has been used fairly extensively in the area. Ashprington and Dittisham, near the Dart estuary, show these materials, though the latter has many whitewashed walls. Ashprington is more evidently stone-built, a sleepy place with church and pub at its centre, and nothing much ever happening there, you might suppose, until you start to pick up little bits of history from the church, the war memorial, one or two imposing mansions and other things that tell us that life exists even when there are no legends to account for it and no tourists to view it.

Beyond Exmouth, overlooking Lyme Bay, Branscombe and Beer bring us to chalk cliffs which have been extensively quarried at the latter village and account for much building in chalk and flint-like 'chert' in both of them. Chalk is most uncharacteristic of the country this side of the Jurassic Boundary, but this isolated outcrop provided much of the stone for Exeter Cathedral and many other Devon churches. It had been used since Roman times and was actually mined rather than quarried – you can see great slits in the cliff-sides where men made their entrances and exits. The stone does not weather too well in external use, however, and is not even very stable in its natural formation, since great landslips – notably a famous one in 1790 – have sunk great masses of the local cliffs into the sea. Caves have also been formed very readily, providing suitable hiding-places for local smugglers. Both these villages are attractive, and the cliff walk between them gives fine views of the bay and surrounding countryside, but Beer is much the more commercialized of the two.

Inland again, to an unlikely spot near Honiton, that bottleneck through which the ship of south-western tourism is so often squeezed before bellying out into full sail to fill all corners of the peninsula beyond the Exe. Awliscombe is not a stone village, though there is some chert here, but perhaps it ought to be, for the churchyard has a stony memorial to one James Pady, "brickmaker late of this parish in hopes that his clay will be remoulded in a workmanlike manner far superior to his former perishable materials". With that thought-provoking sentiment we may leave Devon to pass into Somerset, for whilst much of this county of fine villages is on the limestone belt, some of it is sandstone and thus belongs to this chapter on the south-west.

The cosy villages of Exmoor are too often built of cob and colour-washed beneath their thatch to justify inclusion in this book, but Allerford, on the northern fringe, is a well-known exception, with its tall-chimneyed red sandstone houses and much-photographed arched packhorse bridge beside a ford across the shallow stream. Several other places – such as Porlock Weir – can be found with nice groups of stone cottages. We are also reminded in this vicinity that Somerset is a western outpost of pantile roofing, generally confined to eastern England.

The villages of the Quantocks are also inclined to hide their naked

Allerford, Somerset.

charms beneath veils of plaster and whitewash, and Stogumber and Vellow, which lead us to them, often show the form but not the colour and texture of their stone walls. At Stogumber they lead up the hill to the church of pinky sandstone. The ecclesiastical court here was a zealous vanguard of the coming Puritan revolution in the seventeenth century, it would seem, with a particular obsession about Sabbath sports, for two men were brought before it in 1623, one for playing bowls and the other tennis in the churchyard "on the Saboth day". Meanwhile, Anastasia Wipple's prodigal and unmarried daughter Elizabeth was excommunicated for coming home, after four years absence, rather heavier than when she went away. The archdeacon must have been a hard man to remain unmoved by the mother's gorgeous name – like Russian ice cream.

It was a rather more enlightened church in which the rector of Combe Florey presided for a decade and a half two centuries afterwards. There was never a less dogmatic clergyman. He might advise the local girls to guard their virginity until the seductive flatteries were backed up by marriage certificates, but to threaten them with hellfire and damnation would have been utterly unthinkable to him, for he was a man of wit, and no man of wit can seriously believe in divine vengeance. It was in the summer of 1829 that the admirable cleric

The church of coursed sandstone at Combe Florey.

Sydney Smith came to this beautiful sandstone village, and I came here myself with some reverence, 150 years after him, to one of the high points of my own odyssey. Was this the place that launched a thousand quips? "The Smith of Smiths", as Macauley dubbed him, called it "a kind of healthy grave", for although he had been in rural Yorkshire for twenty years, he was a Londoner at heart, like Dr Johnson, and no country-lover. We have already noted his reaction to the Cotswolds. Smith suffered from hay fever at Combe Florey and said that his nostrils were so irritable that an absurd remark or the sight of a dissenter set him off sneezing that could be heard in Taunton when the wind was in the right direction. And he wrote ironically: "I saw a crow yesterday, and had a distant view of a rabbit today." He saw flowers, grass and birds as "delusions" – "They all afford slight gratification, but not worth an hour of rational conversation: and rational conversation in sufficient quantities is only to be had from the congregation of a million people in one spot."

Still, he rebuilt the rectory and settled down to the life of a country parson, occasionally relieving the boredom by visiting London or Paris and exciting the village by bringing to it such distinguished visitors as Lord John Russell and the Reverend Thomas Malthus. Once he replied to an invitation from a member of the well-known publishing family: "Dear Longman, I can't accept your invitation, for my house is full of country cousins. I wish they were once removed." He should have been a bishop, but bishops, politicians and the House of Lords had too often been victims of his wit to give him such preferment. "I must believe in the Apostolic Succession," he once said, "there being no other way of accounting for the descent of the Bishop of Exeter from Judas Iscariot." So he had to be content with his lot, which, after all, was not too bad. "I thank God, who has made me poor," he said, "that he has made me merry." Amen to that, for wit without merriment is an altogether more serious and self-important matter, as a more recent resident of Combe Florey could show.

The Catholic squire who revived at the manor house the literary associations which the Protestant parson had begun at the rectory, moved in during 1956 and lived there until his death ten years later. Evelyn Waugh had all his best work behind him when he came here, his mind preoccupied with a libel action against the *Daily Express* and intermittently subject to hallucinations. Once, when asked why he did not vote in general elections, he replied: "I do not presume to advise my Sovereign in the choice of her servants." Such snooty wit prevented him from being the widely admired figure that Smith was, and his other eccentricities generally cause guidebooks to tiptoe fearfully through Combe Florey without mention of the village's late and great resident. Waugh had previously lived at Stinchcombe in the Cotswolds, but he was never a man of the stone country in spirit, which fact perhaps accounts in some way for the perverse melancholy which gradually took over the brilliantly funny satirist. Instead of adapting himself to the world, as Smith had done, he expected the world to adapt itself to him.

Cothelstone is hardly more than a hamlet, though it has some fine houses, including the Jacobean manor house with its mullioned windows and gabled dormers, and a church close by, all in sandstone. It is a very attractive, compact settlement, standing back from the road like a private estate. The stone is redder here than down in the plain at Stogumber and Vellow, and up on the hills one may come across the occasional unsightly red gash where the sandstone has been quarried.

Like the soil – sometimes described as wine-red – the stone here is metaphorically, at least, more aptly called blood-red. It is hard to imagine this exquisitely peaceful spot as the scene of blood-lust, but the lord of the manor, Sir John Stawell, raised an army for the king and brought the destructive vengeance of the Roundheads on his house, while forty years afterwards Judge Jeffreys, whom Lord Stawell had taken to task for his cruelty, responded by hanging two of Monmouth's supporters at the manor house gateway.

Bishop's Lydeard, by contrast, is a large village with much ugly modern development, but it still shows much red sandstone and has a church built of it, with a fine Somerset tower, its windows dressed with golden limestone from Hamdon Hill, near Yeovil, which promises some of the pleasures yet to come.

Aisholt and Crowcombe both display some sandstone, although curious mixtures of material creep in, Crowcombe even having some Ham Hill limestone (of which more later) in its manor house, as well as brick. Aisholt might have become the home of Coleridge and fathered 'Kubla Khan' and 'The Ancient Mariner', but the poet feared that his wife would be lonely there, and chose Nether Stowey instead, so Aisholt has to rest content with Sir Henry Newbolt and 'Drake's Drum'.

Crowcombe nestles in a little valley with its warm sandstone church of the Holy Ghost at its centre. It had a spire once, but it was struck by lightning in the eighteenth century and not replaced. It has fascinating carvings in stone on the outside and famous ones of wood on the inside. Beneath the pinnacled battlements are the heads of beasts and humans characteristic of their period, but the finest stone carving here is in the tracery of the Perpendicular windows. Inside, however, are the Tudor benches which form a wonderful collection of curious carvings of the time – uncompromisingly pagan in their imagery and preoccupied with the symbolism of fertility. They include a merman with bludgeons coming out of his ears, a Jack-in-the-Green, and two naked men attacking a double-headed dragon.

East Quantoxhead, near the coast, is a pretty village of grey Triassic sandstone, said to be the only bit of Somerset not sold since the Norman Conquest, for the Luttrell family owned it then and have done so ever since. Guidebooks say that you can see Barry, in South Wales, across the Bristol Channel from here, but that is no big deal. The village's lively duckpond, edged by a stone wall, is a more attractive stretch of water.

We have by no means finished with Somerset yet, but we have done with the sandstone and the granite and can now move on to the limestone belt which supports so much of England's most homely and rewarding domestic building, as well as some of its most spectacular ecclesiastical architecture.

CHAPTER 3

The Limestone – South

The limestone rises out of the sea, white and virginal like Aphrodite – though somewhat more massive – at Portland Bill, forming great cliffs made largely of planktonic algae and the shells of tiny sea-creatures. The so-called Isle of Portland, which is really a peninsula joined to the mainland by the natural ridge of pebbles known as Chesil Bank, is a solid block of limestone four miles long and nearly two miles wide. As John Leland remarked, "Its soile is sumwhat stony." Although its chief industry is quarrying, however, and its villages are unquestionably built of stone (not only the houses, but the fences and the very pigsties, even), it has only marginal relevance to our subject, for it is a grey, bleak and treeless place, salted by the lashing sea and peppered by innumerable quarries, and whilst its product is among the finest building stones in the world, it is not such as can be found in the cottage walls of our country villages, except on the island itself, for its large, even blocks of white ashlar do not lend themselves to vernacular building. The domain of Portland stone is imposing public buildings and ambitious private mansions. Out of the great holes on Portland much of London was built, by such men as Sir Christopher Wren, who used fifty thousand tons to rebuild St Paul's. Wren was Surveyor of the Quarries on the Island of Portland, and quarrymen two centuries after his time have found stones bearing his mark which were finally rejected as unsuitable.

Great valleys are cut into the rock as if it were a gigantic vanilla blancmange scooped out with an enormous spoon. The stone is actually a creamy colour, turning whiter during weathering. Although it has been quarried for many centuries, it was in the seventeenth century that it really came into its own as the supreme British material for large-scale building.

I know of no finer or more dramatic introduction to the delights of limestone than to see Portland and then go a few miles along the Dorset coast to Abbotsbury, where you come upon a village of orange limestone houses with roofs of thatch or slate. The place is most famous for its swannery, established in the fourteenth century by Benedictine monks, in the lagoon called 'The Fleet' formed by Chesil Bank.

Portland: splitting a block of limestone with plugs and feathers.

Thatched cottages of limestone at Abbotsbury, Dorset.

Hundreds of swans nest here each spring and hatch their cygnets in a sort of public maternity ward presided over by the Swanherd, whose job in medieval times included the provision of fat swans for the monastery table. The remains of the tithe barn with its stone buttresses bear witness to the one-time wealth of the monastery.

All of Dorset is famous as Hardy country, of course, but the tall monument on Black Down above Abbotsbury is not to the poet and novelist but to that other Thomas Hardy, the captain of Nelson's flagship *Victory*, who lived in the lovely village of Portesham and to whom the writer was related. The father of Hardy the novelist was a master mason, and his son studied architecture before turning to literature.

The sudden transformation of the scene after Portland also throws us into the complications of limestone at the deep end, for Dorset has been one of the richest sources of a variety of building stones for many centuries. This book is not intended to be a technical one, and I would not be qualified to write it if it were, but it enhances the pleasure of discovery to have at least an elementary grasp of limestone's various qualities.

To the geologist, limestone comes in infinite variety, but only a little of it is suitable for building purposes, and its chief presence is roughly defined by what I have called the Jurassic Boundary. It is found mainly in two belts or ribbons of rock known as the Oolitic and the Liassic limestone. The Oolitic belt provides, as a rule, the best building stone. It sweeps up from the coast of Dorset to North Yorkshire, with the lias accompanying it along its north-west flank. The oolite generally forms softly rolling and flat-topped hills, whilst the lias is characterized by a more erratic landscape with isolated and abrupt hills.

The limestone was formed when the land where it occurs was beneath the sea – hence its composition. The oolite consists of very hard and tiny spherical grains massed together, often likened to the roe of herring. It might equally be compared with frog-spawn on a microscopic scale. The oolite is divided into two strata called the Great Oolite and the Inferior Oolite. 'Inferior' in this context does not mean 'worse': it is the older and lower strata and is often coloured by the presence of iron oxide in the rock. The Oolitic limestone's fine texture means that it can be sawn or chiselled in any direction without splitting, and it is called 'freestone' by the quarryman. When it is dressed to a smooth, flat finish, the mason and the architect call it 'ashlar'. (Stone which cannot be cut and dressed to a fine surface in any direction is called 'ragstone'.)

The Liassic limestone is coarser – more shelly and uneven – and less durable, but it can produce spectacular effects. It is often rich in fossil remains. Much building has been done with Liassic limestone in the past, but with the decline of natural stone as a building material, due to its high cost, those quarries which have survived have, with few exceptions, been those providing the more reliable building stones. Both Oolitic and Liassic limestone can vary in colour, due to both chemical action in the ground and 'weathering' in the open air – from white, cream, yellow and buff tones to gold, brown and cinnamon, and occasionally having pink, green or blue tints.

The so-called Isle of Purbeck, the peninsula to the east of Weymouth, produces a building stone which has been famous since Roman times as 'Purbeck Marble'. In fact it is not marble at all, which is a metamorphic rock, transformed from limestone into a crystallized state by heat and pressure. Purbeck is a hard, shelly limestone which can be given a high polish, and it has thus been used as a substitute for real marble in churches and cathedrals throughout the country. There are other hard English limestones which can be polished to a marble-like finish, but they have little relevance to our stone villages.

The Isle of Purbeck, however, has many quarries, some of which are still working, and in the charming village of Corfe several resident masons fulfilled orders for carved stone in the Middle Ages. The tradition of stone working has existed in some families for many

Jurassic limestone. Cottages in the village of Corfe.

generations, and masons entered their sons as apprentices on Shrove Tuesday each year, when the initiation ceremony for a young lad was to run an obstructive gauntlet of his mates without spilling the mug of ale he had to carry. This ritual was superseded by the kicking of a ball along the haulage route to Poole Harbour, to maintain the right of way. The Ancient Order of Marblers and Stonecutters still gathers on the same day each year in the Town Hall in West Street. Ironically, the upper chamber in which the members meet is built of brick. But some of the village's stone-roofed houses have engraved designs in the stones over their doorways – the work of masons who carved the Purbeck Marble.

It is the inevitable fate of our most famous villages that they should be sacrificed at the altar of the tourist trade, and Corfe is a burnt offering smouldering on summer weekends with the fumes of cars, coaches and motor-cycles whose occupants flit around its streets and hilltop ruins like fire-flies on Guy Fawkes night. Both the village and the castle above it, built of the local grey stone, are among the tourist magnets of southern England, in recognition of which the place now sports double yellow lines along its narrow streets.

Worth Matravers, on the Isle of Purbeck.

The castle ruins occupy a spectacular site on their conical hill, but the history of this ancient fortress is a grim one. It was built by Edward I on the site of an earlier building where Edward the Martyr was murdered by his stepmother. King John used the castle as a state prison and starved twenty-two French noblemen to death there. In the Civil War the castle resisted attack by the Roundheads until Cromwell's troops were admitted by treachery, and then it was mostly demolished, its stone finding fresh occupation in the village buildings. Legend has it that when Edward the Martyr was killed, his body was dragged along the ground by his horse. The corpse was taken to a blind woman's cottage in the village, and her sight was restored. She saw white broom flowering and vowed that she would regularly place some on the King's grave. Walking to Shaftesbury each year, she dropped seeds along the road and established the plant there which became known as Martyr's Broom.

Worth Matravers lies between Corfe and St Aldhelm's Head in this treeless and much-quarried peninsula. The remains of strip lynchet fields on the steep cliff slopes tell a story of poor farmers struggling to grow crops on bad soil with wind, landslips and salt spray to add to

Cottages at Sutton Poyntz.

their problems. The village is a little austere, like the country around it, but its church is worth seeing, with some Saxon stonework among the largely Norman fabric, and a fine chancel arch.

Weymouth was itself a stone village once, with some importance as a port ever since the Roman occupation, but of course it has never been the same since George III addressed his retinue there, crying "Once more unto the beach, dear friends, once more." Sutton Poyntz and Osmington, not far away, have been more fortunate. Rubble walls of grey Portland and a duckpond edged with willows distinguish the former, which is inside Weymouth's borough boundary but just out of reach of the worst development. Osmington is a little-known neat grey village where John Constable spent his honeymoon with his long-awaited bride, Maria Bicknell. They were the guests of Constable's closest friend, the vicar, the Reverend John Fisher, who had married them in London. They stayed for six weeks, and Constable painted several pictures of the bay and the village, some of which are now, alas, in the United States. There is a memorial tablet to John Fisher in the church, as well as the Latin couplet on a monument which, not surprisingly, pleased Thomas Hardy: "I have entered harbour. Goodbye Hope and goodbye Fortune. I have done with you. Play with someone else."

Along the coast road beyond Abbotsbury, Punknowle, despite its uncharacteristically ugly name (they pronounce it 'Punnel' in these parts), is worth a slight diversion. Its cottages of stone beneath thatched roofs are neat and attractive, but the village as a whole is rather spoilt by the dominating presence of farm silos. Its church is interesting, however.

Burton Bradstock is an attractive large village, again of the warm-coloured stone in contrast to the grey of Corfe. It should not be passed through quickly on the main road but lingered in, through back lanes like Donkey Lane and Shadrack. The Chesil Bank, beginning at Portland, ends here, fifteen miles distant, and the pebbles at this end are smaller as a result of their constant bombardment in the ocean currents.

Dorset is a kind of geological maelstrom and is dotted with so many villages of stone that we must be selective. Few counties of England have such varied and unspoiled scenery, resulting from the complicated rock formations that make the land, and the absence of raw materials to create extensive industry. Much of this agricultural county is chalk and clay, but limestone reaches out through Dorset like an outstretched hand. The villages are delightfully informal on the whole – the 'planner' has rarely had a hand in their development. Gabled houses with mullioned windows and roofs of thatch or stone tiles are the characteristic buildings here, the mullions often supporting stone lintels in the larger houses.

There is a belt of Corallian limestone which supports several sandy-coloured stone villages overlooking Blackmoor Vale. Marnhull, where this stone has been quarried, is one of the largest of them. It is a stylish and prosperous place of houses with mullioned windows, which Hardy called 'Marlott' and designated as the birthplace of Tess of the d'Urbervilles. It was very much a working village of farmers and quarrymen then but has since become a fashionable residential place. The church of St Gregory has a particularly fine tower.

Stour Provost and Fifehead Magdalen are among other good villages on the red soil of the Corallian limestone, and they remind us of the intriguing names to which Dorset is delightfully prone, like Winterbourne Zelstone, which is not a stone village, and Ryme Intrinseca, which was once but has allowed the intrusion of other materials to spoil it.

The names fit the Dorset dialect like gloves. Before Hardy, the great poet of Wessex was William Barnes, sometimes called 'the Dorsetshire Burns' – a teacher and clergyman who sang hymns of praise to the local life and landscape, as when he invites us to go walking with him:

We'll wind up roun' the hill, an' look
All down the thickly-timber'd nook,
Out where the squier's house do show
His grey-wall'd peaks up drough the row
O' sheady elems, where the rook
Do build her nest; an' where the brook
Do creep along the meads, an' lie
To catch the brightness o' the sky;
An' cows, in water to their knees,
Do stan' a-whisken off the vlees.

Dorset's best stone villages occur across the River Piddle and the Cerne valley in the western half of the county. It is characteristic of forthright Wessex that those with fastidious sensibilities have not been allowed to change good old Anglo-Saxon names like Piddle to something less graphic, though they have tried hard enough, and some of the villages to which the river gave its name have been corrupted to Puddle. Ralph Wightman mentions an aunt of his who ignored the prefix altogether when referring to Piddletrenthide. In Rutland the oversensitive were more successful. The one-time Pisbrook is now Bisbroke.

In the Cerne villages flint is much in evidence, mixed with stone, brick and timber, for here is Dorset's belt of chalk – hence the famous gigantic landmark carved on the hillside above Cerne Abbas: that exalted graffito reverently preserved by the National Trust. (The chalk hills of England are almost as irresistible as lavatory walls for creating unsaleable works of art.) We are to believe that this pin-headed policeman on point duty, with a knobbled club like a parody of all the cave-men ever dreamed up by newspaper cartoonists, is a representation of some pagan god so superstitiously revered that neither the Benedictine monks of the village monastery nor the Puritan officers of Cromwell's army allowed it to be defaced. We are not meant to laugh, either at the Victorian author who cautiously drew the attention of the "observant" visitor to the giant's "uninhibited masculinity" or at the modern writer who solemnly informs us that "A sight-line taken vertically up the middle of the penis on May Day would have pointed directly at the rising sun as it came over the crest of the down." (The observant visitor to Trafalgar Square might notice that a sight-line taken vertically up the middle of Nelson's cockade on the summer solstice would point directly at the sun as it reached its meridian.) Barren women were said to conceive if they spent a night on the potent member, and learned men argue that the figure represents Hercules or some forgotten deity. Personally, I should opt for the hunter Orion, who is up there in the night sky flashing his mighty weapon as he lecherously chases the virgin Pleiades. He was renowned as a rain-maker and deserved overtime pay as a fertility figure. This would explain why the giant is carved so enormously on the curved hillside that he can only be seen properly from the heavens. Pagan imagery is part of the character of this area, however, whether genuine or fictitious, and as elsewhere the stone itself is part of the folklore.

From Dogbury Gate, a little way north of Cerne Abbas, a road leads west to Evershot, with fine views from High Stoy and Gore Hill – among Hardy's 'Wessex Heights' – the latter looking down on the Cross-and-Hand on Batcombe Down. It is an isolated, eerie monolith, about which various legends have gathered, but is probably only an ancient signpost. Hardy represented Tess as swearing an oath of fidelity on it.

Sydling St Nicholas is a peaceful street village, tucked away from main roads, and although there is an intrusion of brick, there is much flint and stone in the walls of its thatched cottages, and a long village pond opening out from the stream flowing through. The large tithe barn is built of flint, with stone buttresses, but the old roof, sad to say, has been replaced by corrugated iron. Celtic field systems have been traced on the hills surrounding the village.

Rampisham is another quiet place, watered by a clear stream in a valley with church and manor house in close company and a village school of stone which, like so many others, was being sold for conversion into dwelling-houses when I was there a few years ago.

The road through Evershot continues to Beaminster, near which town is Stoke Abbot, a beautiful village nestling along deep lanes in an amphitheatre of hills, with several thatched houses. It does not get a lot of attention in the guidebooks, and perhaps that is what makes it so attractive. In an area where communicating roads between villages are not plentiful, it is off the beaten track and seems to me everything that a traditional English village should be. It is muddy in winter, because no main road is anywhere near it, and its traffic is in farm vehicles. Its building is of haphazard growth, unplanned about its Norman church, but lovely in its effect, with roofs of thatch keeping dry the mullioned windows of warm limestone, and even the odd perversity of a corrugated-iron shed roof cannot spoil its cosy indifference to the ordered chaos of life beyond the village confines, which seems like a different world though only a mile or two away. The place never begins to look, as some of our more enthusiastically adored villages do, as if it had been specially created out of a heap of stones and set up for our admiration like a work of art, and thus it is all the more admirable. There was a thickish fog the last time my wife and I negotiated the lane from Beaminster to look at it, but even then it seemed warm and welcoming – not posing like a prima donna – and in summer it is the

Coursed house walls and random boundary walls at Stoke Abbot.

Calypso of my odyssey: an island nymph promising immortality in its sun-drenched arms.

Powerstock and Netherbury both have some attractive stone building. Powerstock is largely Victorian, but its church of St Mary has a richly ornamented Norman chancel arch, and a little way outside the village a motte-and-bailey earthwork is known as Powerstock Castle. Netherbury is neat, with its church standing above houses which are mostly on the west bank of the River Brit.

Melplash is no more than a hamlet between them, and unfortunately on the main road, but the gabled Tudor manor house was the home of the More family whose most illustrious member was the saintly Sir Thomas. One of their monuments is in Netherbury church. The house has been much altered and extended since those distant days.

Farther south, near the coast again, is Chideock (pronounced Chiddick) which is built, for a change, of yellow sandstone, protruding in from Devon. This village also suffers from its main-road position, but to the south of it is Golden Cap, the highest cliff on the south coast, with the sandstone forming the flat top that gives it its name.

It is around Sherborne, in the north-west corner of Dorset, that the limestone villages of this county perhaps reach their climax. I have already mentioned Ryme Intrinseca, and, like it, its large neighbour Yetminster is on the 'cornbrash' limestone, but, unlike it, it is still

The Dorset style at Yetminster.

composed almost entirely of the native material – a coarse yellow stone now considered inferior for building purposes. But this village makes a very stylish picture and a study in local architecture, with mullioned windows of three or four lights in serried ranks all along the main street, whether manor house, school, farm or humble cottage, and most of these buildings of the sixteenth to the eighteenth century.

Much of the stone building in this corner of Dorset has been carried out with material from just over the border in Somerset – the gold Liassic limestone that makes Sherborne one of the cosiest-looking small towns in England. Its satellites are Bradford Abbas, Trent, Nether and Over Compton and Sandford Orcas. Each has its delights, but collectively they are like a golden tiara about the head of this princess of English towns. How I wish it were a village so that I could dwell on its charms.

Trent is perhaps the best of the local villages, with its old stone houses grouped near its fascinating church and completely without any formal village plan, in contrast to Nether Compton, which makes a slight concession in having a village green, although its warm stone cottages are not arranged round it. Sandford Orcas has a charming small manor house of the mid-sixteenth century, little altered since it was first built. It is supposed to be haunted by many ghosts, and the apes carved in stone have been heard laughing in the moonlight.

Bradford Abbas is a very appealing village, to my mind. Its church has a fine tower, and the west doorway is protected by a porch with a cusped arch and a curious little gable, but it all, alas, shows the sad gradual disintegration of the soft golden limestone. There is some modern building in stone in the area, however – an encouraging sign, perhaps, though it is difficult to be optimistic about the future of stone building. Ralph Wightman was able to write in the sixties that in recent years there had been "some realisation that the building stone of Dorset is within easy reach and since it is good enough to be exported across the Atlantic it might as well be used at home". But it is still expensive, compared with the mass-produced modern building materials.

Passing over the border into Somerset, the villages around Yeovil provide some of the greatest delights of all the limestone country of England, and I do not except the Cotswolds from this judgement. The Ham Hill quarry which has provided the golden stone glowing so warmly in the local cottage walls is situated a little to the west of Montacute. The proper name of the site in Hamdon Hill. It adjoins the hill from which Montacute takes its name, *'mons acutus'* ('pointed hill'), now known as St Michael's Hill and topped by a folly where once a castle stood. The top of Hamdon Hill itself bears Iron Age earthworks, but the disused quarry pits dominate the scene. The stone is described sometimes as Oolitic limestone, sometimes as Liassic, sometimes as a shelly sandstone, but whatever it is, its effect in buildings is beautiful. It has been quarried since Roman times. Ham Hill stone is a freestone readily given a fine ashlar finish and amenable to intricate carving. Although it tends to wear and split after a long life in buildings, and thus to cause some trouble to the owners of ancient houses, it continues to delight the eye. Tinted with iron and mottled with lichens, it radiates warmth and happiness like a golden girl on a sunny beach.

Montacute is itself a tribute to the unrivalled attractions of Ham stone. The open square of the large village is flanked by weathered Ham stone houses, and if the place is a little showy and formal, that is understandable, for it boasts one of England's finest Elizabethan mansions, Montacute House, which was built of the same stone nearly four hundred years ago. The house was built for Sir Edward Phelips, a Speaker of the House of Commons and Master of the Rolls, and the prosecutor of Guy Fawkes. Its architect is not known with certainty, but what he achieved here is a classic of Tudor craftsmanship, not large by the standards of most stately homes but exquisite in its use of the stone, both inside and out, unadulterated by later extensions in contrary styles. Great balustrades, terraces and towers stand above the lawns and yew hedges, with curved gables, oriel windows and obelisks all drawing the eye toward this honey-coloured treasure of the

Garden wall and gazebo of Ham stone at Montacute House.

National Trust in grounds scented by roses and shaded by cedar trees.

Beneath Hamdon Hill is Stoke-sub-Hamdon, and scattered around this southern fringe of Somerset between Yeovil and the Blackdown Hills are several other villages in which cottages, houses and churches display the mellow qualities of Ham stone – East Coker, Middle Chinnock, Hinton St George and Barrington among the best of them, with Odcombe and Haselbury Plucknett as 'also rans'.

East Coker – once preoccupied with making sailcloth – was the birthplace of William Dampier, the seventeenth-century mariner to whom piracy, shipwreck and privation were all part of his experience of the sea. He was aboard the ship that rescued Alexander Selkirk from the island of Juan Fernandez, giving Defoe the seed from which *Robinson Crusoe* grew. Dampier sailed round parts of the Australian coast seventy years before Cook and was alarmed as much by the kangaroos he saw as by the Aborigines. His navigational skills and scientific observations were admired by Nelson, among others, and there is a brass to his memory in the village church of St Michael, which also contains the remains of a more recent repatriate to the land of his fathers.

A cordwainer, Andrew Eliot, who was also a Puritan, left this village to sail to America before Dampier was born here. He became the Town Clerk of Boston, Massachusetts, and took part in the Salem witch-hunt of 1692. His descendant Thomas came to England in 1914 to study at Oxford and stayed for the rest of his life, becoming a naturalized British subject. T. S. Eliot made East Coker the subject of the second part of his *Four Quartets* and asked that his ashes should be buried in this church:

> Here, whence his forbears sprang, a man is laid
> As dust, in quiet earth. . . .

Near the church is the old manor house, Coker Court, which is now a school, and below it a row of almshouses, all built with the local stone that makes East Coker one of the loveliest villages in the area.

Hinton St George, towards Windwhistle Hill, is its chief rival, although some modern housing not entirely sympathetic to the old village has crept in. Hinton House was for centuries the home of the Poulett family, whose members included that Sir Amyass Poulett who was rather put out at Queen Elizabeth's suggestion that he should quietly murder his charge at Fotheringhay, Mary, Queen of Scots. His conscience was mocked as 'daintiness' by the Queen. A later Poulett must have been caused some embarrassment by a later queen. The Lord Poulett who became MP for Bridgwater in the eighteenth century had the Queen for a godmother and was given her name as his own – Anne. The monuments of all the Pouletts are in the village church, and the village inn is called the 'Poulett Arms'.

The last Thursday in October is the time to be at Hinton St George. This is 'Punkie Night' when local children parade around the village with their punkies, singing

> It's Punkie Night tonight.
> Give us a candle, give us a light,
> If you don't, you'll get a fright.
> It's Punkie Night tonight.

The 'punkies' are hollowed out mangolds or turnips, strung at the top and decorated with faces or other designs and with candles burning inside them. This pagan tradition is undoubtedly a local variant on the Hallowe'en Guisers ritual, in which the figures with their lanterns represent those who have come back from the dead.

It is typical of the stone villages of England that the dead refuse to lie down, for when a new village policeman, unfamiliar with the area, tried to ban the ceremony just before the Second World War, strong complaints to the Chief Constable secured the right of the village to carry on with its tradition. The Chief Constable of Dorset, not many years afterwards, was similarly driven to overrule an officer who tried to stop a ceremony at Abbotsbury called Garland Day, held on 13th May, when children go round the village with garlands of flowers on poles, to bring luck to the householders. This is a relic of an ancient tradition which was originally intended to bring good luck to Abbotsbury's fishing fleet.

Barrington is another lovely village of Ham stone, chiefly notable for the large house, Barrington Court (National Trust), with its twisted chimneys and mullioned and transomed windows, standing in remarkable harmony with the thatched cottages of the villagers. It was built by the first Earl of Bridgewater, and one of its curiosities is a stone basin at the original front door for visitors to wash their hands in. It was the later owners, the Strode family, who perversely introduced red brick to the scene in their seventeenth-century stable block.

"The apples aren't much good," a man at Crock Street told me as we stopped at the old apple tree in his garden. I looked at him doubtfully. Could there be such a thing as a no-good apple in scrumpy country? The tree, at any rate, had mistletoe growing on it – that parasitic plant held in such reverence by pagan peoples that it was banned from Christian churches. Frazer thought it was the mythical Golden Bough with which Aeneas ventured into the Underworld. It is supposed to give protection against lightning, epilepsy, witchcraft, barrenness, ulcers, nightmares and poison, among other things. The snag is that a sprig of the stuff has to be broken off by throwing stones at it when the sun is in Sagittarius and the moon is on the wane. Its healing properties are nullified if you cut it with a knife blade. Besides, the host tree should be oak, not apple. But there is no law, ancient or modern, to say that you cannot cut a sprig and kiss a pretty girl under it, and that might be as good a cure as the stuff the doctor prescribes.

Yeovil is the only industrial centre in this area, and many of its surrounding villages – over the border in Dorset as well as in Somerset – have become expanded dormitories for its workers, with the inevitable result that what were once stone villages have often become nondescript places spoilt by modern housing in unsympathetic building materials. All the more praise is due, therefore, to those villages which have resisted such development. Yeovil supplied many of them with employment before the growth of factory industry, for it has long been a leading centre of the leather glove-making trade, and before the Industrial Revolution this was a cottage industry, employing many women and children in the surrounding villages to cut and stitch gloves in their homes. Women and girls living in unhealthy cottages were forced to work long hours to supplement the wages of their menfolk, who could not support their families on the fourteen or

The golden ensemble at Brympton d'Evercy.

fifteen shillings a week they received as agricultural labourers. Besides, the farmers were turning arable land into pasture and needed fewer workers, so young men and boys were deserting the villages to go to the towns, or even to South Wales to work in the pits. It is not easy, when we stand in these villages today making admiring comparisons with the ugliness of our large towns, to imagine the social hardships their stones have witnessed.

Brympton d'Evercy is arguably not a village – nor even a hamlet – at all, but no one who has seen it will complain that I should not have sneaked it into this book. It lies just west of Yeovil and was a private estate, reached by a long avenue of oaks and consisting of manor house, church, dower house and stables, all standing together in a breathtakingly picturesque group of golden stone. It is one of the outstanding sights of the southern limestone belt. The manor passed from the d'Evercy family to the Sydenhams, who owned it for many generations and built the manor house beside the older church. The story goes that John Stourton, a Somerset Member of Parliament, owned three manors and had three wives and three daughters, so he was able to give each daughter a manor, and Joan Stourton got Brympton d'Evercy as a wedding gift when she was married to John Sydenham in 1434. The dower house was built for her to live in during her old age. Nowhere is the mellow beauty of Ham Hill stone more dazzlingly eloquent than in this ensemble of Tudor buildings.

The limestone continues northwards beyond Yeovil – past the apple orchards of the scrumpy country – where we come to tiny places with lovely names such as Queen Camel, Chilton Cantelo and North and South Cadbury. Each has its various attractions, with much yellowy-grey stone building. Queen Camel is a well-cared-for village, with a narrow stone packhorse bridge over the stream, whilst North Cadbury is built mainly in Ham stone, but its southern neighbour has allowed much brick to intrude. To the west of the latter village, however, is the famous hill of Cadbury Castle. Flat-topped, with its slopes well wooded, it is formed of Oolitic limestone. This is one of the largest Iron Age hill-forts in Britain, with ditches and stone ramparts whose remains are now buried. The graves of many men have been found in the vicinity, and folklore attributes the fortress to King Arthur, whose legendary Camelot this is often supposed to be. "At South Cadbyri," wrote Leland in 1542, "standith Camallate, sumtyme a famose toun or castelle. The people can tell nothing thar but that they have hard say that Arture much resortid to Camalat." It is less stark and intimidating than the great looming mass of Maiden Castle, near Dorchester, but it has as much mystery about it. Four hundred years after the Roman invasion, the 'fire of vengeance' blazed in the Celtic peoples of the west, and they rose to defend their land against the Saxons under the leadership of a mighty warrior who is fondly supposed to have been Arthur.

Cadbury Castle has been the scene of much activity by archaeologists in recent years, spurred on by the discovery, in the fifties, of sherds of Tintagel ware on the site. Many interesting finds have been made, but so far the existence of Arthur has not been proved. Personally, I am sceptical of the advantages to be gained by discovering the truth. The destruction of myths by science is not wholly to be applauded. We trade in romance for information in an age when many of those who have abandoned belief in God have merely set Truth up on the same altar and worshipped that instead, thus substituting fear of probable nuclear war for fear of possible hellfire. Wisdom is what we should be seeking, not Heaven, nor Truth-at-any-price.

North Cheriton, Horsington and Temple Combe are strung out beside the main road south from Wincanton, none of them among the best that Somerset can offer but each built of the warm limestone and having its individual charm. Temple Combe was a home of the Knights Templars, but hardly anything remains of their chapel.

Butleigh, westward on the fringes of the Polden Hills, is associated with the Hoods of illustrious memory in the annals of the Royal Navy. The stone is distinctly cooler now, but the village has much interesting

The grey limestone tower of
St John Baptist at Pilton.

Castle and church at Nunney.

old building and some new, in stone with pantile roofs, round the green which used to be an apple orchard.

Moving further north, Pylle and Pilton, just south of Shepton Mallett, bring us to the fringes of the Mendips, and the roads rising up the slopes give us a view of the larger village in a hollow below, with its fine church and cottages among magnificent chestnut trees, and the ruins of an ancient tithe barn on the hillside above it. The barn belonged to Glastonbury Abbey, Arthur's Avalon, and the well-known landmark Glastonbury Tor, five miles away, can be seen from here. Medallions of the four Evangelists on the gables of the barn echo those on the abbey barn below the Tor.

The stone is no longer the yellow, honey or gold of Ham Hill, however, but is unequivocally grey. It came from the quarries at Doulting, only a mile or two away, which supplied the stone for Glastonbury Abbey and Wells Cathedral. Until the dissolution of the monasteries, Glastonbury owned the quarries, which are just north of the village. It is a coarse-grained Oolitic limestone, still worked on a small scale, for it has been used to face motorway bridges in the area.

Doulting stone can be seen at its best at Nunney, five miles east. Although brick and rendering have found their way here, it is a fine village with its church and castle on either side of a street which is spanned by the inn sign of 'The George'. Actually Nunney's 'castle' is a fortified mansion, crenellated under licence by Sir John de la Mare, but it had its moments in history. During the Civil War, under siege by Cromwell's troops, its Royalist occupants tortured their only pig each day to deceive the enemy into thinking from the squeals that they were well supplied with livestock for slaughter. The ruse failed, with what results we can now see.

As the Mendip Hills rear up from the valley here, we are obliged to make a slight diversion, for this range supports a few stone villages not to be missed. The character of the rock here changes from oolite to the more ancient Carboniferous limestone, sometimes helpfully called Mountain Limestone. This is the stuff of Cheddar Gorge and Wookey Hole. It is hard, rough and of a cold grey colour, and though it has not been used as extensively as the Jurassic stone in domestic building, it can be seen in some villages and in isolated farmhouses and field walls.

Croscombe, between Shepton Mallet and Wells, is still too near the Jurassic limestone to be consistent in its use of one or the other, but it is an interesting village of assorted colours beneath its pantile roofs. The church of St Mary has one of Somerset's finest spires, but it had to be rebuilt after being struck by lightning in 1936. Great care was taken to obtain matching stone, and the masons did such a good job that you can hardly tell where work of the fifteenth century ends and that of the twentieth begins. The interior is full of richly carved Jacobean oak, adding to the overall impression of prosperity here, for the village had a thriving woollen and other textile industry.

Wedmore lies in the flat landscape of the Somerset Levels, between the Polden Hills and the Mendips, on an outlier above what was once marshy waste, and so it is called the Isle of Wedmore. It shares the grey stone of the Mendips and some of the appearance of a town, having been a royal residence once, long ago, and though its prosperity and population have declined, it still calls its centre 'the Borough'. Alfred the Great lived here, and in 878 he signed the Treaty of Wedmore which brought short-lived peace between Danes and Anglo-Saxons.

One unusual village building bears the inscription "John Westover, chyrurgeon". It is a house with mullioned windows, built in 1680 specially for the surgeon's mental patients, and must have been, for the time, an enlightened establishment, for the insane then were still, as a rule, thrown into cells like pigsties, always ill-treated and frequently chained, and abandoned to the evil spirits that were thought to possess them.

Churchill is on the northern edge of the Mendips in Avon county and was the ancestral home of the family whose name it bears. It is a commuter village for Bristol workers now, but Churchill Court still stands, which Ralphe Jenyns sold to an ancestor of the Duke of Marlborough way back.

Chewton Mendip, back in Somerset, proclaims the capabilities of the local limestone in its typically splendid church tower. It was built with the profits from lead mining by Carthusian monks of the Bethlehem House of Sheen and shows really superb stone carving in its pinnacles, tracery and figures – one of whom appears to be a bagpiper, a long way from home, one might think, but the Romans introduced pipes into England, whence they spread to Scotland and Ireland and survived there after mercifully groaning themselves into oblivion in most of England. A seat in the chancel is reckoned to be a 'frid stool', where criminals could claim sanctuary from their pursuers. Also in this church is the tomb of Countess Waldegrave, whose family occupied the house on the site of the old priory. Lady Waldegrave was a leading society hostess, whose dinner guests in Carlton Gardens laughed merrily at the nonsense of Edward Lear and nodded solemnly, I dare say, at the nonsense of William Ewart Gladstone.

Kilmersdon has another fine tower at its solid stone centre, as well as a stone lock-up which must have detained many a drunken villager for a night beneath the sobering gaze of stone beasts and gargoyles on the church.

Back on the main course of the Jurassic limestone, the oolite again supplies the stone for some fine villages and is seen to perfection at Mells, scattered about low hills which bear several prehistoric camps. The village itself has more than one green and many trees intermingled with the stone buildings. 'Elm, Mells and Vobster', a signpost says, and if this sounds like a firm of solicitors, Mells does have a kind of formal dignity about it, and those who prefer stylishness to homely informality call it the most beautiful village in Somerset.

The Benedictine monks of Glastonbury owned the estate until the Dissolution, when one John Horner, bailiff to the abbot, reputedly acquired the manor for himself by subterfuge – hence Little Jack Horner who "put in his thumb and pulled out a plum". His descendants enjoyed the plum for centuries afterwards, and their memorials are in the Horner Chapel of the majestic church of St Andrew, specially noted for its fine Somerset tower. One of the Horner daughters was married to Raymond Asquith, the Prime Minister's son, who was killed in action in the First World War. The church contains work by Burne-Jones, Munnings and Lutyens, who also designed Mells Park House, beyond the church and manor house. The latter, a splendid stone mansion in gardens graced by hedges of yew, has a Catholic chapel attached to it. Ronald Knox, the priest and scholar, lived here during his last years as a guest of Lord and Lady Oxford, whilst working on his translation of the Old Testament, and his grave is in a corner of the churchyard.

Father Knox (who was alleged to have said at the age of four, when asked what he did at night if he could not sleep, that he lay awake and thought about the past) was no less witty than his brother E.V., the professional humorist and one-time editor of *Punch*, who once made a comment about English villages that we should perhaps take to heart: "I cannot choose a favourite, because directly I remember the one that I admired the most I remember another that I admired still more."

Wellow is at the edge of the oolite in Avon county, one of Somerset's sadder losses in the administrative reorganization of 1974, for it is an attractive place owing much to the Hungerford family who built its church, unspoilt and full of interest. Farther west, on the north side of the Mendips, Cameley is worth notice. It sports red pantiles above its grey stone walls, rare occurrences in the west of England but profuse in this particular area. It is hardly more than a hamlet, but it has a church with an odd notice at the churchyard gate: "Although visitors are most cordially welcomed to the church, treasure hunts are forbidden in its precincts."

Most of the treasure hunted in this region has been coal, lead and building stone, and the scars of industry share the landscape with the villages here as the workers of Bristol share them with the countrymen. Much of medieval Bristol itself was built of Oolitic limestone from the quarries on the saddle-backed Dundry Hill (from which fine views can be enjoyed) just outside the city, and this stone can be seen in the church and cottage walls of Dundry village. A great variety of local stones, in fact, is visible in the villages south of Bristol, including some sandstone. We have veered westward from the main limestone belt, however, and our proper course will take us into the Cotswolds, but first we must turn eastward to look at the villages we have missed in Wiltshire.

Like Dorset, much of this county is chalk, which forms Salisbury Plain and the Marlborough Downs, and on which there are villages with much building in combinations of flint and brick, or flint and other stone, such as Tilshead, very characteristic of Wiltshire, with cottages whose walls are of chequered patterns of stone and flint with roofs of thatch. If it were not that the road between Amesbury and Devizes bends through it, this would be one of the most isolated villages in the south of England. It was a prosperous town once, as can be seen from the size of its church.

The limestone proper begins farther south, at Chilmark and the villages round it in the Nadder valley. The quarries at Chilmark, still operating on a small scale, have been famous for many centuries, producing a sandy glauconite limestone which is creamy white in colour at first but weathers to a greeny tint. Some of this stone was mined, rather than quarried, and the tunnels of the old workings, closed before the Second World War, are fenced off and in use by the Ministry of Defence. A quarry has since been re-opened to provide Chilmark stone. The greatest monument to Chilmark stone is Salisbury Cathedral, and the second greatest Wilton House, but the villages hereabouts are also built of it, and Chilmark itself displays it well enough in its church, houses, cottages and the little bridges crossing the stream.

Stone bridges feature prominently in Teffont Evias too, crossing the stream to give access to each house on the other side, and this village forms a delightful group with its larger neighbour, Teffont Magna, and Dinton, a little farther east. Dinton is a trifle showy compared with the sleepy Teffonts. No less than four of its houses are owned by the National Trust. Philipps House stands in beautifully landscaped grounds on the hillside, in neo-classical design by Jeffrey Wyatville. It is leased to the YWCA and used as a conference centre. The Old Rectory is on the site of what is believed to have been the birthplace, in 1608, of Edward Hyde, the first Earl of Clarendon and historian of the Civil War. He also lived at the creeper-covered Tudor mansion known as Little Clarendon, whilst his contemporary Henry Lawes, the composer, who collaborated with his friend John Milton on the masque *Comus*, lived in rather humbler circumstances at Lawes Cottage, close to the church.

Fonthill Gifford, a few miles west of Chilmark, is a tiny place straddling a crossroads, but it occupies a bizarre niche in the story of English stone building by virtue of that folly to end all follies (one might have hoped) Fonthill Abbey. William Beckford, the son of a Lord Mayor of London who had grown immensely wealthy from West Indian sugar-cane plantations, was a spoilt boy who had graduated to megalomania by the time his father's Palladian mansion, Fonthill Splendens, came into his possession. In 1796 he employed James Wyatt – that much-belaboured exponent of Gothic Revivalism – to build him a 'ruined' convent, of which sufficient should *remain intact* for him to live in it occasionally. During the next few years he hastened to have the building expanded until it was a hair-raising fantasy as eccentric as the sham castles built by Ludwig of Bavaria. A central octagon tower rose 276 feet into the air, above the cruciform wings of this architectural wonder, and the estate was surrounded by a twelve-foot-high wall. The whole was built of local stone, and Beckford reputedly spent half a million pounds on his enchanted abbey. Nelson came to stay with Sir William and Lady Hamilton, and Beckford lived in the place for fifteen years, but at length his money ran out, and he sold Fonthill to another eccentric, John Farquhar, for little more than

'Fonthill from a Stone Quarry' by J. M. W. Turner.

half of what it had cost him. Two years later the walls came tumbling down, as proper foundations had not been provided under the great tower. The whole fantastic building, a sham ruin, became a real one, and little now remains of what Hazlitt called "a glittering waste of industrious idleness".

The Oolitic limestone again breaks out in Wiltshire north of the Avon, where Broughton Gifford, Monkton Farleigh and South Wraxall stand clad in their grey stone between Bath and Melksham. Monkton Farleigh's own quarries at Farleigh Down produced the stone for these villages. This one stands on a little hilltop and introduces us to an architectural oddity of the district, the saddle-backed church tower. South Wraxall has two more. I say 'oddity' because saddle-backed roofs are far from being an architectural speciality of the region, yet there is a small crop of them in this vicinity. South Wraxall's chief attraction, however, is the medieval manor house built by the Long family, whose tombs are in the church and whose arms are on the village inn. The manor's gatehouse has an oriel window in the upper room and stands at the entrance to a fifteenth-century house round three sides of a courtyard, making a picturesque group. Broughton Gifford spreads itself expansively round a large green on which is Gifford Hall, an attractive house of 1688.

The stone from Monkton Farleigh is of a variety of oolite called Bath

Overleaf: Castle Combe, Wiltshire.

stone, and it has been mined, more often than quarried, from the rock spread over a fairly wide area. It was mined because the cost of removing the 'overburden' would have been greater than the cost of digging tunnels. Bath stone was immensely popular at one time, and no greater tribute could be paid to its qualities than the city of Bath itself. Its great drawback is its porosity, resulting in a lack of long-term durability. Nash used it on Buckingham Palace, which had to be refaced later with Portland stone. It was Ralph Allen, the philanthropic 'Man of Bath', who exploited some of the existing local quarries and owned others in his great collaboration with the John Woods, father and son. The most reserved of men, Allen was taken by Fielding as the model for Squire Allworthy in *Tom Jones* and was complimented by Pope (which was quite an achievement) who said that he "did good by stealth and blushed to find it fame". He built a tramway to transport stone from the Monkton Down quarries, which were subsequently linked with the Kennet and Avon Canal.

The construction in 1841 of the Box Tunnel, on the Great Western Railway, gave added impetus to stone mining and quarrying in the area, which had hitherto relied on transportation by horse-drawn carts or by river and canal. Most of the quarries have closed down now, but one or two still operate, notably those at Hazelbury and Monks Park, Corsham. The former is an open-cast quarry, the latter a mine. Many miles of shafts were excavated in the hillsides here from a huge cavern which became known as 'the Cathedral'. The quarrymen held their meetings in it when there were industrial disputes, and when it was finally closed, it was much used by courting couples and youngsters searching for bats' nests. Then mushroom growing was carried on in some of the galleries, but now these mines, like the one at Chilmark, have been taken over, rather ominously, by the Ministry of Defence. The stone which came from them is honey-coloured at its best and hints at the pleasures of the Cotswolds to come, but before we reach the hills of Avon and Gloucestershire, Wiltshire has one or two more treasures in store.

Biddestone – note the suffix – is the first of them. It is an extremely comely village. Its long green is terminated by the village duckpond and flanked by fine houses in which the stone is still grey – not yet the honeyed tones of the Cotswold oolite. But the roofs are of stone tiles: the thatch has gone, and one knows that this is different country from that farther south. Yatton Yeynell, with its seventeenth-century manor house, is likewise grey, but a mile along the B road on which it stands, the warmer soft brown colour emerges in one of the most famous of English villages, which is not of the Cotswolds in nature but belongs to them in spirit.

Castle Combe has arguably been 'shot' by photographers more often than any other village in the country, and at first sight it looks as if it might have been built for the purpose. It has posed sedately not only for tourists' snapshots but for cinema and television cameramen and is so self-consciously picturesque that you almost feel that, if you walk beyond the three-arched bridge over the By Brook and look behind its huddled cottages and church, it will turn out to be a film set, designed in Hollywood and propped up at the back with timber scaffolding. But Castle Combe is real enough, and as a beautiful fashion model has a personality behind her exaggerated pose, so this village's incomparable façade disguises an ancient community. The Romans knew the spot, for the Fosse Way passes by, and various remains have been found in the vicinity.

It was a prosperous weaving centre once – Defoe called it a town. The villagers wove cloth in a cottage industry and then delivered it to the Weavers' House, which is still there, by the stream that trickles through the little wooded combe where the village nestles. The castle which gave the settlement its name was built by Walter de Dunstanville in the thirteenth century. Little of that remains, but there is an effigy of its builder in the Perpendicular village church built by the wealthy clothiers, with a fine turreted tower, fan tracery in its vaulted roof, and a splendid chancel arch. It stands near a little square in which the market cross, covered by a roof supported on stone pillars, also holds aloft a crocketed spire, and nearby is the manor house, originally built in the seventeenth century but subsequently Victorianized and now converted to hotel use.

Aye, there's the rub. For such a village, with a population of five hundred, to require a hotel, when Chippenham is but a stone's throw away, it must set up house as a showplace and spread its favours as the model might, and in the hotel's wake have come car-parks and gift shops and double yellow lines which shine brighter than the mellow stone in its cosy old walls, to say nothing of the M4 motorway, which misses it by a whisker and jettisons sightseers popping in as casually from London, Wales and Birmingham as if they were next-door neighbours. Castle Combe is undeniably beautiful, but it has the air of a ham actress trying to upstage her rivals. Making an exhibition of herself, she gets everyone to stare at her, but in the end it is the quiet naturalness of more modest performers that makes the best impression.

CHAPTER 4

The Limestone – Cotswolds

Beyond Bath the Oolitic limestone gradually widens out in a northern direction as far as the Gloucestershire border, then veers eastward, its southern limit heading toward Oxford. The Cotswold Hills begin north of Bath, rising gently from the clay plain, and define the northern limit of the oolite along the steep escarpment facing the valley of the Severn, until they swing eastward past Cheltenham, petering out on the lias near Banbury, a distance of a little over sixty miles. The hills are mainly in Gloucestershire and Oxfordshire, with one end just trailing into Avon and Wiltshire, and the other into Hereford and Worcester. Although the limestone belt as a whole is much wider in the East Midlands, the oolite itself is at its widest in the Cotswolds.

Generally speaking, the farther north you travel in the Cotswolds, the warmer the stone becomes. The cool grey of the southern hills gives way to a buff-grey in the central areas, and the iron content enriches it to a browny-grey at the north-eastern end. For the convenient arrangement of this book, I shall use the term Cotswold a little loosely, to include some villages in their vicinity which, though not strictly of the Cotswold Hills, belong to them in spirit.

The hills themselves have an average height of five to six hundred feet, reaching their highest point at Cleeve Hill (1,134 feet) between Cheltenham and Winchcombe. Hillsides clad in beechwoods shelter winding valleys with villages nestling in them, and the sheep which made the Cotswolds wealthy graze fields defined always by dry-stone walls of grey or yellow limestone. "Anything so ugly I have never seen before," wrote Cobbett in the 1820s, expressing a distaste which was by no means unusual in those days, as we have seen.

The natural fracturing of the rock near the surface produces flattish rectangular stones of two or three inches thickness, which are laid to build walls usually about three feet high. The walls taper slightly for stability, being a few inches narrower at the top than they are at the foot, and the stones are arranged to tilt downwards to the wall's faces, so that rainwater runs off and does not collect in the wall to become a cause of frost damage. The top of the wall is traditionally capped with a row of vertical stones called 'combers' by some and 'cock-ups' by

Oolitic limestone: Stanton, Gloucestershire.

others. It deters animals from attempting to get over the wall. Built in this way, a wall will last for many generations with little attention apart from minor repair. The man who does the job is a 'waller'. Alas, some walls nowadays are being given flat coping stones and even, sometimes, cement cappings.

Such is the undisputed superiority of vernacular building in this region that 'Cotswold stone' has come to be regarded as a thing apart, although it is geologically no different from that in Dorset or Yorkshire and indeed is inferior to the products of these counties in certain respects, particularly when used outside its natural environment, as it often has been. It does not take kindly to a smoky atmosphere and is less durable than several harder oolites. In its proper context among the Cotswold Hills themselves, however, the grey stone looks so right that many people regard the settlements here as the epitome of English village building. In terms of picturesque qualities and consistency, it is difficult to argue with that view.

Part of the secret is the abundance of easily worked freestone, which is used on roofs as well as in walls, and for churches, barns, houses, garden walls, cow sheds and pigsties, bridges and the very gravestones in the churchyards, so that there is a splendid and stylish harmony in everything we see. The floors of the cottages were laid with stone flags a century ago, and the kitchen sink was carved from a solid block. Even barns here can have an elegance that one would hardly expect in other parts.

There were so many quarries here at one time, and so many thousands of quarrymen and masons employed in them, that you would think they must have dug the hills flat, but a mere handful of men now work in the few quarries to have survived.

The village names lose the double-barrelled lyricism of Somerset and Dorset, for we are approaching the down-to-earth, no-nonsense Midlands, where a spade might be called a bloody shovel, and 'Great' and 'Little' are the only prefixes when neighbouring communities share the same name. Such names are ancient, and it is not unusual to find that the village called 'Little' has outgrown the one called 'Great', owing to more favourable economic or social circumstances.

Hill country can always be counted on to harbour religious dissent, but chapels are not as much in evidence in the villages as might be expected, for the Cotswold folk did not make a show of their Nonconformism. They are country people in whom the wine of paganism permeates the blood of more formal beliefs. There is a dark side to the Cotswolds, if only judging by the frequency of plays on radio and television set in the region and dealing with occult and macabre practices. Those intimidating survivals from a mysterious and awe-inspiring prehistory in the south, like Stonehenge and Maiden Castle,

Wallers at work in the Cotswolds. The soft limestone can be dressed to regular shape and laid in courses like bricks.

A barn at Upper Slaughter, Gloucestershire. The walls are of thin courses of limestone and the roof of graded stone 'tiles'.

Bisley, Gloucestershire, from the church lych-gate.

give way here to a strong current of more recent country lore, much given to ghosts, witches and religious rites, more often associated with fertility and the harvest than with petrified symbols.

Most of the smaller houses and cottages in the Cotswold villages date from the seventeenth and eighteenth centuries, when the prosperity which had made wool towns like Chipping Campden and Cirencester so stylish in earlier centuries spread to the valleys with the weaving industry and enabled the villagers to build their homes of stone to replace the poor country hovels of medieval times. Cotswold architecture, however, possesses a remarkably consistent and immediately recognizable style, present in the humble cottage as well as in the fine town house. Gabled roofs, built at a steep pitch, are covered in stone tiles, and subsidiary gables have dormer windows in them, bedrooms usually being in the roof space. The steep slope of the roof has the same purpose as in thatched buildings. The limestone tiles are porous, so the rain needs to be run off rapidly.

Windows nearly always have stone mullions supporting heavy lintels with moulded drip-stones above, and decorative carving of the stonework is frequent. The nature of the stone shows itself clearly in the churches, so often built by wealthy wool merchants and decorated with precise and detailed carving. The churches rarely have spires. Those villages fortunate enough not to have a single brick wall, iron railing or concrete lamp-post to disturb their elegant uniformity of style and colour, are certainly the most tasteful and natural of all the villages of England. As J. B. Priestley put it unbeatably half a century ago: "Even when the sun is obscured and the light is cold . . . these walls are still faintly warm and luminous, as if they knew the trick of keeping the lost sunlight of centuries glimmering about them."

One of the curiosities of this region might lead one to think that those mushrooms grown in underground quarry tunnels had swollen to enormous size and become petrified like stalagmites. In fact, the stone mushroom-shaped objects one sees so frequently in the Cotswolds, used as garden ornaments or finials on gate-posts, or as bollards to restrict parking, were originally made as 'rick-staddles' or 'staddle-stones', for farmers to support their haystacks on. They allowed air to circulate beneath the hay and prevented rats from getting in.

It might well be the Cotswolds that gave us the word 'stone' as a measure of weight. In medieval England, farmers had stones weighing fourteen pounds to test the weight of the fleeces they sold to wool merchants. The travelling merchants carried weights around with them, also totalling fourteen pounds. With these they could check the accuracy of the farmer's stone and, added to it, they balanced the finest fleeces, which weighed twenty-eight pounds.

Many a seventeenth-century Cotsaller gave lusty voice to a popular drinking song in the local inns. It was so popular as to be almost a regional anthem:

> The stones, the stones, the stones,
> The stones, the stones, the stones,
> The stones, the stones, the stones.
>
> The stones that built George Ridler's oven
> And they came from the Bleakeney's quar,
> George he was a jolly old man,
> And his head grew above his hair.

The song goes on for several verses, not making much better sense, at first sight, than the alternating chorus of "stones, stones, stones", but in fact it was a Royalist song with much cryptic symbolism. 'George Ridler' was Charles I, whose head grew above his hair in the form of a crown, and the oven was the Royalist party. 'Bleakeney's quar' was Black Nest quarry near the village of Bisley – a place much given, it would seem, to versification:

Beggarly Bisley,
Strutting Stroud,
Mincing Hampton,
Painswick Proud.

Bisley occupies a fairly central position on the higher ground of the
Cotswold belt and is commonly known as 'Bisley-God-help-us' on
account of its exposure to biting winds. Although the grey Oolitic
limestone is everywhere, it is used in contrasting forms, the poorer
houses built with rubble walls like a bleak mountain village, others
with smooth ashlar. The church with its broach spire stands above the
roofs of this beautiful village where nooks and alleys lead the eye
everywhere, from the church down to the steep winding road via 'Old
Neighbourhood' towards Chalford.

Bisley also has seven springs, which are 'dressed' on Ascension Day
in a ceremony more commonly associated with the Peak District. This
ancient pagan tradition was revived here, ironically enough, by the
Reverend Thomas Keble, who came as vicar of the large parish in 1827
and found a tree propping up the roof of the church. He was responsible for much restoration in the village and surrounding hamlets, and it
was only the rise of Stroud that ensured Bisley's future as a quiet village
on an unclassified road. It was of ancient foundation, as pagan altars
and Roman remains have been found here. Keble seems to have been
the inventor of the absurd tale about a medieval stone coffin, found in
the village with the bones of a young girl in it. It was dug up by
labourers building a village school near the manor house of Over
Court, where the young Elizabeth Tudor was supposed to have stayed.
The theory was circulated that Elizabeth had died here in her youth,
and as no one dared to tell her father, a local boy took her place and
became queen.

A little to the west of Bisley is Slad, where a girl named Rosie
occupied a similarly exalted position in the mind of a lad called Laurie
who was brought up here and educated at the village school. He came
across Rosie one day sitting behind a haystack:

'You thirsty?' she said.
'I ain't, so there.'
'You be,' she said. 'C'mon.'
So I stuck the fork into the ringing ground and followed her, like doom.
We went a long way, to the bottom of the field, where a wagon stood
half-loaded. Festoons of untrimmed grass hung down like curtains all
around it. We crawled underneath, between the wheels, into a herb-scented
cave of darkness. Rosie scratched about, turned over a sack, and revealed a
stone jar of cider.
'It's cider,' she said. 'You ain't to drink it though. Not much of it, any rate.'

Huge and squat, the jar lay on the grass like an unexploded bomb. We lifted it up, unscrewed the stopper, and smelt the whiff of fermented apples. I held the jar to my mouth and rolled my eyes sideways, like a beast at a water-hole. 'Go on,' said Rosie. I took a deep breath . . . Never to be forgotten, that first long secret drink of golden fire, juice of those valleys and of that time, wine of wild orchards, of russet summer, of plump red apples, and Rosie's burning cheeks. Never to be forgotten, or ever tasted again . . .

The well-deserved fame of Laurie Lee's evocative recollection of a Cotswold childhood has brought to Slad a procession of American tourists whose cameras click away at the crumbling stone walls of the village houses to form a cute collection back home, with Bourton-on-the-Water and Castle Combe, in a sort of New World museum of the olde worlde, understanding little of the real life that created these places on bare earth, despite their own, very different, pioneering ancestry. All museums are the same. Literature, alas, is only a temporary experience like music and theatre and snapshots, reminding but not recreating. The pain and tears, the flooded kitchen floor, madness and suicide, mystery and experience, missed altogether by the camera, can be recalled with truth and beauty but never resurrected. The stone itself is a better silent witness than a snapshot for those who understand its language. Laurie Lee hardly mentions the stone in his autobiography, but he was born and brought up with it and took it for granted in a way that I, brought up with red brick, cannot. A blind man could read a stone wall like Braile if he had been brought up with it. Its shapes and textures, and the way it was held together, would tell him what sort of stone it was, what part of the country he was in and what kind of a building the wall belonged to. Stone speaks to the seeing eye in a way that other materials cannot. Timber can be beautiful, but not eloquent; brick is sometimes stylish, but usually dumb; concrete is a village idiot.

The village inn at Slad is called 'The Woolpack' and a nearby village in the Painswick valley is Sheepscombe. All the villages hereabouts were once busy in the cloth industry, and mills and weavers' cottages survive at Sheepscombe, where the beeches in nearby Cranham Wood are rich with russet, cinnamon, copper and gold in autumn, and the stone is golden all year round. But on Sheepscombe Green there used to be a gallows, and Laurie Lee relates an awful story about the derelict hangman's house in which he played as a boy.

You could hardly say that Paradise is round the corner when you read the history of these benighted villages during centuries of hardship, but oddly enough there is a hamlet with that very name on the Cheltenham road near Sheepscombe. The ludicrous story goes that Charles I – who scattered compliments indiscriminately to his Royalist subjects as modern politicians kiss jam-faced babies – arrived here during the Civil War and declared "This is Paradise." Further face-tiousness reduced Paradise to a local joke, which is a great pity, for it is a charming place. The Plough Inn, which matched the level of royal wit by changing its name to the 'Adam and Eve', would have done better to call itself 'The King's Head', to remind everyone that monarchs should not be taken seriously.

Moving down the tail of the Cotswolds, Nympsfield and Uley lie at the edge of the oolitic uplands, the former high and dominant, with the Severn Vale and the river itself below, much as they were seen by neolithic and Celtic settlers whose burial mounds keep their spirits with us. The most famous of the long barrows is Hetty Pegler's Tump, just north of Uley. Hester Pegler was the landowner whose ground the 120-foot-long barrow stood on in the seventeenth century, but the barrow itself is more than four thousand years old. The stone burial chamber was excavated in the nineteenth century, when fifteen human skeletons were found.

Horsley and Avening lie to the east, grey stone hill villages which have not changed much in two or three hundred years. Queen Matilda, the Conqueror's wife, founded the living at Avening, where they still make 'pig's face sandwiches' on the local feast day, to commemorate her dining there on brawn. Avening Court was the old manor house occupied by Henry Brydges, the pirate son of Lord Chandos of Sudeley, and there is a monument to him in repentant posture in the beautiful church of Holy Cross.

When William Cobbett passed through Minchinhampton and Avening in the autumn of 1826, he admired the distant prospect of Gatcombe Park and was told by a local man that it was owned by "One Squire Ricardo, I think they call him". David Ricardo, then recently deceased, was an economist and Member of Parliament, the son of a Dutch Jew. He is all but forgotten now, but through his interest in science he became one of the promoters of the Geological Society. Gatcombe was built by Edward Shephard, a wealthy manufacturer of the famous Uley Blue cloth, and it was his son who sold the place to Mr Ricardo. It is now the home of Princess Anne and her husband, situated conveniently for Great Badminton.

The stonework of so many 'Cotsall' cottages and farmhouses, whether in village streets or isolated in secret valleys, displays the craft of the mason and the prosperity of the original owner, the first arising from the malleability of the freestone and the second from the backs of the sheep. Woollen cloth made in the Cotswolds clothed country gentlemen in Stroudwater Scarlet for the winter hunt and Uley Blue for the Sunday service, while lesser mortals wore broadcloth of duller hue at school and on the battlefield.

Six thousand sheep grazed the parish of Beverstone in the thirteenth century. It is an ancient village, with a castle that was once occupied by King Harold's father, Earl Godwin. The names Shakespeare and Hathaway occur in the parish registers. But much of the village was rebuilt in Victorian days when it came into the ownership of Robert Holford, and its terraced cottages of warm limestone, with barge-boards and Gothic porches, may be, as Gillian Darley has written, "an excellent example of the best combination of good design with improved standards", but their deliberate uniformity of style does lend the village a look of superimposition on the landscape rather than that natural growth which is so much a part of the Cotswold character.

Across the Gloucestershire border into Avon, Little Badminton is very different from the ducal formality of the Beaufort estate at Great Badminton, where horses replace sheep in local affections. The hamlet is older than its neighbour, and thatched cottages and farmhouses surround a village green with good news for pigeons – a dovecote which is said to have as many nesting holes as there are days in a year.

If the expressive name of Marshfield hints that the Cotswolds are petering out at this southern end, it might also be disputed whether it is a village at all, but it does in fact stand on a ridge, a long, stylish street village or small town on the road between Bristol and Chippenham, and thus a coaching station at one time, as can still be seen from its inns. The M4 motorway has rendered it a relatively quiet place now. Its grey church tower, of Somerset heredity, with a gold weathervane, is a distinctive landmark, but the Three Shire Stones here, once marking the junction of Somerset, Gloucestershire and Wiltshire, have become redundant since the début of Avon county. They have the appearance of a prehistoric tomb but were only put up in the eighteenth century.

Moving north again, along the edge of the limestone escarpment beyond Sheepscombe, is Birdlip, looking down upon Gloucester and at the Malvern Hills beyond. The Hill is much more famous than the village itself, presenting the traveller with spectacular views on fine days and unnerving problems on bad ones, for frost and fog gather about its hazardous slopes and earn it frequent mentions in despatches from weather forecasters. It also has a reputation for apparitions. Folklore preceded science in advising caution in hairy weather conditions.

Deeper in the folds of the hills, flanking the Roman road between Gloucester and Cirencester, villages such as Miserden, Elkstone, Bagendon and Duntisbourne Abbots are worthy of attention. Miserden is a tidy place with remains of a motte-and-bailey castle and a Saxon church, much restored. Bagendon and Duntisbourne Abbots both have saddleback roofs on their church towers, and water at their feet, for they are low-lying villages. Bagendon's church has been variously altered in attempts to prevent flooding, while Duntisbourne Abbots diverted its stream along the village street to keep the hooves of horses and the wheels of wagons clean.

Bagendon has a more important claim to fame, however, for it stands on the site of the headquarters, or *'oppidum'*, of the Belgic tribe of the Dobunni, who occupied the area from about AD 10 onwards in houses which had foundations and floors of stone. An old quarry remains beside the arrow-straight Akeman Street. The Dobunni were an advanced Iron Age people with skills in metalwork and a mint which produced coins bearing the names of their kings and the symbol of a three-tailed horse.

Elkstone's name is believed to derive from Ealac's Stone, which some say is in the walls of the fine church, the highest in the Cotswolds, for this is a windswept upland village. There is much carving of grotesque figures and animals, and a dovecote was built into the central structure when the original tower collapsed, or was demolished, in the thirteenth century. More humble use of the local stone earns a mention in David Verey's volume in the *Buildings of England* series, for the yard at Manor Farm has a privy with an oval window, inscribed "P.T.M. 1697". I suppose an oolitic loo is as worthy a monument to vernacular building as many another stone structure. The window tax had only been introduced in the previous year, so the owner must have considered it very important to shed a little light on the proceedings.

Sapperton lies to the west of Cirencester. This compact grey village stands at the head of beech-clad Golden Valley, down which the River Frome flows, whilst the village outskirts are reached on the east side by Cirencester's huge Oakley Park. When Lord Bathurst developed his estate, he demolished the manor house, in which Charles I reputedly slept, and drew criticism from his friend Alexander Pope, who had a hand in planning the grounds.

Much of the woodwork from the manor house was used in the village church, and in the churchyard there are several brass memorial plates on slabs of Oolitic limestone bearing many common fossils. The fixing of a brass plate to a headstone or table tomb was a common practice in the Cotswolds, because although the local stone could be sculptured to decorative shapes, it was not suitable for fine lettering to be engraved on it with any hope of long-term legibility. One such plate marks the grave of Ernest Gimson, who is the chief cause of Sapperton's modern fame.

Gimson came of a great engineering family long established in Leicester. They were Quakers of old but helped to found the Secular Society in the 'metropolis of heresy'. Ernest heard William Morris lecturing there and became his disciple. He made furniture his chief interest and, after a period in London, came to the Cotswolds. He found several wheelwrights in Sapperton and surrounding villages and turned them into cabinet-makers in a sort of Utopian crafts workshop at Daneway House, lent to him by the presiding Lord Bathurst during the early years of this century. Gimson produced beautiful furniture of simple design by hand, steadfastly refusing to have anything to do with mass production, and he was active in William Morris's Society for the Protection of Ancient Buildings.

Sapperton and Coates are linked by a 2½-mile tunnel built towards the end of the eighteenth century. Its object was to link the Stroud-water Navigation with the Thames, the source of which is nearby, and thus provide an inland waterway from the Black Country to London via the Severn. Many men were killed during construction of the tunnel, which was the longest in the country at that time, but the Thames and Severn Canal was quickly superseded by the Oxford Canal, and although it was not finally abandoned until 1933, it was never a profitable venture. In Hailey Wood large mounds of earth and rubble topped with beech trees are spoil-heaps marking the points where shafts were driven in the course of building the tunnel, the stone portal of which can still be seen at the Coates end, near the Tunnel Inn, built at the same time for the navvies who populated the village. Coates enjoys a lovely setting among the meadows, but perhaps not surprisingly in view of its past, its good stone buildings are forced into unhappy companionship with much rendering and painting.

East of Cirencester is a cluster of villages called the Ampneys (the p is silent) with a stand-offish sister a little to the south, Down Ampney, who wears thatch to keep herself dry instead of the stone tiles common to the snug trio. But it is Down Ampney that has the modern distinction, though its sisters may have fairer faces, for here in 1872 was born Ralph Vaughan Williams, the son of the vicar. He became an organist in London during his studies there, but most of his music is one great hymn to the English countryside he loved – *Norfolk Rhapsody, Pastoral Symphony, The Lark Ascending, On Wenlock Edge* and, of course, *Greensleeves*. As an old man, he told Sir Gerald Kelly, who painted his portrait by tying him to a chair (as he was apt to fall asleep), that he had slept through more good music than any other man who ever lived, but the music he created is among the finest ever composed by an Englishman. There is a memorial to him in the village church.

Ampney Crucis has a fine gabled early fifteenth-century churchyard cross, the head of which was found walled up in the church for protection and restored to its original position in 1860. Only at Somersby in Lincolnshire is there another such complete survival of a pre-Reformation monument. The Puritan parishioners here in the seventeenth century were much put out by their Royalist vicar and petitioned Parliament to have him removed. He was accused of being scandalous, quarrelsome, ignorant, drunken and lecherous. His name was Benedict Grace.

Between Ampney Crucis and Ampney St Peter is an isolated church among the meadows by Ampney Brook. Once it was at the centre of Ampney St Mary, but the villagers long ago moved to a new site, and their cottages disappeared, leaving the ancient church on its own. What was the cause of this desertion? Perhaps the Black Death reduced the population so drastically that fear or superstition prevented the survivors from staying on, but we cannot be sure.

Barnsley lies across the Roman road (Akeman Street). It is a tidy street village which earned praise from the *Architectural Review* some years ago for "doing everything in a country way" and "resisting all efforts to import alien elements". But there are two ways of looking at such carefully protected villages. Barnsley was built and owned by the family who built the mansion of Barnsley Park, and the limitations on development also imposed a severity which does not make the shopless place especially welcoming to the visitor.

Like so many Cotswold villages, Barnsley and its great house were built of warm-coloured stone from their own quarry, long since deserted. Quarry Hill is east of the village, and nearby are some cottages and an inn converted into a country house at a junction of several roads, called Ready Token, where weird stories are told of a former innkeeper who murdered travellers and robbed them. Eight skeletons are said to have been dug up there, and a deep well allegedly led to subterranean passages wide enough for horses and carts to pass through. But the Romans were active here, and it may be that the skeletons were theirs, and the passages only old shafts of the nearby quarry.

Barnsley had a white witch in the sixteenth century, one Alice Prabury, who "useth herself suspiciously in the likelihood of a witch, taking upon her not only to help Christian people of diseases strangely happened, but also horses and all other beasts".

A couple of miles along the road is Bibury, one of the best known of all Cotswold villages. William Morris called it the most beautiful village in England, but each of us has his own opinion on that point. Even when it is crowded with coach parties, however – as it frequently is – Bibury is delightful, and its string of weavers' cottages known as Arlington Row, rising gently uphill from the marshy meadow, must have a strong claim to be among the most photographed houses in the country. The stream is actually the River Coln, which sparkles alongside the street, passing under a couple of stone bridges, and has a compelling fascination for the visitors who spot trout swimming in it.

One of the bridges gives the residents of Arlington access to the

Bibury, showing Arlington Row.

church and shops, but it was not always a solid stone bridge, and in 1638 someone made a complaint to the ecclesiastical court that one Richard Tawney had damaged it by digging, but the defendant claimed not only that it had been necessary for him to clear a passage for the stream to prevent his house being drowned but that he had "caused that part of the bridge which he dugge downe to be repayred better than it was before". Case dismissed.

The churchyard contains beautifully carved headstones and table tombs, and the church itself is a testament to the wealth of the medieval community, earned from the wool trade. Arlington Mill, now a museum, was both a corn and fulling-mill, and the weavers of Arlington Row made cloth in cottages which were converted from a fourteenth-century monastic sheephouse and which are now almshouses owned by the National Trust. Nowhere can the Cotswold association of stone and wool be more graphically symbolized than by the old stone walls of Arlington Row. During five hundred years they have seen the stuff grown, woven and worn within their confines.

Down the River Coln a little way from Bibury one comes to Quenington and Hatherop in a close group with Coln St Aldwyns, and the three share a school and a vicar between them. Quenington, however, has its own church, noted particularly for its richly carved Norman door-ways and tympana. The tympanum over the north doorway repre-sents the Harrowing of Hell, and that over the south doorway the Coronation of the Virgin. What confidence and imagination those Normans showed in their carving of stone! Jacks-in-the-green, zigzag patterns, beak heads, fertility symbols, limpet shells and farm animals vie for attention on these crowded and amazing doorways in a sort of holy variety show, and if it was a command performance, the masons at least had every incentive to show their skills and extend their repertoires, not in terms of pay-packet and public applause but in spiritual well-being and private satisfaction.

Despite the presence of a factory at one end of the village – the agri-cultural engineering firm of Godwin's, which employs many people from the neighbourhood – Quenington is an attractive place with stone garages blending respectably with its old houses, but Hatherop presents a more formal picture, for although its origins are ancient, it was largely rebuilt in the nineteenth century as a model village. Hatherop Castle, so far from being a medieval ruin, is a Victorian girls' school.

Hatherop and Southrop are pronounced 'Atherup' and 'Sutherup' by the locals. 'Sutherup' is an attractive village whose church has a famous and beautifully carved Norman font and herring-bone masonry in the walls of its nave. The vicar here at one time was John Keble, the shy and unambitious divine and poetry professor who became the chief author of the Oxford Movement in company with Newman, Wilberforce and others. There is some modern development in the village and one or two of its buildings have rendered façades, but it is worth seeing for its fine cottages and farm buildings and a veritable crop of ball finials.

Eastleach comprises two former hamlets, Eastleach Martin and Eastleach Turville, separated by the little River Leach, and the stone footbridge that joins them is called Keble's Bridge, for John Keble's ancestors were lords of the manor, and John himself became curate of both hamlets after his ordination. The churches at either side of the stream are interesting, one with a saddleback tower, but much of the other village building is Victorian, though carefully in keeping with the Cotswold style.

The Second World War brought to this village from London an unlikely, lonely and frightened but very talented lady, who settled here and happily became one of the villagers for the rest of her life. 'Nadia' Benois, born and brought up in Russia, the daughter of a French professor, was really named Nadezhda Leontievna Benois, and she became an artist and theatre designer, doing much fine work particularly for the ballet. She lived in Eastleach, where she was visited by many people famous in the performing arts, and when she died in 1975, her ashes were scattered in the churchyard by her son, Peter Ustinov.

Farmworkers who protested at the Industrial Revolution's interference with their way of life a century and a half ago, gathering into angry mobs to destroy threshing-machines despite sentences of death or transportation, would perhaps not be so surprised as we might imagine if they saw today not only that machinery was the thin end of the wedge they feared but that its offspring has nothing to do with the land at all, for the cornfields of Fairford have become a huge aerodrome, with concrete runways that Concorde has risen from like a monstrous son of Dumbo, a great white elephant whose monstrous trumpeting rattled the solid old stones of these Cotswold villages as if they were but flimsy huts in the African jungle.

Perhaps some reassurance can be found at Filkins, over the Oxfordshire border, for not only is this an unspoilt Cotswold village, with roofs as well as walls of stone, but it possesses a small folk museum, partly in the old village lock-up, created by George Swinford, a former stonemason, who worked in the local quarry and supervised the building of several modern council houses in the village, built in traditional style at the expense of Sir Stafford Cripps. Mr Swinford's own handiwork on village houses can be seen in the form of carvings of a shepherd and a stonemason, appropriate symbols of the guardianship of Cotswold tradition.

In this low-lying country among the meadows, Kencot, Broadwell and Langford meander along a road crossing several brooks which flow into the Thames. The villages all have their churches on the west side of the road. We are plainly not in the Cotswolds now, but these villages share their spirit, lying beyond the Great Oolite, but not too far away to be built of the stone. Broadwell has a large church for such a small village, but Langford's is more notable, having Oxfordshire's most important Saxon remains. We can continue on this course to Little Faringdon, beside the River Leach, and thence to Lechlade, where the river joins the Thames. Beyond this town to the south is Inglesham, just inside Wiltshire, where the Coln also joins the stripling Thames, and to the east Kelmscot, a justly famous Oxfordshire village.

Inglesham is a deserted, tiny place of honey-coloured stone, with a plain little towerless church which was preserved from the restorer's over-eager hand by the efforts of the sage of nearby Kelmscot, William Morris, artist, author, designer, craftsman printer and philosopher. Here Morris and his wife Jane entertained poets and Pre-Raphaelite painters – Dante Gabriel Rossetti, Edward Burne-Jones, Ford Madox Brown, William Butler Yeats, Christina Rossetti – all of them came here by coach or on horseback and walked the grounds of the manor house in animated conversation.

Kelmscot itself wears a kind of grey woollen shawl around its shoulders that makes one understand Rossetti's remark that it was "the doziest clump of grey old beehives", but Kelmscott Manor (the inconsistency of spelling is absolved by tradition), where Rossetti flirted with Jane Morris in the intervals between painting her portrait, is a place of pilgrimage for artists and craftsmen of all kinds, and it gave its name to the most famous and influential of all private presses, on which Morris printed his beautiful books in London. Morris lived for twenty-five years at the manor house tucked away among quiet lanes and high stone walls. He, unlike Rossetti, always thought of Kelmscot as a "heaven on earth". In his Utopian story *News from Nowhere* the travellers arrive in this village at the end. When Morris died, a farm cart brought his body from London for burial beneath an unusually simple monument which is now rapidly deteriorating.

Farther south, way off the Cotswolds in the Vale of the White Horse (in Berkshire until 1974), but essentially grey villages of Cotswold stone, are Coleshill and Great Coxwell, the former a nineteenth-century model village, and the latter famous for one of the finest buildings in all the stone villages of England. Coleshill was built of coral rag, faced and roofed with Cotswold limestone. The village is owned by the National Trust. It is invariably William Morris who is quoted in likening the Great Coxwell tithe barn to a cathedral, but he cannot have been by any means the first to be impressed by the resemblance. If our cathedral cities possess the greatest architectural wonders of building in stone, then the barn at Great Coxwell, also owned by the National Trust, is among the closest we shall come to them in village England. The Cistercian monks of Beaulieu Abbey in Hampshire, who were granted the manor of Faringdon by King John, built this great barn in the thirteenth century, of stone quarried near the site. It stands fifty feet high and over fifty yards in length. Stone buttresses reinforce the roughly coursed walls, and the roof is of graded courses of Stonesfield stone tiles, borne on massive beams, bracing struts and oak posts on seven-foot-high stone bases. What colossal amounts of grain must have been kept in this vast storehouse once! For seven hundred years it has remained a barn – host to rats and mice below and Death Watch beetle above – but as you step into its lofty interior, the dim light, the towering roof, the silence, the sheer spaciousness, all combine to induce a feeling of reverence.

It is a satisfactory proof to the atheist that the awe with which people view really great buildings is induced by monumental scale and human genius and is nothing to do with religious feeling, even when the building is a cathedral. Tithe barns were built by the Church for the exploitation of peasants. But that in no way diminishes our marvellous admiration for the way in which the builders of the barn at Great Coxwell did their work.

We must now return northwards, to look first at a pair of villages on the oolite east of Burford – Asthall and Swinbrook beside the River Windrush. Such close proximity to a water supply implies very early foundation, and Roman and Saxon remains have been found in the valley. A Roman road ran through the site of Asthall, and the graves in the churchyard of St Oswald's, standing isolated in a field at Widford, are said to have been dug through a Roman pavement. The Windrush marked the southern boundary of the ancient Wychwood Forest, much loved by Henry II and his successors as a hunting forest, in which the villagers were permitted to graze horses and cattle other than oxen.

Asthall is as pretty as a picture, with a typical Cotswold ghost story to tell, and we might easily pause in it for a while if it were not that just along the willow-lined river across a stone bridge, is Swinbrook, which is just as pretty and thrice-blessed with eccentricity. The Fettiplace family owned the manor for many centuries, and Swinbrook's church is famous for their effigies. Half a dozen of them are stacked up on shelves, in sets of three, against the north wall of the chancel. Both monuments are of the seventeenth century. The earlier one is of local stone and shows the recumbent figures in armour, each stiffly leaning on one elbow, as if they were about to perform a dance routine in a Tudor cabaret. The later group, sculptured in alabaster and without armour, look slightly more comfortable but no less extraordinary – a trio of old soldiers in bunk beds, waiting for reveille.

Another trio familiar in this parish may well have been the Tom, Dick and Harry whose names are so freely taken in vain (for they were hardly, at the time, the insignificant nobodies their names represent today). The Dunsdon brothers were born at Fulbrook nearby and took to the forest as bandits. They became widely known when they robbed the Gloucester Mail coach of £500 and bragged about their successes. They were said to store their booty and keep their horses in an old quarry passage. But the butler of Tangley Hall got wind of their plan to rob the place while the squire was away, and a constable and several other men waited for them inside the house. At midnight – so the story goes – an arm came through the Judas shutter in the front door and felt around for the key, whereupon the butler grabbed the arm and tied it fast with rope. Among the oaths and mutterings heard outside the words "cut, cut" were distinguished, and after a series of awful moans the severed arm dropped inside the door. It was Dick Dunsdon's, for he was never seen again. Tom and Harry, undeterred, continued with their robbery and pillage until at last they were arrested and duly

Nancy Mitford's grave at Swinbrook, Oxfordshire.

hanged at Gloucester in 1785. Their bodies were brought back to Swinbrook and hung in chains on the gibbet tree which still stands near Widley Copse.

If it is the Fettiplaces who populate Swinbrook church, it is the Mitfords who claim precedence in the churchyard. Lord Redesdale brought his large family to Swinbrook and practically rebuilt the manor house in which his several famous daughters grew up. Nancy was the eldest of them. Her satirical novel *The Pursuit of Love* is set in the neighbourhood. Sister Jessica, who wrote *The American Way of Death*, is supposed to have said: "I have nothing against undertakers personally. It's just that I wouldn't want one to bury my sister." One buried Nancy, however, beneath a thick block of stone bearing the mason's chisel marks and a mole in relief. She had said she did not want a cross, that symbol of torture, and had been especially fond of moles. I expect she lies too deep for them to keep her company now. The sisters had kept mice, rats and snakes, among other things, as pets, which set them apart from most girls even as children. Unity Valkyrie Mitford was also buried here after a tempestuous ride through life in which she became one of Hitler's friends and attempted suicide at Munich by shooting herself in the head and giving herself nine years of brain-damaged existence before dying at thirty-three. Was it an Act of God, or what, that laid a German land-mine in this village in 1940, to explode and blow out the church's east window? Sir Oswald Mosley, Evelyn Waugh and the Duke of Devonshire form other unlikely links in the chain of the Mitford clan's associations.

On the west side of Burford are Westwell and Taynton. Westwell is a picturesque village with a green and duckpond at its centre, and a war memorial in the form of a monolith on a stepped base. Taynton's name must appear on every roll of honour in the stone industry, for although the village itself looks a little the worse for wear, its quarries helped to build Oxford, Blenheim Palace, Windsor Castle and Eton College. The quarries, on the Great Oolite, lie north of the village and are mentioned in Domesday Book, but they were in use for centuries before the Normans came. They produce a coarse, shelly limestone of brownish hue with streaks of a lighter colour. Closed down once, they have been reopened in recent years to be operated again on a small scale, but overgrown hollows and spoil-heaps mark the extensive workings of over a thousand years.

One Richard Taynton was Clerk of Works to William of Wykeham at Windsor, when great cartloads of stone were hauled by teams of horses or oxen the whole sixty miles from Taynton because the river above Wallingford was too erratic for transportation by water. Among Sir Christopher Wren's master masons at St Paul's was Christopher Kempster, who had his own quarry at nearby Upton, called Kit's Quarry. There is a monument to him in the church at Burford, made by his son William, who followed his father in the profession and himself carried out work for Wren.

Other quarries were scattered along the valleys of the Windrush and its tributaries to the west, across the border into Gloucestershire again – Barrington, Windrush, Sherborne and Farmington among them. Windrush and Sherborne are contrasting villages on the south banks of their respective streams – one of haphazard growth and the other a formal development. Windrush consists of stone houses and barns round a triangular green; Sherborne is spread out on either side of the great house and the church, which sports monuments by Rysbrack, Westmacott the Elder and Bacon. Westmacott's monument to James Lenox Dutton shows a life-sized and bare-breasted angel trampling on Death. The house, which was partly demolished when the present one was built in the nineteenth century, had been at least partly put up by a Taynton mason, Valentine Strong, and it was said that the old house "was so solidly built that the greatest difficulty was experienced in pulling it down".

The stone from the local quarries was whitish in contrast to Taynton's, and it gave the river its name, for 'Windrush' comes – surprisingly perhaps – from the Celtic *'gwyn'* and *'riasc'* – 'white marsh'. The stone was mined here, not quarried, and donkeys were sometimes used like pit-ponies to haul the stone to the surface along sloping tunnels, then to the little wharf on the river at Little Barrington for loading on to barges.

Little Barrington, Gloucestershire.

Barrington's stone, as well as Taynton's, was used at Blenheim, and its superb weathering qualities can be seen very well there. The local Strong family of masons owned the quarries at Barrington for several generations, and Valentine Strong left money in his Will for a way to be made between the two bridges at Barrington "that two men may go a front to carry a corpse in safety". It is still known as Strong's Causeway. One of the mine shafts ran beneath the New Inn at the Little Barrington crossroads, and the innkeeper's wife would stamp on the floor to let the quarrymen know that their dinner was ready. Farmington quarry is open-cast and is still worked near the Roman road, Fosse Way. Its stone was used to build London's Inner Temple church.

There is some stylish building in both Great and Little Barrington: hardly a house that is not well dressed in matching outfits of warm stone walls and fine roofs. In Great Barrington's church there is a beautifully carved eighteenth-century marble monument to the children Jane and Edward Bray, being led to heaven by an angel.

Aldsworth lies in its own great tract of peaceful country to the south of Sherborne, near the River Leach. You see at once that there is no pressure at all on its space as it lies sleepily indifferent to the world beyond. The noisiest things in this village, next to the residents' lawn-mowers, seem to be the Norman grotesques on the string course round the nave of the church, which is itself quietly tucked away from the village centre. These are roaring, shouting monsters of some mason's vivid imagination, which Massingham called a "Rabelaisian riot".

Chedworth, Yanworth and Withington sprawl on the hillsides west of Pancake Hill and Fosse Way, watered by trickling streams and shaded by beautiful woods beyond the charming little main-road settlement of Fossbridge, where the Roman road crossed the River Coln. Most celebrated among them is Chedworth, for the fine remains of a Roman villa in a beautiful rural situation north of the village. It was discovered in 1864 by a gamekeeper searching for his ferret and is now preserved by the National Trust. Across the old railway track on the other side of the wood, however, more recent earthworks bring us up to date with a jolt, for the decorative mosaics of an ancient civilization suddenly give way to the overgrown criss-cross concrete runways of a modern one.

Withington also had its Roman villa, a large church and several fine houses belonging to the Bishops of Worcester; but William Cobbett, passing this way in 1826, found nothing good in it: ". . . here, in this once populous village . . ." he wrote, "you will see *all* the indubitable marks of most melancholy decay." Why, the place did not even possess an inn! "I asked two men, who were threshing in a barn, how long it was since their public-house was put down or dropped. They told me about sixteen years. One of these men, who was about fifty years of age, could remember *three* public-houses, one of which was what was called an *inn*!" Well, Withington has its public house back again, Bill, so rest in peace on that account, at least.

The catch with all those rural writers who see, or saw, the ruination of English country life in the Industrial Revolution is that they do not fully face up to life as many lived it *before* the coming of industry. June Lewis notes the inventory of Ann Coates of Chedworth, which amounted to little more than a bed, a table and a few pots and pans. We smile at the quaint spelling when we read of a "litel cetel" and "a pear of And Irns", but we do not easily imagine the awful reality that such a list represents.

Northwards, the wolds rise towards their highest point on the escarpment near Cheltenham. Sevenhampton, Brockhampton and Charlton Abbots stand alongside a country road running parallel to the ancient salt way, and prehistoric and Roman remains lie thick on the ground towards Winchcombe. Along the Edge the presence of a hawthorn hedge, instead of the usual dry-stone wall, and woods of ash betrays the change from the Oolitic limestone to the clay of the lias.

Deeper in the hills, Naunton, Guiting Power and Temple Guiting are totally Cotswold in character along the River Windrush, Naunton having a large quarry nearby from which its stone was taken. Temple Guiting was a preceptory of the Knights Templars, and it possessed the earliest known fulling mill in England.

The village inn at Guiting Power is called 'The Farmer's Arms', and not far away is the Cotswold Farm Park, run by Joe Henson. Joe's upbringing in a show-business family was not lost on him when he turned to farming, but there is a much more serious purpose to his establishment than the entertainment which his collection of animals and birds undoubtedly provides. For these are rare breeds of British farm animals which have been close to extinction and now thrive here where farmers can study their ancient virtues. It is a remarkable fact that our dependence on nature shows signs of coming full circle despite the Industrial Revolution. As we begin to look afresh at the sun and the wind as sources of power, and the stone that built these villages begins to look a better proposition than architects have thought for a couple of generations, so the advantages of reliable farm animals of old are being looked at with a fresh eye as against the costly and troublesome machinery of modern agriculture. Great credit is due to Joe Henson for the energy and foresight he has put into his labour of love.

Stanton and Stanway stand in stony alliteration along the western edge of Cotswold, with Snowshill nearby, above the steep escarpment which few roads attempt to scale. A half-timbered barn among the grey stone reminds us, once again, that we are at the limit of the oolite, and the honey colour of the buildings at Stanway hints at greater pleasures to come. Stanton is a beautifully preserved pure Cotswold village in which the local authority has built council houses totally sympathetic in style and material.

Both villages have much of interest in their stonework. Stanton's church of St Michael, beloved of Wesley, has a churchyard cross, erected as a war memorial in 1919 by Sir Ninian Comper, who was also responsible for the alabaster figures of the reredos and much of the stained glass. A wild strawberry in the corner of the east window is his signature, or trade mark. The altar in Stanway's church of St Peter is also his work.

There is fine lettering by Eric Gill on the war memorial in this village, which is somewhat grander than its neighbour and well known for the gatehouse of Stanway House, with its three bell-shaped gables topped by scallop shells, the symbols of the Tracy family who owned it. It is not known who designed and built this extraordinary structure, but it could well have been one of the aforementioned Strong family of master masons.

Snowshill, Gloucestershire.

The village hall was once a tithe barn, and the cricket pavilion, supported on rick staddles, was built by Sir James Barrie, that unlikely cricket fanatic from north of the border, who was a frequent guest at the big house. Above Stanway is the huge amphitheatre of Coscombe Quarry, from which a great deal of the stone in north Cotswold villages has been taken.

Snowshill perches on a slope round a central green on which its church is built. Its exposed position on the high wolds gives it a name which belies its cosy look on summer weekends when tourists gather round the village inn. The church is over-restored, but the manor house is a fine building, preserved as a museum by the National Trust. A group of burial mounds near the village – one long and five round barrows – yielded a skeleton with a stone battle-axe and a dagger, a spear and a pin of bronze, all but the spear being of Continental origin.

A country road runs down from Snowshill across the border of Hereford and Worcester into the Vale of Evesham and Broadway, somewhat ambiguously known as 'the painted lady of the Cotswolds'. Broadway has been given a lot of stick by writers who despise what is popular, and Massingham actually advised his readers to avoid this "unpleasantness" by taking a different route to the northern extremity of the wolds. It must be admitted at once that the place is rather self-conscious, and the easiest thing would perhaps be to say that it is a town and not a village and pass on. After all, the place had a railway station once. But Broadway demands respect and admiration from anyone looking at stone buildings and deserves the benefit of any possible doubt. What is tragic about it is not that a lot of people come to see it but that it lies on busy main roads between Evesham and Stow-on-the-Wold, Cheltenham and Stratford-on-Avon. It thus has a flow of noisy and heavy traffic and a parking problem for its visitors, neither of which it had when Henry James and John Singer Sargent knew it and gave it a reputation among their fellow-Americans as the most beautiful village in England, while Alfred Parsons, Jean-François Millet, Edmund Gosse, William Morris and the actress Mary Anderson also did their bits towards spreading its fame.

It is not the literary and artistic Broadway Set and their evenings of chamber music that draw the majority of visitors to this village, however, nor is it the ruthless show-biz commercialism that has ruined many other places, for although 'Broddy' has its souvenir shops and cannot be accused of looking a gift-horse in the mouth, it has not sacrificed a scrap of its dignity and style in appealing to coach-parties from the Midlands and elsewhere. When Nikolaus Pevsner called it *the* show village of England, he meant, of course, architecturally, and the pleasing fact is that thousands of people who have not the slightest conscious interest in architecture are nevertheless touched by its sheer aesthetic qualities. Its wide main street comes down the hill, lined on either side by a succession of mellow old buildings of golden Guiting stone with gables and dripmoulds, mullions and transoms, stone roofs and garden walls combining to produce a dazzling display of beautiful village construction. It takes a particularly brutal snob, I think, to cock a snook at Broadway.

Cleeve Prior, beside the Avon, has cottages of stone with roofs of red tile round its triangular green. The priors of Worcester were the landowners here, and an avenue of yews leads to the manor house which has a priest's hole where Charles I's banker hid during the Civil War. No doubt whose side this village was on. The fifteenth-century local is called 'The King's Arms'. The churchyard contains some finely engraved headstones, including one to a local mason, Michael Campden, which shows the tools of his trade and the arms of the Masons' Company. It was cut by John Laughton.

Whilst we are in Hereford and Worcester, on the lias a little off the main course of Cotswold villages, we must take note of Overbury. It is quite uncharacteristic of both Worcestershire and the Cotswolds, with some timber-framed and even brick building in it, but it qualifies for

Broadway, Hereford and Worcester – 'the painted lady of the Cotswolds'.

mention here by virtue of its predominantly stony nature. It lies below Bredon Hill, and its big house, Overbury Court, has been the home of the banker family of Martins for near three hundred years. The village is a model of refinement, despite its assorted building materials, and as if to prove it, it has no public house.

Back in Gloucestershire, Saintbury and Blockley stand either side of Chipping Campden, hugging like a grey woollen glove the outstretched thumb of the Cotswolds. Both villages show to perfection the way in which the old masons fitted their houses to natural contours in the days before bulldozers and giant excavators could flatten a hillside for a new housing estate in a few days between tea-breaks. Blockley, with its switchback road and its unexpected history of industry, has received most publicity (Angela Rippon has done for Blockley what Henry James did for Broadway), but I find Saintbury the more appealing of the two, with its seventeenth-century houses linking the Norman church, with its slim broach spire, at the top of the hill and the fourteenth-century village cross at the bottom.

Blockley, by virtue of the brook which flows apace from the hill above the village, begat water-powered mills which have at various times produced silk thread, soap, iron and, of all things, pianos, and it claims to have been one of the first electrically lit villages in England, but its prosperity was built partly with child labour, for in 1836 the Reverend F. E. Witts found that the silk operatives were mainly "young females and boys from 8 to 10 years of age".

On the slopes of an island of lias above the plain to the north are Hidcote and Ebrington, with Tredington, in seeming isolation in Warwickshire's Red Horse Vale, like a stone that has rolled away but gathered some moss in the form of modern development. The stone becomes deeper in colour, and the hamlets of Hidcote Boyce and Bartrim, in particular, look slightly foreign to the Cotswolds, as if they had strayed over here from Northamptonshire. But Hidcote is famous for the gardens of Hidcote Manor, which are among the finest to be seen. Now the property of the National Trust, they were laid out over nearly half a century by Major Johnston, who presented them to the Trust after the Second World War, since when they have become one of the chief tourist attractions of the north Cotswolds and an inspiration for many other garden designs. Lawrence Johnston was an architect, and his layout is based on straight lines and formal hedges and walls separating the different sections of the gardens, but everywhere the eye is led from one source of interest to another, with open views, long vistas, shaded pathways, steps and waterfalls, and every part has its own character in the plants and features which make it such a delightful place for every garden-lover.

Formal hedges of yew and hornbeam give way to wild ones of

Tredington, Warwickshire.

hawthorn around Ebrington, where dry-stone walls become a little scarcer on the clay, and the hedges themselves have a curious place in local folklore. One of the stories told among the ancients of this village, which is supposed to be famous for the folly of its inhabitants, is that they once let the hedges round their fields grow tall so as to keep the cuckoo in and ensure permanent spring-time. This same tale is told of Borrowdale, in the Lake District, where they built a wall to trap the bird, and when it flew over the top, they shook their heads ruefully, muttering: "By gow, if we'd nobbut laid another line o' stanes atop, we'd a copped 'im!" Actually, the wags of both Ebrington and Borrowdale borrowed the tale from the Wise Men of Gotham, before the days of easy communications, and nurtured it as their own, along with several other anecdotes of medieval parentage. In the same way superstitions about ghosts, stone circles, giants and so on travelled the country centuries ago and can now be heard as identical bits of local folklore as far apart as Dorset and Cumbria.

Back along the Fosse Way from Tredington, Bourton-on-the-Hill lies west of Moreton in Marsh at the edge of the oolite, with its much more famous big sister, Bourton-on-the-Water, seven miles south. I do not know what is specially feminine about the latter, but I hesitate to call it a big brother lest I seem to imply some tyranny in its nature. Here is Massingham, predictably, on Bourton-on-the-Water: "Bourton has been called the Venice of the Cotswolds, but this is obviously a misreading for the Wigan of the Cotswolds. The only thing to do at Bourton is to stand and stare at those lovely bridges and pray for the death of the Progress all round you. . . ."

Well, with a motor museum, bird zoo, model (i.e. miniature) village, souvenir shops and cream teas on offer, it does rather make an exhibition of itself, and the double yellow lines along its road sides are like medal ribbons awarded in the crusade against the infidel motorist. I have left the place with great relief myself on crowded summer days. But before we label Bourton as a kind of English Disneyland and rush away, it is worth noting that the place does have some fine stone buildings, apart from the charming foot-bridges which cross its most un-Venice-like stretch of the River Windrush, and in winter, before the kiss of the sun wakes up the sleeping beauty and takes her to the ball, its warm stones and back alleys are delightful.

Between the hill Bourton and the vale one are two more pairs of twins, the Swells and the Slaughters. The first pair are on the River Dikler and the latter on the Eye, both of which run into the Windrush at watery Bourton. The curve of the wolds from Broadway down to Bourton-on-the-Water is undoubtedly the most crowded area of the Cotswolds during summer weekends, and it is hardly surprising that these villages attract day trippers from the backstreets of Birmingham,

Coventry and Wolverhampton. Broadway and Bourton, for all their seaside atmosphere, represent an escape from the dreary city to nature and fresh air. The Swells and the Slaughters attract a lot of visitors too, but they are not in the same league when it comes to show-business, being essentially small farming villages with more barns than shops. Lower Slaughter is the most formally picturesque among them, with bridges over the bisecting stream like Bourton. It is a magnet for amateur water-colour artists who can cope with its scale and paint it without impossible obstruction from people and traffic. For all four of these villages are 'quiet' places in spite of the tourists – a little bemused by the presence of so many strangers in their midst and indifferent to the allure of commercial exploitation. Upper Slaughter and the Swells, especially, are in many ways the epitomes of Cotswold hamlets, with their respective streams flowing between green fields of cows and willows to millponds and marshy meadows, while the low hillsides with their sheep and dry-stone walls slope down to the back doors of the old stone-roofed cottages.

The higher ground above the Windrush to the east is occupied by the Rissington triplets, Great, Little and Wyck. Little Rissington seems the biggest of the trio in latter days, for it possesses an RAF airfield on its plateau and extensive modern quarters, but Wyck Rissington is better known, as the place where Gustav Holst held his first professional engagement as organist in the village church – "a young man of great promise" according to a local dignitary.

Near Gloucestershire's border with Oxfordshire another trio forms an interesting group in the valley of the Evenlode – Oddington, Adlestrop and Daylesford. There are two Oddingtons – another in Oxfordshire. The Gloucestershire one is the larger of them. It belonged to the Archbishop of York centuries ago, and Henry III was a frequent guest here. The church is isolated from the rest of the village now, the village having been shifted farther away from the river bank when the plague swept the area, but Roman and Saxon finds indicate the antiquity of the original settlement, across the river (and the railway line) from Daylesford and Adlestrop. Ah, yes.

> Yes. I remember Adlestrop –
> The name, because one afternoon
> Of heat the express-train drew up there
> Unwontedly. It was late June.
>
> The steam hissed. Someone cleared his throat.
> No one left and no one came
> On the bare platform. What I saw
> Was Adlestrop – only the name.

And willows, willow-herb, and grass,
And meadowsweet, and haycocks dry,
No whit less still and lonely fair
Than the high cloudlets in the sky.

And for a minute a blackbird sang
Close by, and round him, mistier,
Farther and farther, all the birds
Of Oxfordshire and Gloucestershire.

Edward Thomas was the brief, unscheduled visitor, soon to be brought to another untimely halt in the First World War. The train does not stop here any more (it was not supposed to *then*) but it made famous the village that Jane Austen knew through her relations the Leighs, who lived in the big house and whose memorials are in the church.

Daylesford, the smallest of these three villages, is by far the greatest in historical importance, for it was here that Warren Hastings built his mansion before the long impeachment trial began, recovering the estate which his family had lost as a result of the Civil War. He had vowed to do so, according to his own account, when only a child, and Daylesford thus indirectly played a small part in the lives of countless Hindus and Muslims who never knew that such a place existed. The bells of the village church rang out when the lord of the manor was acquitted, at the cost of seven long years and his entire personal fortune. The Indian influence in the architecture of Daylesford House is only slight, and it is a commonplace to say that Hastings must have been thankful for the fact, but he was so far from trying to forget India that in his retirement he tried to breed Indian animals and grow Indian crops here; and the stone used for the house was brown Hornton, more like the colour of the oriental buildings so familiar to him than the material from Whitequarry Hill above the house. When he died, this flawed giant was buried in the churchyard in the company of his ancestors beneath a monument of stone inscribed simply "Warren Hastings 1818". On the north wall of the nave is a tablet recording the history of this village church, since rebuilt by another well-known local family, the Grisewoods, among whom was Freddie, whose voice was also known far beyond his native shores.

Across the border into Oxfordshire again, Cornwell and Churchill lie close to streams running into the Evenlode. Cornwell is undeniably a stone village, but it is hardly a Cotswold one, having been practically rebuilt in the 1930s by Clough Williams Ellis in a theatrical manner reminiscent of Portmeirion. It has both style and prettiness, but of a contrived and artificial sort, far removed from the lengthy natural development of the best local villages.

Churchill was Warren Hastings' birthplace, and also that of William

The Rollright Stones, Oxfordshire.

Smith, a man of no little significance to this book, for it was he who first mapped the rock structure of England, and he was thus the founder of modern geology. He was a canal engineer, and many of the terms still used in geology were borrowed by him from the quarrymen he talked to. Rocks found in thin bands below the clay were called 'layers' or 'liers' by the quarrymen, and thus we get 'lias'. There is a memorial to Smith in the village, in the form of a single monolith. A sixteenth-century vicar of this village was brought before the bawdy court accused by the local gossips of fornication with his housekeeper, and the woman did penance in the old church, but the building has been replaced by a modern one on a new site even more on the hill now than it was when the village got its name.

North of Chipping Norton are Great and Little Rollright, and whatever modern virtues these grey stone villages may possess, it is the Bronze Age megalithic circle near them which captures popular interest here. Standing beside the ancient road along the windswept Cotswold ridge, this great circle of pitted and weatherworn stones of Oolitic limestone, called 'the King's Men', still stands after three and a half thousand years as a witness to the ancient cult of monumental structure with the natural rock. The so-called King Stone on the other side of the road (in Warwickshire) points to the rising sun, as does the Hele Stone at Stonehenge, and folklore ascribes to these stones, as to Long Meg and Her Daughters in Cumbria, and various other such circles, magical properties, such as, for instance, that it is impossible to count them accurately. Long Meg and Her Daughters were locally believed to have been turned to stone for dancing on the Sabbath, whilst the king and his men who form the Rollright Stones were petrified by the local witch, who became an elder tree at the same time. The superstition associating elder with witchcraft and doom goes back to palaeolithic times. It was thirteenth in the Druidic tree alphabet (hence the unlucky number), and its leaf shape was the pattern for arrow-heads found in long barrows.

At one period the villagers came up to the stones on Midsummer Eve and formed a circle round the King Stone whilst one man cut an elder tree with a knife. It was believed that the witch bled and the King Stone turned its head. Village maidens went one by one to listen to the treacherous Whispering Knights, and fairies were also supposed to dance round the King Stone, near which there was once, according to Stukeley, a maze cut into the turf, long since ploughed up. Drovers taking cattle along the ancient track were among those who used to chip pieces from the King Stone for good luck, and gypsies used to sell pieces as talismens at the local fairs. Local tradition says that St Augustine came to Long Compton, in the valley below, to settle a dispute, but it is clear that Christianity has not exercised a more powerful hold, or a longer one, over the minds of local people than these ancient standing stones.

It is arguable, of course, that the witch and God were equally ignorant of geology and slipped up, not for the first time, in turning the Merry Maidens into granite, the King's Men into Oolitic limestone, and Long Meg and Her Daughters into the local sandstone. How much more powerful the divine retribution for dancing on the Sabbath would have been if, for instance, the Merry Maidens had been turned to chalk! But He obviously never thought of that.

Hook Norton – the Hog's Norton of old tales – represents old Christianity here in its large Norman church. It is a straggling village of the deep-coloured lias from which iron ore has been quarried, but the church is its chief attraction, with fourteenth- and fifteenth-century wall paintings of saints and angels, and a primitive but marvellous font with carvings of Adam and Eve in company with signs of the Zodiac and a centaur.

Warwickshire's Cotswold fringe is enhanced by Whichford, Ascott and Sutton-under-Brailes, gathered about their greens on the lias, below the ridge where the king and his men were turned to stone. The

The ancient stone font in the church at Hook Norton.

medieval lords of the manor of Whichford were the de Mohuns, from whom the Earls of Derby descended through the female line.

Over to the west, north of the so-called Four Shire Stone where one county has deserted the former quartet, and not far from Fosse Way, is the site of the deserted medieval village of Broadstone, which was in Oxfordshire when it existed and is in Warwickshire now it does not! Oblique aerial photography shows up clearly the pattern of stone foundations of street and buildings where people lived and moved and had their being, and where now only an empty field enclosed by hedgerows entertains the ghosts of those for whom this was home. It is only one of multitudinous sites of lost medieval villages identified in recent decades, but from the layman's point of view one of the most spectacular, for its soil-covered and overgrown walls remain high enough to be traced easily on the ground.

Across the ridge again to the south some attractive Oxfordshire villages nestle snugly in the soft bosom of the northern hills with the River Glyme as their cleavage. Chadlington and Taston, in the lovely walking country of the downs above the Evenlode, both sport prehistoric monoliths, known respectively as the Hawk Stone and the Thor Stone. The latter gives the hamlet of Taston its name and seems to indicate the site of a pagan shrine. The classical scholars Sir Henry Rawlinson and his brother George were born at Chadlington. George was a clergyman and professor of ancient history at Oxford. Henry was a diplomat and President of the Royal Geographical Society, and it was he who deciphered the inscription in three languages cut into a rock face in Persia (as it then was) to record events in the reign of Darius, the great ruler of the Persian Empire.

The lost village of Broadstone. Oblique aerial photography shows up the pattern of stone walls and foundations.

Spelsbury lies between Chadlington and Taston and is a trim-figured contender in village beauty contests, in country where hedges compete with dry-stone walls for the honour of dividing fields, but the hedges are being ruthlessly torn up by the farmers requiring larger fields for economical use of agricultural machinery. There is much complaint about this widespread recent practice, from conservationists who have never gone short of their daily bread. They have their priorities wrong, of course, and too often confuse change with destruction. The Enclosure Acts gave our agricultural land its present appearance, dictated by economic necessity, and the same needs will continue to change the countryside without undue regard to current aesthetic tastes. The first requirement is to feed the people.

Putting a roof over their heads has brought fame to the graphically named Stonesfield for centuries, for the quarries which produced thin slabs of stone for so many thousands of Cotswold cottages, and for Oxford itself, made what are undoubtedly among the best roofs in England. They were worked from Roman times to the early years of this century. The material was actually mined, not quarried, from a thin seam of oolite about sixty-five feet below the surface – a light brown sandy limestone that splits easily on exposure to frost, although this process was not discovered until the sixteenth century. Medieval masons used what the quarrymen called 'presents' – stone which could be used as it was delivered straight from the workings. From the sixteenth century, however, 'pendle' stone was used. It was quarried in the autumn and spread on the open ground with a covering of soil to await the hard frosts of winter. When the frost came, the church bells were rung and all the villagers got up, in the middle of the night if necessary, to uncover and spread out the stone and water it if it was not already well soaked. The frost then got at the water in tiny fissures in the stone, and all that was needed to split it into tiles was a tap with a mallet.

The roofing materials from Stonesfield and elsewhere in the Cots-wolds and the East Midlands are frequently called 'stone slates', but this seems to me misleading. Slate is a particular metamorphic rock which does not occur in this region, and whilst a tile is, strictly speaking, a manufactured slab, the term 'stone tile' seems more satisfactory than a complete misnomer.

One of the by-products of this village industry was the sale of pieces of stone which contained fossils. Quarrymen used to keep a sharp eye open for them and sell them to scientists from Oxford University, who came to inspect the displays in the cottage windows in the hope of finding some rare specimen.

Shipton-under-Wychwood, to the west, is a fine village teeming with interest. Shipton Court is one of the largest Jacobean houses in England, though it was much altered early in the present century. The mullion windows, rather oddly, are modern, having replaced the earlier sash windows. The Shaven Crown Hotel is a fifteenth-century building, originally a hospice run by the monks of Bruern Abbey, who built it. The guests' lounge – a splendid medieval timbered hall – was once the monks' refectory. Several ghost stories gather round Shipton, not surprisingly, for it was the burial place for the inhabitants of Wychwood Forest.

The road to Taston from Spelsbury leads on to a pair of villages known as the Enstones – Church Enstone and Neat Enstone. The River Glyme separates one from the other. Near a crossroads is the monu-ment from which Enstone probably got its name – the so-called Hoar Stone is actually a burial chamber. A large number of lanes and roads radiate from a central parlour here like a spider's web, and the Enstones stretch their grey legs out lazily, having fed well on fliers of one sort or another for centuries. The coaches from London to Worces-ter passed this way, changing their horses here very often. In modern times, more traffic was brought by a new road between Woodstock and Chipping Norton (now the A34) constructed through the village by

ploughing the whole course of sixteen miles with a team of eight oxen. It brought more than twenty coaches through Enstone every day, travelling between Oxford and Birmingham. And latter-day fliers have come here in the form of RAF pilots using the old airfield north of the village.

One of the roads leading north brings us to Great Tew, a precious village of yellowy-brown stone, thatched roofs and little front gardens. Many of its chocolate-box cottages are very old, but it preserves the village stocks, which do it no great credit, and it looks – and is – too contrived to be a real Cotswold village, for it was largely planned by J. C. Loudon for General Stratton on the basis of the existing cottages built by Viscount Falkland. Loudon was the manager of the estate, and he cooked up a Scotch broth of conifers, hawthorn hedges, fences, deciduous trees and rhododendron in the grounds around the mansion, with drainage channels and wide, winding lanes, partly grassed and partly laid with stone. The village itself, left *in situ* in the valley below the park, was made picturesque as an alternative to moving it wholesale to a new site well hidden from the manor. Alas, the village has fallen into a state of some dilapidation, and though there is constant talk of restoration, and the place has been declared an Outstanding Conservation Area, the process of recovery is slow. What is worth seeing at Great Tew is the monument to Mary Anne Boulton. Matthew Boulton, the Birmingham engineer who formed the famous partnership with James Watt, bought the Great Tew estate in 1815. When his wife died, Boulton commissioned Sir Francis Chantrey to make the monument, for which he paid £1,500. The result was a masterpiece of the period in stone. The lady reclines elegantly with her back resting against a cushion. Her hands rest on an open book, but her eyes, though looking down, gaze into space in reflective piety. It is sentimental, but superb.

Sandford St Martin has also been subjected to some planning but wears grey instead of Great Tew's tawny and does not look quite so much like a fashionably dressed lady of faded beauty fishing for compliments. In Victorian times the village was half owned by Dr Edwin Guest of Sandford Park and half by the Reverend Edward Marshall of the Manor, and between them they rebuilt much of the village to accommodate the workers in decent housing and controlled growth of the 'closed' village to keep the Poor Rate down. The ford which had long ago given the place its name was across the sandy headwaters of the River Dorn.

The so-called Redlands of north Oxfordshire have been extensively quarried in the past for iron ore. Geologically, the local stone is marlstone, from the Middle Lias layer, and it is the iron oxide in the rock which gives such rich tints to the building stone commonly known

Courtyard of the Shaven Crown Inn at Shipton-under-Wychwood.

as ironstone. The red soil above it is exceptionally fertile, and so arable land replaces sheep pastures in the area.

Deddington, Adderbury and Bloxham are all sizeable main-road villages on the west wide of the River Cherwell, built of the tawny-coloured ironstone. Their roads bring heavy traffic through them, and their proximity to Banbury brings modern expansion for industrial workers. Deddington has scant remains of the castle where Piers Gaveston felt the "black dog's teeth" when Warwick captured him there and took him to execution unhindered by the formalities of trial and judgement. The medieval market place at the village centre was once a noisy and bustling place which declined with the growth of Banbury. Deddington had been one of Oxfordshire's wealthiest villages at the time of Domesday Book, and its subsequent prosperity can be seen from its large church, several fine houses, inns and the attractive almshouses in Church Street. It is arguably, like Bloxham, a small town. The church had a spire once, but it collapsed in 1634.

Bloxham and Adderbury still have their spires – "Bloxham for length, Adderbury for strength", as one expression of local rivalry has it, and it does express in a nutshell the soaring height of Bloxham's spire and the solid elegance of Adderbury's. Rivalry between these villages appears to have gone to extraordinary lengths, but occasionally sympathy ot outlook was also without limits. In 1544 the parish priests of Bloxham and Deddington were hanged from the towers of their churches for their opposition to the English Litany. The villagers of Bloxham and Deddington, at about the same time, had no reservations about going to Adderbury, if they were ill, to consult Elizabeth Cracklow, the local wise woman with a widespread reputation for healing, who was far too popular to heed the Bishop of Oxford's warning to cease using charms.

The old pagan images in the village church would have seemed to support her indifference to new-fangled ideas. The same sculptor worked on Bloxham's church as well, and whilst Jennifer Sherwood calls Bloxham's church of St Mary "one of the grandest churches in the country", it is Adderbury's, of like dedication, which has more of a village atmosphere, with carvings of rural scenes and weird monsters both inside and outside the building in a fantastic display of sculptural imagination. Dragons, gryphons and mermaids are among the more identifiable fantasies, while reality is represented by minstrels with pipes, cymbals and other instruments, and a shepherd, a housewife and other figures.

Perhaps the mason's work was among the inspiration of the Earl of Rochester, that witty and profligate Restoration poet who built the seventeenth-century version of the much-altered Adderbury House and died repentant at thirty-three after a reckless ride through life and

Carvings on the church at Adderbury, Oxfordshire.

literature. It was he who first called Charles II "the merry monarch",
but he was up and down like a man on a see-saw in his relations with
the King, of whom he wrote the famous verse:

> Here lies our Sovereign Lord the King,
> Whose word no man relies on,
> Who never said a foolish thing,
> Nor ever did a wise one

Rochester was imprisoned in the Tower before he was twenty for
seducing the heiress Elizabeth Malet, who was supposed to be marry-
ing the Earl of Sandwich's son, and he (Rochester) courted his
second wife, Anne, supposedly insane, by presenting himself to her as
the Emperor of China. But whose mind was unhinged by this affair?

> Womankind more joy discovers
> Making fools than taking lovers.

These villages became centres for making plush cloth in the eighteenth and nineteenth centuries, as a development from the old woollen cloth industry which had provided another expression of rivalry:
"Bloxham dogs come to Adderbury to buy their togs".
Hardly in Lord Rochester's class, these local verses at least have the

merit of genuine country amusements, and the Adderbury Morris dancers keep some of the old spirits alive and kicking in their summer performances, on Cotswold village greens, reviving some ancient fertility ritual that was disappearing even in Shakespeare's day, before Cromwell put his much-maligned foot down:

> The nine-men's morris is fill'd up with mud;
> And the quaint mazes in the wanton green,
> For lack of tread, are indistinguishable.

One quaint maze that is far from indistinguishable is at Somerton, an unattractive village of grey oolite on the east bank of the Cherwell. It is in the grounds of Troy Farm, outside the village along the road leading to Ardley, and is often said to be of sixteenth-century origin, but that is unlikely. The name indicates that the maze was here before the farm. An ancient earthwork variously known an Ash Bank, Aves Ditch and Wattle Bank ran along the eastern edges of the parish boundary, within a few yards of the site of the maze. It was probably used as part of the boundary between Mercia and Wessex, but the dyke was already there when the Saxons came and is likely to be of pre-Roman origin. The chances are that the maze has been there as long as the ditch and is Celtic. Ash and spirals both had magical significance in Celtic religion.

Several of these turf mazes remain in different parts of England, and almost without exception they are in the stone country. It is arguable, of course, that the arable land beyond the Jurassic Boundary has been subject to more ruthless ploughing, and therefore more mazes could have been destroyed there, but it seems most likely that the majority of such mazes remain in the stone country simply because there were more there in the first place. We have noticed maze patterns on rocks in Cornwall, and they occur in France, Wales and Ireland, as well as in England.

Another of these turf mazes, identical in design to mosaic patterns in the floors of Chartres Cathedral and other French churches, is preserved at Wing in Leicestershire, and I wrote of this in my book on that county, as follows:

> The origins of the maze go back at least as far as the Minoan civilisation of Crete. It was connected with ideas of resurrection – the centre represented death, to which one went and then made one's way out of. The story of the labyrinth of King Minos, in which Theseus slew the Minotaur, embraces this theme, and may explain its origin. In Britain, on mazes such as this one at Wing, a spiral dance called 'Troy Town' used to be performed in some villages at Easter, and this was the maze's purpose – the enactment of an ancient ritual, possibly arising from the delivery of the Athenian maidens from the dreaded Minotaur. Why the mazes were later called Troy Town is

not clear, but it was possibly because of the old tradition that heroes from Troy founded Britain and France, where the mazes occur. . . . In Wales they were known as 'Caerdroia' – Troy Town, as in England.

At the northern extremity of the Cotswolds near Banbury are Wroxton and Hornton, the latter's famous quarries supplying the warm brown stone of which both are built. The A422 westward from Wroxton runs along a raised bank where the land on either side has been quarried for iron ore and then levelled and reinstated as farm land. Wroxton was the site of an Augustinian monastery, and a Tudor house, Wroxton Abbey, was begun on the site by Sir William Pope and completed after his death, with a lake and elaborate water works in the grounds. This impressive building is now a college, but it was owned at one time by the North family, to which the noble and ignoble Prime Minister belonged, and his tomb by Flaxman is in the church, along with Pope's and that of Thomas Coutts, the banker.

Hornton's original quarries were north of the village, but they are now just over the county boundary at Edge Hill in Warwickshire. Cottages stand near the church where the quarries used to be. Hornton's Liassic limestone produced bluish-grey flags much used for the floors of Cotswold cottages, as well as the rich brown stone used for walls. The latter is one of the best of the ironstones, darkening on exposure through the rusting of the iron oxide in the rock, but greenish and golden tints are found in it too. Broughton Castle, near Banbury, is the stone's most spectacular monument.

Well outside the Cotswolds, but belonging to this chapter in spirit, are a few stone villages near Oxford, such as Cassington, beside the Oxford-Witney road, Stanton Harcourt and the villages surrounding Otmoor, whilst north of the city are Glympton and Bletchington, the former only a tiny hamlet but both having big houses in adjacent parkland. The limestone encircling Oxford is a variety known as Corallian, or Coral Rag. It consists of fossilized shells and corals and is a rough, lumpy stone which has to be treated rather like flint – that is, bedded in generous layers of mortar. A number of quarries around Oxford used to supply building stone, not always of good quality, of which the most notorious were perhaps Headington and Wheatley – coarse with poor durability. Much used in Oxford in the seventeenth and eighteenth centuries, it was soon subject to exfoliation, and a great deal of decayed stone has had to be replaced.

The new church at Wheatley, built in 1855-7 by G. E. Street, was the scene of Henry Broadhurst's youth as a stonemason's apprentice. He was born near Oxford, and his father and brothers were stonemasons too. He began learning the craft in the time-honoured manner – making tea for thirty or forty men and fetching beer for them twice a day from a public house a mile away, because the landlord was foreman of the masons' yard. As the completion of St Mary's Church approached, masons began to be laid off, and as there was no work to be had in Oxford, Broadhurst became an itinerant mason, finding jobs in Buckingham, Banbury, Norwich and elsewhere, tramping many hundreds of miles in search of work and earning around twenty-four shillings for a sixty-hour week. Eventually he ended up in London and worked as a 'rougher-out' on the new Houses of Parliament, dressing stones to rough shape ready for the 'carvers' to work on.

Henry Broadhurst came to sit inside the great building he had helped to erect. From being the Stonemasons' Society TUC delegate at the age of thirty-two, he eventually became one of the first working men to be elected a Member of Parliament, and in 1885 he was appointed Under-Secretary of State in the Home Office by Prime Minister Gladstone. Some of the masons and quarrymen who had known him as their tea-boy lived to see him in the company of the Prince of Wales, though not always with full appreciation of his endeavours on behalf of working men, for he was in time expelled from his own union.

Gladstone's Home Secretary, and later Chancellor of the Exchequer, was Sir William Harcourt, and he brings us conveniently back to Oxfordshire and Stanton Harcourt, a medieval manor among the marshes between the Thames and the Windrush. The Harcourts, whose monuments crowd the church (including the eccentric painted mock-Gothic tomb of George, Viscount Harcourt), owned the manor from the twelfth century, and Simon Harcourt lent a room in the manor house to Alexander Pope, so that the poet could leave London and work in peace in the country on his translation of Homer's *Iliad*. Most of the old house was demolished when the family moved to Nuneham Courtenay, but the so-called Pope's Tower remains, as well as the spectacular Great Kitchen, which Pope likened to Vulcan's forge. "The horror of it has made such an impression on the country people," he wrote with tongue in cheek, "that they believe the witches keep their Sabbath here, and that once a year the Devil treats them with infernal venison, viz. a toasted tiger stuffed with tenpenny nails." There might have been slightly more truth in Pope's wit than he realized, for a large prehistoric settlement existed on the marshes nearby, and three standing stones were known locally as the Devil's Quoits.

Pope was mocked himself, by his erstwhile friend Lady Mary Wortley Montagu, when he wrote a sentimental epitaph for a pair of local young lovers killed by lightning whilst getting in the harvest. John Hewet and Sarah Drew, "an industrious young man and virtuous maiden of this parish", were to have been married on the following Sunday, and Lady Mary sent Pope a cynical alternative to his verse:

> Who knows if t'was not kindly done?
> For had they seen the next year's sun,
> A beaten wife and cuckold swain
> Had jointly curs'd the marriage chain.
> Now they are happy in their doom,
> For Pope hath wrote upon their tomb.

Otmoor is a bleak, uninhabited expanse of former marshland to the north-east of Oxford, much associated with mystery and magic in local folklore, crossed by the River Ray and a Roman road and now used by the army as a training area. Round its fringes, however, are a few stone villages of some charm and interest, although it must be said at once that they are something of an anticlimax after the best of the Cotswolds. Not only have brick walls and red tiles found their way into these villages, but barns with corrugated iron roofs stand up prominently from the flat farmland divided by hedges. Still, stone there is in plenty in the older parts.

Islip is an ancient village where Edward the Confessor was born around 1004, at a Saxon palace now completely disappeared. The church of St Nicholas, succeeding that which the Confessor left in his Will to Westminster Abbey, interested Swift, who fancied the living before he went to Dublin. The village was the scene of much fighting during the Civil War, but the best-remembered battles in this area occurred over the draining and enclosure of Otmoor in the nineteenth century.

Oddington and Charlton were two of the seven villages which had traditionally held common rights on the marshes, grazing geese and cattle there, and when the order for drainage and enclosure came in 1829, after forty years of agitation from landowners, who included the Duke of Marlborough, the local people took to rioting and destruction in their efforts to keep the moor as their common land. They broke down embankments, hedges and fences, smashed bridges, harassed magistrates and drove their cattle into the ploughed fields. Troops had to be called in, and there were many arrests, but it was five years before the villagers resigned themselves to the fact that they were fighting a losing battle and gave up. An anonymous author wrote the last ineffectual word on the enclosure of common land by the rich:

> The fault is great in man or woman
> Who steals a goose from off a common.
> But what can plead that man's excuse
> Who steals a common from a goose?

Oddington is a pleasant little village near the canal which was dug to divert the River Ray on a new course. The church of St Andrew contains a particularly unusual and unpleasant memorial – a brass to Ralph Hamsterley, a sixteenth-century parson, which takes the ghastly hint in 'dust to dust' and shows him shrouded and being consumed by worms.

The road through the village skirts the fringe of the moor and comes to Charlton-on-Otmoor, a place of stone cottages and many little bridges crossing streams south and east of its centre. It is the best of the Otmoor villages, with its church tower of bright yellowish stone standing above roofs of thatch or red tile. Charlton was evidently athletic in the early seventeenth century, for the minister was censured by the ecclesiastical court for playing football and wrestling with the village cooper and other men, in what appears to have been a drunken brawl.

Stanton St John lies south of Otmoor, closer to Oxford. It was the home of John Milton's grandfather, a forest under-ranger who disowned his son, Milton's father, when the latter became a Protestant at Oxford. Milton senior's Protestant contemporary, John White, founder of the New England colony of Massachusetts, was born here, and his house can still be seen in the village. As for John Milton himself, he visited his grandfather here and courted Mary Powell, a local magistrate's daughter, secretly. He was twice her age, and the resulting marriage had unhappy consequences, though Mary bore him three daughters before she died in her twenties.

A more recent resident of Stanton St John was A. E. Coppard, the poet and story-teller, who rented a cottage called Shepherds Pit here after giving up his job as an accountant in Oxford to devote his time to writing. He had also lived at Islip. Alfred Coppard spent a couple of years in extreme poverty at Stanton, with little literary success, until Harold Midgley Taylor, founder of the Golden Cockerel private press, cycled twenty-five miles from Berkshire to persuade him to co-operate in the press's productions, and Coppard's stories *Adam and Eve and Pinch Me* saw the light of day. The book, published ominously on 1st April 1921, was hardly a work of art in the William Morris tradition. As Coppard recalled, ''The type was poor, the paper bad, the leaves fell out, the cover collapsed . . .'', but it was the start of his success as a teller of the vivid rural tales which have become more widely known since some were dramatized for television in the series *Country Matters*.

Brief Diversion

Before continuing our exploration northward, we ought to take notice of some stone building in the west Midlands which, although it scarcely provides a single village of pure stone, does deserve mention for the sake of completeness. The stone of the region produces some highly interesting uses in an area where industry has brought too much brick and slate for the survival of any villages which may have been entirely stone-built at one time.

Cottages built of Swithland slates and quarry rubble at Woodhouse Eaves, Leicestershire.

The Charnwood Forest area of Leicestershire has contributed to the character of many villages over a wide area, for both granite and slate have been quarried there and used for building on a limited scale as well as – in the case of slate – for distinctive roofing. Mountsorrel has been known for its granite for centuries, but it is very hard to work and has been used chiefly in road-making. The church at Mountsorrel, however, is built of it, and other isolated buildings in the vicinity have walls of undressed rubble from the quarries.

In Swithland Wood, well known for its spring carpet of bluebells, are the rain-filled pits from which Swithland slate has been quarried for centuries. The Romans were first to exploit the material. It provided roofing slates far more attractive in their variety of colour than the uniform cold grey of the Welsh variety, and rough-hewn stone from the quarries was also used for building houses here and there. A group of cottages at Woodhouse Eaves shows off the material to perfection in both walls and roofs, and several other villages, such as Newtown Linford and Swithland itself, have houses built of local stone.

The most interesting use of Swithland slate, however, was in making gravestones. These can be seen in all the local churchyards and were popular because the slate lent itself to elaborate engraving. A local art form grew up in designing and engraving headstones and other monuments in the material, with fine lettering and flamboyant decoration, and if the villages of north-west Leicestershire do not display as much stone in their buildings as one might have hoped, at least their churchyards still possess ample testimony to the one-time busy-ness of the local quarrymen and masons.

We have already entered Hereford and Worcester on the fringes of the Cotswolds, but farther north-west there is a good deal of stone building in the counties bordering Wales, especially in the villages of south Shropshire and parts of Cheshire. Grinshill, north of Shrewsbury, is one of the notable quarries of the area, still working, and much of its red and white sandstone can be seen in Shrewsbury itself, but the Welsh Marches are famous for their black-and-white half-timbered buildings, and stone makes only intermittent appearances. Shropshire is not a county in which to seek stylishness in village building, in any case, for it was always a relatively poor area, but several places – Cardington, Minton and Munslow, for instance – have plenty of local stone in their houses and churches.

Munslow, near Church Stretton, is one of the best stone villages of the region, for although it has a rather dilapidated look, there is more visible stone in this village than most, for the greenish-brown Silurian sandstone was quarried near here once. Its most stylish building is the Jacobean house which eventually became the village school. It had been the home of the Littleton family, who provided Charles I with his

Sandstone at Munslow, Shropshire.

Solicitor-General in the affair of the Ship Money. The village had both a green and a castle motte once, but both have been lost – rather carelessly, as Lady Bracknell would have said – for what was once a green village is now a street village, and a good deal less attractive as a result. Some traveller to distant parts once brought back a stone from the Great Wall of China, and this at least survives, a strange relic to be deposited in a Christian church.

Rubble walling is more usual in this area than dressed stone laid in courses, for the Silurian and Ordovician stone here is older and harder than that to the east. Most of it is sandstone, but Wenlock Edge is formed of limestone, and that too has been used for building in the past. It is still quarried, but not for building nowadays. The fine ruins of the priory at Much Wenlock show it to advantage. Quarries to the west, at Hoar Edge, provided much stone roofing material which can still be seen here and there in the area.

At South Tawton, in Devon, we noted a probable sheela-na-gig in the church, and these slightly mysterious fertility figures come back to mind in Shropshire, for the county has no less than four of them – more than a fifth of all those known in England. A sheela-na-gig is a lewd figure found – in Britain at least – almost without exception in the fabric of ancient Christian churches. In Ireland it occurs frequently on castles too. A grinning woman, usually of repellent aspect, crouches to hold

open her hugely exaggerated vulva with both hands passing beneath her bent legs, in a sort of ironic invitation to sex without love.

The best known of the English 'sheelas' is the one at Kilpeck, in Hereford and Worcester, which is frequently reproduced in books about Celtic art to back the theory that these are cult figures of the Celtic religion. Nearly all those surviving in England occur this side of the Jurassic Boundary, but my own belief is that they are not Celtic at all but have a northern European origin. Humanity tends to attribute to an acknowledged 'dark age' anything it cannot properly account for as a product of a more enlightened period.

I have discussed the Shropshire sheelas in my book on that county and will not repeat the argument here, but it is interesting to note that the stone regions of England (Yorkshire, Derbyshire, Oxfordshire, Avon, Wiltshire etc) are where most of these figures have survived the puritan offensive. They are very much to do with stone villages because, except for one in Oxford, none remains in large towns or cities, and the survival of those we know of, under the noses of increasingly puritanical Christians, is easier to explain than the pre-servation of the Cerne Abbas Giant – they tend to be in small churches in backward and thinly populated rural areas which have escaped the attention of the zealous. Those in Shropshire occur where stone buildings are most in evidence – along Corvedale, at Holdgate and Tugford and in Church Stretton.

The sandstone of the west of England has also been much quarried in Staffordshire and Cheshire, where it is generally red, but not to an extent to provide whole villages of it, for timber and brick have been more readily available in these parts, as in Shropshire and Hereford-shire, and of course brick has become far too prominent in and around all the major industrial conurbations of the Midlands and the north to leave intact any villages worth consideration in the present context, with one or two precious exceptions which we shall notice in due course. But weaving one's way between the centres of manufacturing and heavy industry provides much delight in the northern half of England, and anyone in the south who may still think that stone village building ends with the Cotswolds has many pleasant surprises in store.

CHAPTER 5

The Limestone – Midlands and North

From the Cotswold Hills, the Jurassic limestone continues, decreasing in width, north-eastwards from Oxfordshire, through Northampton-shire, Leicestershire and Lincolnshire, turning gradually northwards in a wide arc towards the Humber. The wider belt of oolite, accom-panying the lias, also crosses Buckinghamshire and the fringes of Bedfordshire and Cambridgeshire. It would seem a little ungracious not to add Rutland to the list, for although it no longer exists as such – being part of Leicestershire since 1974 – the former tiny county was, *par excellence*, a region of stone villages, and within its boundaries were two quarries of great importance. The word 'stone' occurs frequently in the old village names throughout the region – Adstone, Farthingstone, Radstone, Shalstone and so on.

The characteristic scene in this part of England is rolling country populated by sheep and cattle, with always the tall spire of a distant church in view. There is a relative scarcity of trees, and the dry-stone walls of the Cotswolds give way here to an abundance of hawthorn hedges, carefully maintained, for this is fox-hunting country, where the illustrious hunts of the Shires – Quorn, Belvoir, Cottesmore, Fernie – hold their meets in many a village where cottages and inns of grey or rust-coloured stone form picturesque backgrounds to scarlet coats and the hunters of bay and chestnut.

It is a comparatively dry region, with less rainfall than the south, its chief rivers being the Nene and Welland, rising in Northamptonshire and Leicestershire respectively and flowing to the Wash. Stone bridges cross many a brook trickling through the valleys, but the relative scarcity of water is the explanation of the surprising fact that this area – for so long one of the major sheep-rearing parts of the country – never became an important centre of the wool trade, like the Cotswolds. The sheep bred here, Defoe observed, "are, without comparison, the largest, and bear not only the greatest weight of flesh on their bones but also the greatest fleeces of wool on their backs of any sheep in England . . .". But the 'fulling' of wool was dependent on an adequate water supply, so the fleeces went elsewhere.

The fine pasture land remains important for the supply of both wool

The Eleanor Cross at Geddington, Northamptonshire – carved from Oolitic limestone seven hundred years ago.

and mutton, however, and also for beef and leather, the limestone belt being flanked by the two largest boot and shoe manufacturing centres in Britain – Leicester and Northampton. At the turn of the century a third of all workers in Northamptonshire were engaged in leather manufacturing industries.

Apart from the building stone, the other most obvious bounty from the foundations of this region, to anyone driving through it, is iron ore. The so-called Northampton Sand ironstone has been dug out of the earth on an industrial scale, by open-cast mining, since the mid-nineteenth century, sometimes from depths of a hundred feet. It is the *raison d'être* of iron and steel towns such as Corby and Wellingborough.

The geology of the whole Midland region determined in prehistory that the modern preoccupations of the small, dark people of Celtic origin who settled the area would be engineering and mechanics. The descendants of those pioneer settlers – Celts, Romans, Saxons, Vikings – who laboured to mine the earth's mineral riches and cultivate its intractable clay soil, have inherited a philosophy of hard work and independence. They have included men of iron resolution such as George Fox and Hugh Latimer. There is little romance or sophistication in their make-up. They believe in 'good, solid food' and are nonconformists in both religious and secular matters, tending to keep their own counsel and indifferent to both southern affectations and northern ebullience. Insensitive and unimaginative (this area lacks the grandeur to feed imagination), they suffer perhaps from a too inward-looking existence induced by factory life, which is relieved only by mass evacuation to the seaside for a fortnight each summer.

It might be supposed that these facts have precious little to do with the English village, but this is not so. For nestling in the shadows of the foundry chimneys of these Midland industrial centres are beautiful villages built of ironstone. It is hardly fifty years since Corby itself was a pleasant little stone village, and it is the earth's mineral treasures which have made this region the factory community it is. Cars and cycles, boots and shoes, hosiery and knitwear, as well as the iron and steel works, consume the vast majority of workers in the area. If nature had not provided the iron ore, man could not have built these villages, and it was quite unreasonable for anti-industry men like H. J. Massingham to rage against the ugliness of the one whilst wanting to preserve the beauty of the other. Idealism does not give us our daily bread.

In this area the ironstone has been used for centuries for building houses and churches, often of a rich cinnamon colour, lending a lovely mellow quality to numerous villages which are, perhaps, the least known of all those discussed in this book, since the East Midlands are devoid of the more obvious tourist attractions. Right on the doorstep of Corby, almost literally within a stone's throw of the town where blast furnaces, explosives, drag-lines and unemployment loom large, one of the most charming villages in the region, Rockingham, climbs up its little hill lined with warm ironstone houses, some thatched and some tiled, towards the church and castle overlooking the valley of the Welland below.

It is as good a place as any in which to start an exploration of this region's villages, and perhaps better than most, for it was William the Conqueror who built its hilltop castle. Alas, Rockingham is a street village standing along a busy main road, but it manages to hang on to its country character, which was so important at one time that the village gave its name to a vast royal hunting forest covering the north-eastern part of Northamptonshire. The area is still known as Rockingham Forest.

The strategic importance of the Norman castle, overlooking a vital crossing of the Welland, gave way in more peaceful times to the importance of the village itself as a staging post, and indeed Rockingham once progressed to the status of a small market town but declined after the Civil War.

The castle has been owned by descendants of the Weston family since Elizabethan times, when it was rebuilt, and among the friends of later Westons Charles Dickens was a frequent guest here when he was at the height of his creative genius, writing *David Copperfield*. "Of all the country houses and estates I have yet seen in England," he wrote, "I think this is by far the best." Perhaps he was unduly influenced by the warmth of his friendship with the owners, but at any rate he was sufficiently impressed by Rockingham Castle to base 'Chesney Wold' on it when he wrote *Bleak House*. The surviving Norman gateway and adjoining walls are of the local ironstone, quarried nearby when William of Normandy occupied the English throne.

If Rockingham has a disappointment, it is that its church is not the typical noble village nucleus one expects of this region. Not only is it rather separated from the village itself, but nineteenth-century rebuilding and restoration are all too evident, and instead of a tall broach or recessed spire, its tower is surmounted by a curious octagonal pyramid, as if the masons started to build something but, forgetting what it was supposed to be, abandoned it.

If we want a superb village church, we shall do better at Warmington, due east, or at Geddington, between Corby and Kettering, and in this area there are many other interesting villages, such as Rushton, Great Oakley, Wadenhoe and Brigstock, all deserving attention which space forbids, to say nothing of Barnwell, where the Duke of Gloucester has his home. The predominant warm buff stone of which they are all built is from the quarries at Weldon, immediately east of Corby, which supplied stone for the upper part of King's College Chapel at

Cambridge and for the best-preserved of the three surviving Eleanor Crosses – the tall, restrained monument of grey oolite at the centre of Geddington. Old St Paul's, destroyed in the Great Fire of London, was also built of Weldon stone, which was carried to the capital in panniers on the backs of donkeys.

In Great Weldon itself is a curiosity of a building called Haunt Hill House. It was built of Ketton limestone in the seventeenth century by the mason who lived in it, and it is a minor monument to the mason's craft, even if a trifle eccentric.

Barnwell St Andrew has in its churchyard a headstone to three tragically short-lived children of Daniel and Ann Stevens. Daniel was one of a family of stone-carvers, and he made this lovingly carved memorial in Ketton stone.

We must not by-pass the villages at the south-west end of Northamptonshire. There are many, but Aynho is particularly distinctive and attractive with its great house, Aynhoe Park, at its centre. In the sense that it is a model village, and thus one man's creation, Aynho is a masterpiece. Standing on a hill overlooking the countryside of Northamptonshire to its north and Oxfordshire on its other sides, its neat cottages often sport apricot trees on their walls, along sloping lanes, one of which is called Skittle Alley. There is some shelly limestone in the garden walls of this dove-grey village, which presents a quite startling contrast with Adderbury, just across the Cherwell and the Oxfordshire border.

Evenley, round three sides of its large square green, is now being spoilt by expansion, as is Staverton to the north – a village which, twenty years ago, I came to by chance and found a delightful surprise. Moreton Pinkney suffers from its main-road position, and Adstone is overgrown and uncared for, but it is interesting to compare these ironstone villages in the hilly country south-west of Daventry with the grey stone of Mixbury, farther south in Oxfordshire, where the houses, built a century ago, are given uniform dressings of red brick.

Silverstone's name is a clear enough indication of its situation on the limestone, but its only attraction now is for motor-racing enthusiasts, little of its pale silvery stone remaining visible nowadays. Weedon Lois is also losing its silvery stones to boring bricks, but the village cemetery contains the grave of Dame Edith Sitwell, with its monument designed by Henry Moore. Alas, the choice of stone for the job was not wise – it has been there less than twenty years and is already wearing badly. Another curious distinction of the villages in this vicinity is the style of the village signs – admirable with their unusual Roman lettering.

Stratton Audley is another Oxfordshire village of yellowish-grey oolite, and others in this area, such as Cottisford and Hardwick, used to be nice before landowners largely rebuilt them in brick. This is the

A corner of Aynho, Northamptonshire.

country of Flora Thompson's famous autobiographical trilogy *Lark Rise to Candleford* – the author's father was the village stonemason.

Across the northern boundary, just in Warwickshire, Priors Marston is altogether more pleasing. It comes as a surprise if you approach it via the long Welsh Road from Southam, since all before it is brick, and then suddenly brown ironstone greets you in the attractive houses all round the village green.

Another Northamptonshire village which cannot be overlooked is Ashton, near Oundle. Even more worthy of note than the prettiness of the village itself is the manner of its creation, for this is another modern village, built at the turn of the century. The Honourable Charles de Rothschild, son of the first Lord Rothschild, was an enthusiastic entomologist, and the Rockingham Forest vicinity was noted as the habitat of the Chequered Skipper, a rare butterfly. In one of those extravagant gestures which earn those who can afford them a reputation for eccentricity, Rothschild bought the village with much surrounding land and gave it to his wife as a wedding present. The villagers benefited from the purchase, for Rothschild, as well as building himself the mansion, Ashton Wold, rebuilt the village in local stone, putting a bathroom in every cottage and burying all the village's electric cables underground, thus saving Ashton from those hideous

Priors Marston, Warwickshire – the seventeenth-century 'High House'.

poles and wires that disfigure so many of our otherwise unspoiled villages – though nowadays, of course, even Ashton has sprouted a luxuriant crop of television aerials on its thatched roofs. A great annual event takes place on Ashton's village green in October when the chestnut trees have shed their fruits – the Conker Championship of Great Britain.

Fotheringhay is a little to the north, a tiny village once lorded over by the castle – now only a mound – which brought birth to Richard III and death to Mary, Queen of Scots. What remains at Fotheringhay, however, is much of the old church, built by the master mason William Horwood under contract to Richard, Duke of York, from 1434. Its most distinctive feature is the octagonal lantern surmounting a square tower, and flying buttresses and fan vaulting add to the rare elegance of the village's oldest stonework. Stone monuments were erected in the church by Elizabeth I to Edward and Richard, the second and third

The stone-built Duddington Mill on the River Welland.

Dukes of York. Among other attractive villages in this part of Northamptonshire are Deene, Apethorpe and Duddington.

At the northern tip of the county, a village of more direct relevance to our subject is Collyweston, for here the famous Collyweston tiles have been made which roof the houses in this village and many others in the East Midlands. Collyweston tiles were made and used by the Romans and are still made and used today. The material is mined (not quarried) from the Inferior Oolite, and the resulting tiles are thinner, and therefore considerably lighter, than those produced in the Cotswolds, though they still need strong timbers to hold them up. The ingenious stoneworkers at Collyweston let nature do most of the work. Large blocks of the fissile limestone are left out during the winter with the bedding planes upright instead of flat. Rain penetrates between the layers, and when it freezes in icy weather, it expands, splitting the rock into thin slabs just right for making the tiles. They weather to a greeny-brown colour and have been used extensively at Cambridge, among other places.

Along the borders of Buckinghamshire, Bedfordshire and Cambridgeshire there are several limestone villages, such as Ravenstone and Weston Underwood in Buckinghamshire, Odell and Turvey in Bedfordshire, and Helpston, Peakirk and Sibson-cum-Stibbington, now all in Cambridgeshire. Sir Peter Scott's Wildfowl Trust owns waterfowl gardens at Peakirk, but Weston Underwood, where William Cowper lived quietly at the Lodge, is now blessed with an incongruous 'Flamingo Garden and Tropical Bird Zoo', where the poet visited his friends the Throckmortons at the big house, Weston Park, since demolished. It is a *very* stylish and well-kept model village, though, in spite of one brick house at each end of the street. The cottages have cobbled pavements in front of them. The village inn is called 'Cowper's Oak' after the tree in Yardley Chase which inspired one of William's poems, and Weston Lodge itself is a respectable house, in which Cowper had window seats, a walled garden and views over the fields, "for you must always understand," he wrote, "that when poets talk of cottages and hermitages, and such-like things, they mean a house with six sashes in front, two comfortable parlours, a smart staircase and three bedchambers of comfortable dimensions. . . ." Ravenstone – Weston's neighbour – is not in the same class, showing not only much more haphazard growth but more various materials, with some brick, some thatch and some brick dressings in its creamy stone cottages.

Just over the Leicestershire border from Rockingham is a string of attractive stone villages which make the tourist neglect of this rich county incredible. Massingham entirely ignored Leicestershire in his pre-war book on the limestone country, and many another author rushes off likewise into what was Rutland without bothering to see what Leicestershire has to offer. Have I actually read somewhere (or am I dreaming it?) that Leicestershire is not a county where village building has flourished? The villages in the county's south-east corner may not be as pretty and photogenic as those of the Cotswolds – the plain architecture is in line with the no-nonsense character of the people – but Great Easton, Medbourne, Glooston and Bringhurst are good villages of the rust-tinted lias stone of the area and are often graced by fine broach spires on their churches.

Horninghold is another village which must be seen by the connoisseur. Although it is of ancient origin, its modern development was as an estate village, built mostly in the early twentieth century by T. A. Hardcastle of Blaston Hall, and in a most picturesque setting. It has a look of tidiness and prosperity which, though far removed from the haphazard growth of older villages, and therefore a trifle inhospitable, without shops or public houses, certainly qualifies it for a place in any book about domestic building in stone. The graceful spire of Horninghold's ancient church of St Peter, moreover, draws attention to a building which, remarkably in the circumstances, remains free of extensive restoration.

Farther north there is much limestone of a cooler hue in the villages of the Leicestershire Wolds. Places such as Waltham on the Wolds, Croxton Kerrial, Stonesby and Chadwell have their particular charms, but they are not, on the whole, specially attractive villages and are now somewhat under the shadow of imminent coal-mining development in the Vale of Belvoir. Croxton (pronounced Crowston) Kerrial has a church in which the use of different stones can be clearly seen, the chancel being of warm ironstone and the rest of grey oolite. Legend has it that the long-vanished chapel of the local abbey contained the viscera of King John, the abbot (who was the King's physician) having prudently removed them before he was buried at Worcester, so as to avoid suspicion of poisoning.

Back to the south-east of Leicestershire, however, and one village of the old county which absolutely demands attention – Hallaton. It is easily the prettiest of Leicestershire villages, set among rolling hills heavily populated by sheep. There was once an iron-working site nearby, of ancient origin, and a motte-and-bailey castle was built to protect it, probably during the troubled reign of King Stephen. Perhaps this was the earliest source of Hallaton's prosperity, for it grew into an important market town, as the size of its church indicates. It later declined to village status again with the rise of Market Harborough.

St Michael's is one of the most impressive village churches in Leicestershire, with a splendid broach spire surmounting its big Norman tower (surrounded by grotesque heads), Saxon coffin lids on display and stone carvings of evil beings inside. A certain pagan

The market cross at Hallaton, Leicestershire.

presence insinuates itself on the visitor even without further information about the goings-on at Hallaton, and he only needs to walk to the triangular green to see the curious conical market cross and hear the church bells ringing their melancholy tune every three hours, for the impression to seem complete.

> Old Dunmore's dead, that good old man,
> Him we shall no more see.
> He made these chimes to play themselves
> At twelve, nine, six and three.

Does the clock go backwards, or is this poetic licence? Never mind – the visitor has heard nothing yet! On Easter Monday each year the ritualistic extravagance of Hallaton takes wing and flies to its spirited climax.

When the open fields here were enclosed in 1770, a piece of land known as Hare Crop Leys was awarded to the rector and his successors on condition that, each Easter Monday, he would provide two hare pies and a quantity of ale for the traditional ceremony called Hare Pie Scrambling, which has continued up to the present day. The bizarre events begin with a procession to church, led by a band. Later the participants enjoy a rowdy lunch at the local inn, after which the pies are collected from the Rectory. Made of more readily available meat than hare nowadays, they are cut up into pieces by the rector, as part of the ritual, and put into sacks. The ale is put into two small casks. The procession now forms up again and marches – or totters – to Hare Pie

Bank, where the sacks are emptied and those who wish join in an uncouth scramble for a fistful of pie. This ritual is accompanied by the Bottle Kicking routine, in which men from Hallaton and neighbouring Medbourne compete in kicking the casks of ale across the village stream. The frothy ale is then drunk at the village cross, which looks like nothing so much as a phallic symbol.

That these customs have their origin in some ancient pagan ritual is obvious, and it is hardly surprising that local rectors have occasionally expressed deep misgivings about taking any part in such proceedings. But when one incumbent went so far as to refuse to supply the hare pies, notices were soon posted up in the village with the simple ultimatum: "No Pie, no Parson."

The Celtic survival is as plain here as in the south-west, where we noticed three hares appearing in churches and where symbols such as the Padstow Hobby Horse have wider fame, but I doubt if there is any more blatantly erotic than the Hallaton Hare Pie Scramble, in which that sinister animal sacred to the dawn-goddess Eostre is actually a witch in disguise, being torn to shreds, or symbolically raped, by the Devil in the form of greyhounds. It might be that the pre-eminent sport of hunting in the Shires is connected with this eruption from the collective unconscious, for the sport certainly existed long before the unfortunate red fox became the traditional quarry. Pagan or not, hunting has carried many a Leicestershire sporting parson along with it, happily intoning Biblical injunctions about the holiness of all God's creatures in church on Sundays and yelling 'Tally-ho' with the Quorn or the Fernie on Mondays during the season. It was, indeed, a rector of this very village once who, pressed to pray for rain during a period of drought, agreed to try it but warned his optimistic flock that "It's no damned good with the wind in this quarter."

Hunting of the fox is not more than two or three hundred years old, but the chase is as old as mankind, and it seems odd that the modern sport is regarded as the God-given right of the rich. Medieval villagers in Rockingham Forest or the Leicestershire Wolds might starve to death while noblemen dined on venison, but let a peasant be caught taking a deer and he would be blinded or have his hands cut off. No one wants to eat foxes, but the expensive snobbery of the sport, particularly in the Shires, puts it beyond the reach of ordinary mortals and thus encourages their outrage. Nevertheless, a meet in one of the local stone villages on a crisp November morning is one of the great English sights. Foxhunting has contributed to the appearance of the local countryside and to the employment of local craftsmen, for hawthorn hedges have to be 'laid' or 'pleached' to prevent them from growing too tall for horses to jump them.

The creation of Rutland Water – a giant reservoir the size of Winder-

mere – has put on the map, to some extent, the tiny former county whose secrets remained largely unknown except to those who were already familiar with its charming stone villages and fine churches. The whole county possessed only one set of traffic lights and only one obtrusive sign of industry – the chimneys of the Ketton cement works.

This is an appropriate starting-point for Rutland because, although cement production is now the priority at Ketton, the fine-grained Oolitic limestone for building, which has been famous for over four hundred years, is still quarried here. It has gone into the building of Cambridge as well as into local village churches, although ironically the church at Ketton itself is not built with it, stone from Barnack having been used instead. The quarries near the latter village (once in Northamptonshire, then in Huntingdonshire, now in Cambridgeshire) produced a coarse limestone known as 'ragstone' which was quarried by the Romans and widely used throughout the Middle Ages – the cathedrals of Ely and Peterborough contain much of it. The quarries at Barnack were owned by the monks of Peterborough, and they granted quarrying rights to several other abbeys – for a consideration, of course. The Benedictine Abbey of Ramsey, in Cambridgeshire, paid a tribute of four thousand eels a year, during Lent, for the privilege of taking stone from Barnack in the eleventh century. But the seams were exhausted by the eighteenth century, and the old quarry pits, deserted and overgrown, are now known locally as 'Hills and Holes'. The village itself is exceedingly attractive at its old centre but just as hideous at its outskirts, where brick and concrete flank the main road.

To return to Ketton, its stone is a little more yellow than Barnack, as well as being of finer grain, but some Ketton has a pinkish tinge, and it can weather to buffs and greys as well, whereas the stone from Clipsham, to the north, has a cooler creamy or blue-grey appearance. These limestones of east Leicestershire, Northamptonshire, Lincolnshire and Cambridgeshire are generally harder than those of the Cotswolds, as can readily be seen by comparing the degrees of weathering in the two areas. It generally takes about eight years for the dark quarried freestone from Ketton to lose its sap and weather to the familiar colours we see in the village buildings.

Clipsham stone graces many famous buildings in London, notably Buckingham Palace and the rebuilt House of Commons, and it has been used extensively for restoration work on the Oxford colleges. It is buff when freshly quarried and has a looser formation than Ketton stone. The quarry has been in continuous operation since 1906, except for the war years, and is still open, though with a depleted work force. Fifty feet of overburden has to be removed to get at the seams, and much of the modern waste has been used to infill workings of the

Ketton, Leicestershire.

Clipsham Quarry, showing the depth of overburden above the workable seams of limestone.

fourteenth century. The village itself is quiet and attractive, the only jarring note being some new houses built of Guiting stone from the Cotswolds which, of course, do not match!

The cluster of limestone quarries in the area where Leicestershire, Northamptonshire, Cambridgeshire and Lincolnshire meet – with the stylish stone town of Stamford as their focal point – continue to produce, as they have for centuries past, very fine building stones which are superior to the Cotswold stones in some respects and second only to Portland for their durability; and they have been carried far and wide, by Ouse, Nene and Welland, by horse-drawn cart, by canal and by rail.

All these local stones are known collectively, and confusingly, as Lincolnshire Limestone, and it was at Stamford in 1947 that a society was formed called 'Men of the Stones' to encourage the use of stone in building and to preserve existing stone buildings. Twenty years after its foundation, the society supported the Orton Trust in acquiring the disused Norman church of All Saints in the tiny village of Orton, near Kettering, and set up a craft centre there where stonemasons and carvers could be trained. This work continues, and the redundant church at Little Oakley has also been acquired recently for the same worthy purpose. The Orton Trust is a registered charity, founded specifically for the training of masons, carvers and other workers in stone. The Society does much good work in advising and otherwise assisting in the preservation of existing stone buildings, but although one also hears of a revival of interest in *building* with natural stone, it is difficult to avoid the suspicion that this is wishful thinking in these days of mass-produced materials and a depressing lack of architectural style and individuality.

There is no lack of style in the villages of Rutland. Not only do they possess a great variety of stone, differing in colour as well as in texture, but the steeply-pitched roofs of thatch, or of variable-coloured Collyweston tiles, add extra interest to each scene. Brown marlstone is sometimes mixed with grey oolite in the same buildings. Though many of the villages have good broach spires on their churches, no two of them are alike. There could hardly be a greater contrast than between the squat and solid spire of Clipsham and the tall and elegant one at Ketton, but both are characteristic of the area, and there is an amazing variety between these two extremes.

If one travels east or west across this region, the changes in landscape and architecture, from the brick-built industrial half of Leicestershire to the Lincolnshire fens, are frequent and dramatic. But the changes along the stone belt, travelling north or south, are more gradual and subtle. As one moves northwards from Northamptonshire, Collyweston tiles and mullioned windows with dripstones over them slowly give way to heavy oak lintels and pantile roofs. Pantiles are confined almost exclusively to the eastern half of England.

There is hardly a single village in the Rutland part of Leicestershire which is not worth looking at for one reason or another, though one or two like Langham and Whissendine have been ruined by brick. Ridlington and Caldecott are very attractive villages of ironstone, whilst Tickencote is well known for its Norman chancel arch, so spectacular as to be almost vulgar; Morcott for its predominantly Norman church; Ryhall for its nice little square and the very old 'Green Dragon' inn; Exton for the magnificent collection of monuments to the Noels and the Haringtons, by such as Grinling Gibbons and Nollekens;

Wing for its ancient turf maze, bringing Celtic ritual back to mind, and so on.

My own favourite among them all is Preston, standing to one side of the Oakham-Uppingham road. Built of the ubiquitous ironstone, its finest houses date from the Stuart period, in particular the tall gabled manor house of 1600. Much of Preston's church is Norman, and whilst connoisseurs of Rutland churches get excited over its marble mosaic from Constantinople and its candlesticks from Damascus, I find a stone head on the outside wall more intriguing. This is not one of those anonymous heads of kings and saints that later masons turned out on a production line to adorn so many indifferent churches ("A gross of kings sent up from Kensington," as Ruskin put it). The face has the character and penetrating eyes of an old man painted by Rembrandt, and it is surely a portrait of the master mason of this church, carved in good humour by one of his craftsmen.

Historically, perhaps, the most interesting of the Rutland ironstone villages is Lyddington, secluded in the southern corner. Its church of St Andrew was a peculiar of the see of Lincoln, and the bishops had a house there (now a museum known as the Bede House) until the beginning of the seventeenth century, when it was converted into a hospital by Thomas Cecil, Lord Burghley, of nearby Stamford. It has a superb banqueting hall, reached by a stone staircase, and a ceiling of richly carved oak panelling. The church, meanwhile, contains some rare clay acoustic jars, set high in the chancel walls, and the old stone houses with their mullioned windows gather round the green with its crumbling cross.

At the northern tip of the Rutland part of Leicestershire, Market Overton is a village of great antiquity and not a little interest. Roman earthworks surround the church of St Peter and St Paul, which has Anglo-Saxon remains in its tower arch, and some fascinating finds have been made here, including ornaments of gold and silver and a 'clepsydra' – a bronze bowl with a hole in the bottom used as a clock by the Anglo-Saxons. Floated on water, it took an hour (more or less) for enough water to leak through to make the bowl sink.

Coincidentally, a boy lived here who became one of the world's great scientists and revolutionized our understanding of time, among other things. Isaac Newton's mother, Hanna, came from Market Overton and gave birth to him at Woolsthorpe, over the Lincolnshire border, on Christmas Day 1642, six months after his father died. Hanna said her baby was so small she could have cradled him in a quart mug. When she remarried, Isaac came to live at Market Overton with his grand-mother, and who can tell what influence the stones and the life of this village had on that great man.

Market Overton, like so many places throughout the country, un-

The manor house at Preston, Leicestershire.

Carving in limestone on the
church at Preston.

accountably preserves its village stocks, those relics of a more barbarous age that serve only to remind us that our post-industrial nostalgia about the former charms of village life is a delusion. It was George Crabbe, the Duke of Rutland's unhappy domestic chaplain at Belvoir Castle, not far away from here, who swept away poetic sentimentality about an England that never was in his grimly realistic poem 'The Village':

> Yes, thus the Muses sing of happy swains,
> Because the Muses never knew their pains. . . .
>
> Can poets soothe you [Crabbe asks the poor villager] when you pine for
>   bread,
> By winding myrtles round your ruined shed?

Where the oolite flattens out beneath clay soil in the eastern half of Rutland, the arable land is among the country's most important barley-growing regions. Much of the barley is supplied to the breweries of Burton-on-Trent, which then sends them back to the village inns to be consumed as ale on hot summer days by gasping travellers who have sought in vain the cool shade of hedgerow trees.

There are many deserted medieval villages in the uplands of east Leicestershire, which qualify for mention because their stone foundations remain below ground level as evidence of their one-time existence. Ingarsby and Lowesby, for example, can be traced through history despite the fact that nothing remains above ground but bumpy fields where their streets and houses once stood. Both villages had twenty-five taxpayers at the end of the fourteenth century. Leicester Abbey owned the manor of Ingarsby after the Black Death had in all probability reduced its population to a mere handful, and the abbey no doubt turned arable land, for which local labour no longer existed, into pasture for sheep. The village had disappeared by 1563. Lowesby hardly fared any better in the ownership of the Ashby family, but the thirteenth-century church there has survived intact.

Not all the lost stone villages were decimated by plague or depopulated by medieval capitalists. Nether Hambleton has recently been submerged by Rutland Water, and at the eastern extreme of Leicestershire is perhaps the most poignant of Midland lost village sites, Pickworth – a casualty of the Wars of the Roses.

Tradition has it that after the Battle of Losecoat Field, fought in 1470 beside the Great North Road, where a little wood is still called Bloody Oaks, the routed Lancastrians fled, shedding their tunics to avoid being recognized. The little village of Pickworth is said to have been destroyed by the ravaging Yorkists. It may well be that the Black Death had already devastated it so much that there was little left to destroy, for another village called Hardwick, nearer the main road, had already been decimated before the Roses clash. But whatever the causes, Pickworth was a ghost village by 1491.

One defiant fragment remains above ground level, in an uneven field where the stone foundations of medieval houses and streets have prevented the land from being ploughed for five hundred years. It is a solitary Gothic arch of stone, with carved capitals – bleached by sun and washed by rain for half a millennium – which was once the entrance to the south porch of All Saints Church, built in the fourteenth century with a fine Midlands spire, deserted and derelict in the fifteenth. What remained of the church building in 1731 was finally demolished in order to make use of the stone in bridge-building and for a farmhouse, for a vestige of life was continued or revived here, and some cottages were put up near the arch for the farmer's labourers, but the subsequent repopulation of Pickworth took place a little to the west of the former site, and the villagers built themselves a new church away from what they called "the old foundations".

To this resurrected community in 1817 came a poor young peasant to work as a lime-burner. Out of the scanty wages his employer paid him, the young man hoped to save a pound to get a prospectus printed for some poems he had written. His name was John Clare. Born at Helpston, not far away, he came to Rutland to work, brought by the stone, and met his future wife, "Sweet Patty of the Vale". The publication of his *Poems Descriptive of Rural Life* brought him the attention of wealthy and well-meaning patrons, but his sensitive and humble spirit could not cope with the practical business of life, and he was soon set on the road to mental breakdown. He lived in asylums for twenty-three years until his death, deserted by Patty, who was afraid to visit him. "If life had a second edition," the lonely and tormented poet wrote, "how I would correct the proofs."

Clare wrote an 'Elegy on the Ruins of Pickworth', from which come the following verses:

> Ye scenes of desolation spread around,
>   Prosperity to you did once belong;
> And, doubtless, where these brambles claim the ground,
>   The glass once flowed to hail the ranting song.
>
> The ale-house here might stand, each hamlet's boast;
>   And here, where elder rich from ruin grows,
> The tempting sigh – but what was once is lost;
>   Who would be proud of what this world bestows?
>
> How contemplation mourns their lost decay,
>   To view their pride laid level with the ground;
> To see, where labour clears the soil away,
>   What fragments of mortality abound.

Clare ended his elegy by comparing his own fate with Pickworth's:

> A few more years and I shall be forgot,
> And not a vestige of my memory left.

But he, like the village, left a defiant and finely wrought part of himself above ground, and happily neither is forgot.

The stone villages of Lincolnshire lie on the narrow limestone belt running due north through the districts of Kesteven and West Lindsey to Humberside. The Roman road we call Ermine Street runs straight up the line, known as Lincoln Edge, with the best villages scattered either side of it and Lincoln itself standing in a gap at the centre. This country lies at the edge of the Fens, where stone walls and hawthorn hedges both disappear in favour of dykes. The ridge itself, though hardly more than 150 feet in height, forms a distinct escarpment from the wide, flat and treeless fenland to the east.

Architecturally, as well as socially, we have come to the point where the transition is being made from the elaborate decoration of the south to the plain – not to say austere – building of the north. The Midlands, as so often, compromise. (I like the Opies' discovery that school children take a 'swig' from a bottle in the south and a 'swag' in Yorkshire, whilst in Lincolnshire they take a 'swig-swag'.)

Greatford, where a stone bridge crossing the River Glen leads past lime trees to the village church with its broach spire of Ancaster limestone, is the first of the local villages worth seeing, a few miles north-east of Stamford. It is a spacious village of grey oolite, with some style, but spoilt by the introduction of alien materials in new building. Farther north, west of Bourne, is Edenham, a model village of stone houses built by the lords of the manor of nearby Grimsthorpe, where the thirteenth-century castle still stands, modified by Vanbrugh, at one end of huge parklands in which fallow and red deer roam and through which a splendid long avenue of chestnuts runs. The 'Black Horse' inn is nice (and hospitable) but there is too much brick in the village.

Belton is another model village, built in the nineteenth century and attractive, despite its position on the main road just north of Grantham. The big Stuart house in Belton Park, the home of the Brownlow family, is attributed to Wren, though James Wyatt made alterations to it. It is notable for some exquisite woodcarving thought to be the work of Grinling Gibbons. In the church there are monuments to the Brownlow family by such sculptors as John Bacon, Antonio Canova, Baron Marochetti and Richard Westmacott.

Denton, on the other side of Grantham close to the Leicestershire border, is a village of mellow, warm stone and red pantile roofs,

The only remaining part of the ancient church at Pickworth.

dressed in the Leicestershire fashion in its coat, as it were, but wearing a Lincolnshire hat.

Welby, Kelby and Oasby are but three of many villages of Lincolnshire whose names testify to Danish occupation of the area when they were founded. Oasby is the largest and most stylish with its well-kept gardens a blaze of colour in summer, and its stone a slightly greyer cream than the local norm.

Braceby and Haceby accompany Newton and Sapperton in a nice little group east of Grantham. Stone mullions grace large and small houses in Braceby, while Sapperton's winding street, though a little neglected, sports some attractive old buildings, and Haceby shows red pantiles in profusion. Newton is scattered and more nondescript. It had a central green of oval shape once, with a stream running through it, and it was built around a bit of high ground called Newton Bar which is claimed to be the highest point between Grantham and the Ural Mountains. Similar claims are made for several high points in the East Midlands, and Leicestershire folk are fond of telling you that the east winds blowing here come unimpeded from Siberia.

The pale limestone imparts a deceptively youthful look to Castle Bytham, near the Leicestershire border, and this could easily have been one of Lincolnshire's most impressive villages. Alas, its lovely hilly setting does nothing to save it from the disastrous effect of buildings such as the village hall and shop being in brick. Markery Wood, to the west of the village, recalls Earl Morcar, the brother of King Harold, who owned the castle here, and a fine view of the village is obtained from the massive earthworks where one castle was destroyed by Henry III and another in the Wars of the Roses, subsequently providing stone for village houses.

Ancaster supplied the stone for most of these villages. The unprepossessing village itself sits astride the important Roman military road, now degraded to B6403 at this point, and in consequence of its industry has much brick and a Railway Inn. The stone from Ancaster's quarries has been used since the Roman occupation, and a great many local churches are built of it. Its colour is generally creamy yellow, and it is hard oolite of very fine texture, sometimes capable of being polished like marble. The stone is seen to good advantage at Normanton and Fulbeck – the latter among Lincolnshire's prettiest villages, where the street runs gently uphill from the valley of the River Witham to the hilltop green and church, with pinnacled tower and gargoyles looking over stone cottages of warm hue with orange pantile roofs – though once again the place has resigned itself to some building in brick.

Scampton, above Lincoln, has its attractions, but its associations are not such as seem apt in a book about rural England, for the flat landscape of much of Lincolnshire is dotted with airfields, and north of

The church at Fulbeck, Lincolnshire.

the village towards Cammeringham is the base from which 617 Squadron's 'Dambusters' took off during the Second World War. In fact near Dunston, on the other side of Lincoln, is the decapitated Dunston Pillar, which was erected in the eighteenth century by Sir Francis Dashwood (of Hellfire Club notoriety) as a sort of lighthouse for landlubbers. And such is the scarcity of helpful road signs in these parts that one wishes it were still there. But the lantern was replaced in 1810 by a statue of the king, George III, on the occasion of his jubilee. During the war it had to be taken down because it was considered a hazard to low-flying aircraft. Thus indirectly the landscape dictates to kings as well as commoners.

Formerly in Lincolnshire but now in Humberside is a stone hill village, somewhat bleak and uninviting, called Alkborough, overlooking the confluence of Ouse and Trent with Humber. On the west side of the church is Julian's Bower, another of those ancient turf mazes, the pattern of which is repeated in the church porch and in one of the stained glass windows. We have noticed several of these mazes, cut in turf or carved on stone, and the sites of other turf mazes are known to us, though many have been ploughed up. What is specially interesting about Alkborough's is that the repetition of the pattern in the church porch was probably meant as a defence against evil spirits, since it was believed that they could only travel in straight lines.

The limestone belt itself travels straight from the north bank of the Humber, reduced to a pencil-thin line which peters out altogether beyond Market Weighton but supporting on the way there North Newbald, a neat village built round a sloping green, with a fine Norman church. The priest's door bears the mason's marks on one of the jambs. Some of the houses are whitewashed, but much grey stone is still visible.

The Oolitic limestone, suffering an understandable nervous breakdown in passing through Humberside, recovers its composure in North Yorkshire to produce some of the finest of all English villages along a narrow band running north-westward through the Hambleton Hills until it veers suddenly eastward and rushes into the sea between Scarborough and Whitby. The North Yorkshire Moors are its most obvious contribution to the landscape. The Jurassic rock itself is somewhat erratic, and the moors are too high and exposed for more than an isolated hamlet to be found on them, but in the dales and round the fringes are such beauties as southerners rarely suspect in what they too often dismiss as the industrial north.

It *is* rather surprising to find gracious villages of oolite in this territory of the Celtic Brigantes, who gave the Roman civilizers such a hard time and whose descendants mixed with the equally aggressive Vikings to produce a concoction which has never gone soft. They count it a virtue in these parts to speak bluntly and will have none of the deviousness and dissembling which southerners like to pass off as tact and discretion. "Who pulled *your* chain?" you are liable to be asked if you speak out of turn.

Stonewalling here has little to do with boundaries. It is rather a matter of putting a straight dead bat to every ball that swings, breaks or bounces towards the wicket you are stolidly defending against fierce attack from the fielding side (curious how the language of cricket borrows from the agriculture of the stone country). A certain namesake of mine was a past master of it, even though he belonged to Essex, beyond the Jurassic Boundary. It is, incidentally, a curious fact about cricket, little remarked on by the most conscientious statisticians in all sport, that the areas of England fielding first-class county sides fall into a very distinct geographical pattern. One group is formed of the south-east of England from Hampshire to Essex and the other along the limestone belt from Somerset to Yorkshire, with only Lancashire standing out in isolation from the rest of the company. (So that every reader does not now write to the publisher to take me to task, I repeat that I am talking about England – Glamorgan is in Wales.)

Before we reach the moors, we must progress from Humberside up the narrow belt forming the Howardian Hills, where harsh northern names like Scackleton, Crayke and Scawton Moor do nothing to dispel the idea in southern minds that Yorkshire is cold and bleak.

Another of the country's few surviving turf mazes occurs in these hills, near the village of Brandsby, and again it is known as the City of Troy. Among our national parks, nature may impart a grimness to Dartmoor but it is man whose sinister character pervades these moors, for the old North Riding has long traditions of superstition, embracing the miracles of Catholics and Quakers and the fear of ghosts and witches. If you hung out your washing on Good Friday, chances were it would be spotted with blood when you fetched it in, and soup made from nine frogs was considered the best cure for whooping cough. Witchposts made of rowan were kept beside fireplaces for protection, and at Goathland they used to stick pins in a cow's heart and roast it at midnight to conjure witches from their secret hide-outs. Now that such beliefs have faded away, their places have been taken by sightings of unidentified flying objects.

Wharram Percy, just on the Yorkshire side of the new Humberside boundary, is a lost village which can only be reached on foot, by a footpath from Wharram-le-Street which passes a dismantled railway route and a disused quarry before reaching the deserted village site. Is there a jinx on the place? Extensive excavation has taken place here, where little more than a farm and the old church of St Martin remained above ground level when archaeologists discovered the village be- neath sheep pastures and began their patient work in the early fifties. The site stands on chalk, and the medieval villagers quarried the material near the spots where they built their houses, virtually taking the chalk from their back gardens. They cultivated nearly fifteen hundred acres of land here in the thirteenth century. The manor house of the Percy family had been abandoned by that time, and with succeeding generations new houses were built on the sites of the old, and the ancient parish church was improved and extended. The villagers burnt coal, ate cod and suffered from rheumatism, just as they would today if their descendants were still there. But in the fifteenth century parts of the church were demolished, houses were deserted and left to decay, and the place gradually became a ghost village. What happened to the people?

The Black Death was the major catastrophe. It was after that unspeakable devastation that the church was reduced in size and the arable land given over to sheep. Manpower was scarce and expensive, and it was cheaper to keep sheep on grassland than to cultivate crops. Such men as were left in Wharram Percy drifted elsewhere to find new jobs, and the village was never rebuilt.

The thatched roofs and mullioned windows found so often in villages hitherto all the way up from Dorset disappear this side of Humber, to be replaced by roofs of the recently more familiar pantiles over wooden windows picked out from the stone walls, more often than not, with white paint.

Defoe found the Yorkshire Wolds generally "thin in towns and people" but abundant with sheep in the eighteenth century. Farmers and shepherds had had to contend with wolves ravaging their flocks to within a hundred years of his travels. Yet such is the resilience of *Homo sapiens* that where one village died, another was revived not far away. Langton was developed as an estate village in the nineteenth century, and it has a refined air about it, its cottages of grey limestone forming a sort of guard of honour along the village green for the manor house, where stone greyhounds on the gate piers represent the Norcliffe family who built it.

Howsham, on the wooded east bank of the notoriously unpredictable Derwent, also has some modern building, and not surprisingly, for this warm-coloured village of Liassic ironstone was the birthplace of George Hudson, the draper who became the 'Railway King' and whose 'magic touch' revolutionized the world, according to the electioneering puffs of the time, when he became MP for Sunderland and three times Lord Mayor of York, before it turned out that his magic touch was a little trickier than had been realized, and he lived on the charity of friends and died a broken man. The quiet village street, tucked away from main roads, has cottage walls of squarely dressed brown stone laid in neat courses and picked out with light mortar. Howsham Hall, in startling contrast, is a battlemented Tudor palace of light grey, as bold as George Hudson's brass.

Beyond that imposing pile Castle Howard, built by Vanbrugh – aided and abetted by Hawksmoor – in sandstone, which might seem slightly alien in present company, is Hovingham, distinguished by the Italianate hall built for George III's Surveyor-General, Sir Thomas Worsley, whose descendant Katharine became Duchess of Kent in York Minster in 1961. The entrance to the mansion opposite the village green is via a unique gatehouse which was built as a riding school, and it seems fitting that a Roman villa once stood in this delightfully

Howsham, North Yorkshire.

The church at Coxwold, North Yorkshire.

peaceful spot where Tuscan columns of mellow limestone quarried nearby grace the house and its park.

The Ryedale village of Stonegrave, where the poet and critic Sir Herbert Read lived, not far from the farm of his birth, is also a quiet place. Stonegrave House is set back beyond a wall of brick, but its red pantile roof shelters honey-coloured limestone walls like those which protected Read in his childhood innocence. Nunnington, nearby, is a pleasant place of grey stone with its church on top of a hill which commands wide views over the Vale of Pickering to the east. There is some interesting old stonework at Nunnington Hall, a seventeenth-century manor house now owned by the National Trust.

Beyond the long street village of Ampleforth and the creamy hamlet of Wass, near the beautiful ruins of Byland Abbey, Coxwold stands at the opposite edge of the narrow oolite, built on a hillside with its slightly flamboyant church at the top, and here we enter the North York Moors National Park. Coxwold's creamy-coloured walls and stone-tiled roofs, wide street, grass verges and trees give it so un-spoiled and serene an aspect that you might think the village aspires to go to the Cotswolds when it dies, but what would prevent it from passing the entrance examination would be its most famous house, which is built partly of brick!

Exactly a hundred years before that splendidly controversial York-shireman Dean Inge was born in the brick-built village of Crayke, Coxwold's splendidly eccentric curate arrived and took up residence in a brick farmhouse because there was no vicarage. He had just won instant fame with the first volumes of a long novel called *The Life and Opinions of Tristram Shandy*, and the Reverend Laurence Sterne called his new home Shandy Hall. He spent little time here during the eight years of his curacy, for he had become a lion of London society, though in debt and ill-health and practically separated from his wife, and when he died of consumption he was buried at Bayswater, mourned only by his publisher. A few days later his exhumed corpse made a remarkable reappearance – on the dissecting table of the Professor of Anatomy at Cambridge, who had acquired it at a price from resurrection men and begun to dissect it before someone in the audience recognized the face. As if that were not enough, his restless bones were exhumed yet again in 1969 when the Bayswater graveyard was to be demolished and the Sterne Trust had him re-interred in the churchyard at Coxwold.

One's mind goes back to Dorset for the similarly gruesome fate of another great writer. Thomas Hardy was intent on being buried among his relations in Stinsford churchyard, but well-meaning admirers were insistent that Westminster Abbey was the proper place for him. The classic English compromise was duly arrived at. His heart would be buried at Stinsford, and the rest of him at Westminster. Rumour has it, however, that his heart was eaten by the surgeon's cat. No one would have laughed more heartily at this tale, one feels, than Hardy himself, the tragic novelist. Atheists are generally less in awe of death and its attendant rituals than Christians are. Sterne, the comic novelist, would not have been amused at all.

It was Lord Fauconberg, of nearby Newburgh Priory, which his ancestors had acquired after the Dissolution, who bestowed the living of Coxwold on Sterne, and *his* family had its gruesome side too, for it is said that Mary Cromwell, who was married to Thomas Bellasis, Earl of Fauconberg, brought the headless body of her father, the Lord Protector, or perhaps only his heart, for burial here at Newburgh, where it may still be in a bricked-up attic niche. In the church, the overblown monument to Sir William Belasyse, who died in 1603, is inscribed: "Thomas Browne did carve this tombe him self alone of Hessalwood stone."

Between Coxwold and the well known one-in-four Sutton Bank, which we failed to negotiate in an aged Austin 8 many years ago, is the grassy slope of Roulston Scar, to which a village schoolmaster, inspired by seeing the Uffington white horse in 1857, came home and induced his boys to help him carve a similar animal here in what was surely an act of vandalism, like the regimental badges carved on the chalk downs of Wiltshire by soldiers during the First World War.

We now turn north-eastwards to Ryedale again, for nestling in the wooded river valley is a village undistinguished in itself but possessing one of the great treasures of stone building in England, Rievaulx Abbey. The houses in the village of Rievaulx are built mainly from the stone of the ruined Cistercian abbey founded in 1131, and one of the loveliest ruins in this county which possessed more monasteries at the Dissolution than any other. (I mean, of course, the old county of Yorkshire with its three Ridings.) And now I must eat my words about Castle Howard, for Rievaulx Abbey too was built of sandstone, and there is nothing perverse about that unrivalled structure. The stone was quarried partly near the site and partly from Bilsdale, three or four miles north, and the explanation is that some of the stone here, whilst still belonging to the Jurassic belt, is strictly a limy sandstone rather than a sandy limestone, according to some geologists. Experts have differences of opinion about it, but who cares? From our point of view it looks the same, and though it may be sandy, it is a freestone which can be carved as well as Oolitic limestone, as is abundantly clear in the lofty and majestic ruins of Rievaulx.

Yet this great building has its perversity. Because of the limitations of the chosen site, the church had to be erected in a north-south rather than the usual east-west direction. It is tempting to suggest that the aesthetic sensibilities of the monks overcame their religious ideals, until we learn that a chronicler of the time described the spot as "a place of horror and waste solitude". Cowper was tempted to live here so that he could gaze at the ruins for the rest of his life, but then the poet was out of his mind, and one is reminded of Clare gazing at the humbler ruins of Pickworth. I wonder if ruined churches struck the same melancholy romantic chord in both these fragile minds and seemed like reflections of their own humbled spirits.

Closer to the oolite is Hawnby on the eastern edge of the Hambleton Hills, and the road through the grey village from Rievaulx is through country of woods and streams, sheep and heather, changing from the valley's beauty to the moorland's spectacle before reaching Osmother-ley on the lias, where a stone slab on five pillars, near the market cross, was used as a pulpit by Wesley when it was not displaying the wares of market tradesmen.

The Lyke Wake Dirge, originating from some ancient belief that the souls of the dead had to cross the moors, launched the deceased on his journey with gloomy predictions:

> If ivver thoo gav owther bite or sup,
> Ivvery neet an' all,
> T'fleames'll nivver catch thee up,
> An' Christ tak up thy soul.
>
> But if bite or sup thoo nivver gav nean,
> Ivvery neet an' all.
> T'fleames'll bon thee sair to t'bean,
> An' Christ tak up thy soul.

Living travellers now "tak up" the journey in the footsteps of the dead on the Lyke Wake Walk, forty miles across the moors to Ravens-car. If they do it in twenty-four hours, they can join the club at Osmotherley, always assuming they can get back again. Half way there they pass the head of Rosedale, and downstream is the village of Rosedale Abbey, with nothing but a fragment of a Cistercian nunnery to account for its name, and an ironstone mine on the hill above, instead of a romantic ruin. A seven-foot-high round barrow on Loose Howe, north-west of the village, was excavated in the nineteenth century and produced a fully clothed corpse in a wooden coffin, as well as Bronze Age daggers and a stone battleaxe, so early man was no stranger to the inhospitable moorland of Yorkshire.

To the south are Hutton-le-Hole and Lastingham, watered by Hut-ton Beck and Hole Beck respectively. Hutton-le-Hole is one of York-shire's showplace villages, with warm grey-walled and red-roofed limestone cottages scattered among winding lanes, little white bridges over streams and wide greens where sheep graze freely. If the village

Hutton-le-Hole, North Yorkshire.

has ancient foundations, it shows no obvious signs of them, although there is an area nearby where flint tools have been found, and a group of what might appear to be burial mounds stands not far away. But would you believe that these might be artificial rabbit warrens, made during the Napoleonic period? At the time of the Luddite riots, when the poor had been brought to the brink of starvation, being able to buy neither bread nor meat, the prospect of free rabbit stew must have seemed worth a lot of trouble to emaciated families in this district.

Quakers were here in some strength in the seventeenth century, when the men were employed in local mines, but now the place thrives on tourism. The village stands at the foot of Farndale, famous in spring for its wild daffodils, but the threat of flooding hung over it in the twenties, when there was talk of a reservoir being created here. Better to be over-run by coach parties than drowned for ever.

Lastingham's glory is its splendid church, refounded in 1078 on the site of an earlier monastery which the Danish invaders probably destroyed. Its first abbot had been St Cedd, according to the Venerable Bede, and when he died of plague, he was "first buried in the open air; but in the process of time a church was built of stone in the monastery, in honour of the Mother of God, and his body interred in the same, on the right hand of the altar". Pevsner calls the crypt of St Mary's "unforgettable", but all crypts are easily forgettable to my mind, and it is the part above ground that gives Lastingham its enduring nobility, even though the church was never completed to the original plan.

To the south-east in the Vale of Pickering, past the red-roofed main-road villages of Aislaby and Middleton, another village with claims to be North Yorkshire's prettiest, and one of those much-photographed places which represent the county on calendars, choco-late boxes and postcards, is Thornton-le-Dale. The twinkling beck pirouettes between warm stone houses and neat gardens reached by little bridges across it, and a little olde shoppe sells pomanders and lavender bags to ecstatic old ladies who pour off coaches on sunny afternoons into this Bourton-on-the-Water of the north. But a different tune is played on the old joanna, as it were, by the Lady Lumley almshouses and the village stocks. The humble single-storey alms-houses were founded in 1657 and consist of twelve tiny homes, each having a door and one window.

Beyond the old local quarry and the quiet hamlet of Ellerburn we can set out northwards across the moors for Goathland, and the cultivated prettiness of Thornton soon gives way to a more awesome scene. Levisham and Lockton sit side by side along the next moorland valley, Newton Dale, and are separated by a deep-cut stream which runs into the long and twisting Pickering Beck, the course of which is followed by the North Yorkshire Moors Railway. To the north is a large natural hollow, called the Hole of Horcum, known to some, not surprisingly, as the Devil's Punchbowl. Levisham, above one side of the dip, is of oblong shape with grey goats on its greens and grey stones in its walls, the stone slightly grubby-looking compared with the showplace villages to south and west. Its lovely neighbour Lockton is a sleepy old place of less formal arrangement, and all the better for that, in my view.

These parts of Yorkshire were the setting for James Cook's youth, but the old cottage where he lived at Great Ayton as a boy was long ago demolished stone by stone and re-erected in Australia. Such trans-portation of stone buildings, as opposed to building stones, seems to me an act of the greatest vulgarity. A building removed from its original site can have no value whatever except as a sort of religious relic to overawe the simple-minded. The United States, of course, are full of such amputated bits of England's flesh and bones.

The bleak and seemingly uninhabited Fylingdales Moor suddenly sprouts a crop of giant puffballs which I cannot but see, so help me, as the fungus of a decaying civilization. This is a place where Death's long shadows stretch backward and forward, for prehistoric burial mounds

Robin Hood's Bay – the limestone's last flourish.

accompany the three great globes standing here to protect radar tracking equipment which will give brief warning, for what good it will do us, of imminent doom. What little minds men have, for all our self-exaltation, that we have come to this! No one need write to tell me that this has nothing to do with the stone villages of England. It has to do with everything. For twenty years these radomes, as they are called, in the language of boys' science-fiction comics, have stood here as symbols of the most appalling failure of humanity, like a pawnshop sign where mankind has left the poverty-stricken remnants of his wisdom and imagination in return for four more minutes of Micawber-ish hope.

Lyke Wake walkers and the villagers of Goathland have good cause to reflect on that old prediction that "T'fleames'll bon thee sair to t'bean." Not that *they* will have the first hints of impending disaster, of course. That doubtful privilege is reserved for the wise men of Westminster, who will use their last moments to ensure that the aggressors are also blasted out of existence in what will be the most negative instant in the whole history of the world. I expect when it happens it will be self-righteously explained, to anyone left alive to listen, as a defence of Democracy against Totalitarianism, or of Christianity against Atheism. Any formula will do to persuade the gullible masses that the act was justified, so long as it is not the plain unvarnished truth – man killing man for reasons of power and greed.

The Jurassic stone belt which we have followed all the way from the Dorset coast expires after Fylingdales Moor and is buried at sea with full military honours, you might say. But one delight remains to us before we mourn its passing. The village street of Robin Hood's Bay swoops down to the stony shore between cottages whose grey walls contrast with their red roofs of tile. No one is sure why the bay was named after the legendary outlaw. Some say the Abbot of Whitby engaged him to rid the coast of pirates, with the promise of a royal pardon in return, others that he had friends here with boats if he should need a quick get-away to the Continent, which seems more likely.

At any rate, the village was notorious for smuggling long after Robin's days had ended. The entire population seems to have been engaged in it at one time, and the Court Leet of Fylingdales dealt out plenty of death sentences. Among the cobbled alleys and flights of stone steps, one alley called The Bolts was planned specially to aid escape from the Excise men. The legitimate business here was herring fishing. Now the place has expanded upwards and backwards from the coastline, with much brick and rendering, into what is called Bay Town, but there is still treasure in the stone of the old village.

Flyingdales village, from which the moor takes its name, is just to the north-west, and the church of St. Stephen in Robin's Hood Bay is really the parish church of Fylingdales, but the present church, completed in 1870 to replace the older church, which had itself only been rebuilt in 1821, was clearly for a growing modern community. This at least materialized, which is more than can be said for Ravenscar down the coast. The stone-faced Raven Hall Hotel, expanded from an eighteenth-century house on the site of a Roman lighthouse, or signalling post, thought to make itself the star of a new holiday resort, but the development never came, and Ravenscar remains no more than a hamlet, though it is the terminus of the Lyke Wake Walk.

The sea pounding away at the soft limestone was what created Robin Hood's bay in the first place, and it has taken its toll of the village, erosion having claimed many houses in the last two centuries. The Liassic limestone cliff recedes three inches a year, imperceptibly changing the shape of Britain, as the sea devours its own progeny.

CHAPTER 6

The English Backbone

The uplands known as the Pennine Chain, or 'the backbone of England', begin between Stoke-on-Trent and Derby and run northward to merge with the Cheviot Hills in Northumberland. The rock of which they are made is still limestone and sandstone, but it is harder and older than the Jurassic belt. For nearly two hundred miles, from the Peak District right up to the Scottish border, we shall find villages built of the two main rocks which form the Pennines, the Carboniferous or 'Mountain' limestone, and the Carboniferous sandstone, or 'Millstone Grit'. Some of this Carboniferous rock is 300 million years old, and its upper strata include the coal measures which provide the industrial landscapes of so much of northern England.

The Mountain limestone is harder and less co-operative than the Millstone Grit, although it is the toughness of the latter which gave it its common name, for it was used for centuries to make millstones for grinding corn. When millstones began to be imported from France in the eighteenth century, because they were supposedly superior to our own, another British industry was killed off, and here and there in Derbyshire one may find heaps of unfinished millstones piled up in old quarry sites, abandoned because nobody wanted them.

The buildings in this region – particularly the churches – are more austere than on the Jurassic limestone belt, because the stone is not so amenable to intricate carving. The Carboniferous limestone is pale grey in Derbyshire, becoming colder and darker as one moves farther north, and its surface always has a rough texture almost as if it were untouched by human hand. Houses built of it are often whitewashed in the Pennine dales. The Carboniferous sandstone is often a dull browny-grey in colour. It can be cut in huge blocks and dressed to an ashlar finish, so that it is used for public buildings in the industrial towns of the north, where it becomes blackened with smoke. This stone is still quarried extensively for building, whereas the Mountain limestone is scarcely used nowadays except for road-stone, cement-making and other industrial purposes. Quarrymen working the limestone were quick to take advantage of gunpowder to free the stone from the rock face. They had to supply the gunpowder themselves in the early days

Carboniferous sandstone and limestone: Hartington, Derbyshire.

Abandoned millstones at Millstone Edge, Derbyshire.

and could buy it from the local ironmonger or general store in the village.

The landscape of the Derbyshire Pennines is generally one of high limestone plateaus with deeply cut wooded river valleys between, and dramatic, craggy and treeless cliffs of sandstone with sheer rock faces called 'edges' rising above the sunny pastures below them. Generally the settlements tend to avoid the high, exposed moorland and reside in the valleys so that, for instance, many are strung out along the Derwent and its tributaries. But some moorland villages of the Peak District are among the highest settlements in England. It is immediately apparent that we have moved out of the country of charming and gracious villages into more rugged and sparsely populated parts of Britain.

We will start, however, with Dovedale, at Thorpe, a village of grey limestone beside that river which Izaak Walton called "the finest river that ever I saw", for it was here where Charles Cotton taught the incomplete angler the art of fly-fishing for trout. Upstream in Stafford-

Milldale, Staffordshire.

shire are Milldale and Alstonefield, the latter a handsome village with stone houses round a green, where Squire Cotton's Beresford Hall stood until its demolition a century ago. Milldale sports the packhorse bridge – still known as Viator's Bridge – which provoked Walton to ask his friend if they travelled in wheelbarrows in this country, for it was not wide enough for anything bigger, and as for Walton himself, he would not ride across it for a thousand pounds but might be persuaded to crawl across on all fours. In those days the bridge did not have the parapets which make it look safe enough now.

Staffordshire's tribute to the Dove is the River Manifold, passing through Ilam, with its Izaak Walton Hotel, before it joins the main stream at the county boundary. I suppose we may call Ilam a stone village. It is an ancient settlement in a lovely setting, which William Congreve and Samuel Johnson both knew before it was bought by a wealthy manufacturer, Jesse Watts Russell, in the nineteenth century. He commissioned George Gilbert Scott to build the model village we see now, with tile-hung gabled cottages of gun-metal colour above ground-floor walls of stone. It is undeniably an attractive place but in no way typical of the area – one of those architectural adventures like Portmeirion and Brighton Pavilion which, though splendid in their own right, are totally foreign to their surroundings and in this case too obviously Victorian. Ilam's saddleback-towered church, however, contains two remarkable pieces of contrasting stonework – a primitive sculptured Saxon font, illustrating episodes in the life of St Bertram, and Chantrey's superb marble monument to Russell's father-in-law, David Pike Watts. To look at one after the other is to pass through about a thousand years of craftsmanship and refinement of feeling.

The southern boundary of the Peak District National Park is a little south of Ilam, and the twisting limestone gorge of Dovedale stretches two miles northward, with strangely weathered rock formations long ago given such names as Jacob's Ladder, Twelve Apostles and Lion's Head, and twenty stepping-stones of ancient rock joining the opposite banks of the river for the convenience of tourists who here, at least, notice the stones beneath their feet.

Hartington is farther upstream in the wider sandstone valley, a village whose pinnacled church tower of red gritstone stands above the smooth-faced limestone houses like an old hen guarding her chickens. Hartington enjoyed town status once and was the centre of a large parish. Its market square recalls its former importance, for it was the first town in the county after Derby itself to receive a market charter.

We are back in dry-stone wall country here, but the walls are built of hard, shapeless rubble far removed from the carefully dressed lime-stone walls of the Cotswolds. 'Cripple holes' or 'creep holes' are left for sheep to pass through in this district, and sometimes mortar is used to

The monument to David Pike Watts by Chantrey at Ilam.

secure the coping stones. The Carboniferous limestone area through which the Dove flows is known as the White Peak. The Millstone Grit farther north forms the Dark Peak.

To the east of Dovedale is Tissington, which some call the most beautiful of all Derbyshire villages. Its mellow limestone houses, with garden walls gathering yellow lichen, are built round spacious greens and duckpond, and the village centre is unsullied by a public house or a main road. One lane reaches it from the west via cattle grids and an avenue of lime trees, and another from the east via what is whimsically described as a 'ford', though you could sink a double-decker bus in it after heavy rain. Tissington is an estate village, built by the Fitzherberts of the Jacobean Tissington Hall, dazzling with Virginia creeper on its walls, and though the village is stylish enough, it does not have that appearance of natural growth which provides the best of English villages.

What is famous in Tissington, of course, is its annual well-dressing ceremony, for it is here that the peculiarly Derbyshire folk custom is supposed to have started, though there is scant evidence for that. The supposition comes from the traditions that the purity of the limestone springs preserved the village from the Black Death and that they never ran dry during the 1615 drought when no rain fell for four months. Probably the real origins of the custom are to be found in more ancient pagan veneration for the local water supply, but five wells here are 'dressed' annually on Ascension Day with intricate floral designs usually expressing Christian sentiments, and attended by Christian clergy whose ancient predecessors threw up their hands in pious despair at such pagan water-worship.

Further east still, as we approach the Derwent valley, are Brassington, Hopton and Kirk Ireton, ranged around Wirksworth, which was once a busy trade centre of the lead-mining industry. A chapel at the northern entrance to Brassington is distinctly nonconformist in more ways than one, breaking the pattern of whitish stone with its buff walls. The profits from lead may have given the villages of the area some fine churches and houses of the local light stone to delight modern tourists, but the story of the working people who produced those profits for the landowners is not such as seekers of pretty villages usually care to dwell on, escapists that we are. It is probable that the Romans worked some of the mines here, and after a break with their departure, the deposits were exploited continuously until recent years. In Defoe's time, men clad entirely in leather worked sixty fathoms below ground to dig out lead ore for five pence a day, battling against hard rock, flooding and disease throughout their working lives. Defoe found the local men to be "of a strange, turbulent, quarrelsome temper . . ." and no wonder. If their bodies were not drowned in floods of water whilst they were down the mines, they drowned their sorrows in floods of ale when they came up, and suffered the harsh justice of the Great Barmote courts for their drunken misdemeanours.

Hopton Wood was one of the sources of the Carboniferous limestone used for building. The quarries are no longer worked, but they produced a fine-grained creamy stone which was used in the great museum buildings of Kensington.

Cromford and Bonsall, near Matlock, are partly linked by the new road which Philip Gell built around 1800 for the benefit of his trade in lead. He called it, somewhat pretentiously, Via Gellia, and so it has remained. But the fame of these villages is not connected with the lead industry. It was at Cromford in 1771 that Sir Richard Arkwright built the world's first mechanized cotton mill, and the village houses are those he built for the workers. These villages were centres of framework knitting, and workshops can still be seen in Bonsall. Arkwright built his mill at Cromford at a time when growing discontent among the knitters was threatening machinery, and the mill looks like a fortress. It was powered by a waterwheel driven by the Bonsall Brook, and though it has been much altered and extended, it was at least built in stone. Much subsequent Arkwright industrial building was done in brick (ironically enough, for the area stretching north from here is one of the great sources of the Millstone Grit). Darley Dale stone is still quarried extensively in Derbyshire, and here and in West Yorkshire is the biggest concentration of still-working quarries in England. Millstone Grit is so massive and durable that it is frequently used for building dams.

The old river bridge at Cromford had on it a chapel for thanksgiving by travellers. It is a ruin now, and the bridge has been widened for modern traffic, but on the parapet an inscription still records the leap of a frightened horse in 1697 into the river twenty feet below, from which both horse and rider emerged unscathed.

Winster, Birchover and Wensley are on our way upstream towards Rowsley, Great and Little, where the dark Millstone Grit is much in evidence, forming huge lintels, painted black, and surrounding windows which sometimes have stone mullions. Little Rowsley is roofed with red tiles, whereas Great Rowsley wears Welsh slate on its head and looks all the duller for it. Winster was an important lead-mining town, now much declined, and industry has given it the usual sprinkling of red brick, rendering and red sandstone among its grey walls, so that even its nice setting does little for it, whilst Wensley, a long uphill village, is more consistent in its use of local material, though gaunt.

The River Wye joins the Derwent at Rowsley, and nothing could seem further from the grim landscape of lead mining than the gracious houses that stand near the flowing waters nearby – Haddon Hall by the Wye and Chatsworth House by the Derwent. Haddon Hall, originally built as a fortified manor house in the thirteenth century, is constructed mainly of the grey Carboniferous limestone with dressings of gritstone. It was for a long period the home of the Dukes of Rutland, before they moved to Belvoir Castle. It has been restored in this century, but the original materials were retained. Chatsworth House, palatial home of the Dukes of Devonshire, and only three miles away, was built of Millstone Grit at the end of the seventeenth century. Nowhere can the relative merits of the two materials be seen more easily and clearly. Haddon's grey medieval walls of random or coursed rubble, of the hard intractable limestone, give it perhaps a more homely look as well as its more obviously ancient appearance; whilst Chatsworth, one of England's great mansions, has a scale and stylishness well served by the smooth walls of gritstone which glow like pale gold in the evening sunlight, almost like the Cotswold stone of Swinbrook whence one of the Mitford sisters came here to roost.

Haddon Hall is isolated from any village, but Edensor lay in Chatsworth's parkland and offended the sensibilities of the sixth Duke, so he had it demolished in 1839 and built a new village out of sight of the great house. Whatever one may say about the morality of such destruction, it cannot be denied that Edensor is one of England's most interesting estate villages. It was planned by Joseph Paxton, with the Duke's approval, on highly eclectic principles. There are neither straight rows of uniform terraced houses nor attempts to fake an olde-worlde village of picturesque cottages. There are spacious detached houses and cottages in a variety of styles, and the only thing that gives them unity is the use of the local gritstone throughout. The church has a broach spire. If Edensor looks deliberately eccentric, perhaps that is a point in its favour against those model villages which are deceitfully sham.

Ashford, to the west, contributed to the building of Chatsworth, for a quarry at the edge of this village on the Wye produced dark limestone which could be polished like marble and was known as Derby Black. True marble is a rock which has undergone a metamorphosis through immense and prolonged heat and pressure, and there are no real marbles in England, but Ashford's stone was one of the best imitations, and it was used for inlay work, particularly in the chapel at Chatsworth. The quarries now lie beneath the A6 road. The narrow three-arched Sheepwash Bridge, one of three across the Wye here, has a stone sheep-pen built into its side where sheep were herded (there is no other word for it) into the river to bathe in getting back to the other side.

The Vernon, Manners and Cavendish families who built the great houses here were among those who made huge profits from lead mining, and Sheldon has been one of the industry's hells in life and heavens in death, for it is paradise now for industrial archaeologists who seek out the ruined buildings and winding gear of Magpie Mine. The grey village itself expanded in the nineteenth century when miners came from Cornwall to find work here after the decline of the tin-mining industry. It was no paradise then.

Baslow stands beyond Pilsley – another attractive place tucked away from the main road and quiet round its green – above the Derwent at the fringe of the High Peak, or the Derbyshire Dome, and the search for heaven and hell here is undertaken in a slightly more literal sense, if you like, by rock climbers and pot-holers, for they must be searching for *something* among the great crags and caves that provide such an adventurous playground in this region. Baslow itself was extended by the interests of Chatsworth and is now a tourist village with hotels at a junction of roads north of the great estate. It is a well-sited place, but the landscape around it is more interesting than the village itself, despite its random rubble walls of warm stone, its Victorian Jubilee church clock and the little stone toll house where the trade in mill-stones was duly taxed. Among the natural rocks on the moors above are stone monuments to Nelson and Wellington and an old guidestone

Dry-stone walls enclosing curiously shaped fields at Litton.

indicating the way to 'Cheste-rfeild' (*sic*). Baslow Hall was the some-time home of Sebastian Z. de Ferranti, who turned the place into a sort of domestic power station during weekend breaks from his works in Lancashire.

In all this country around Stoney Middleton quarrying is still very much alive, not for building stone so much as for roadstone or ground limestone for chemical industries. There is hardly a corner turned which does not reveal a quarry, hardly a hill surmounted which does not expose a massacred hillside.

Monsal Dale lies west, and the village of Little Longstone boasts the great stone viaduct across the Wye ravine, built for the Midland Railway in 1862 so that, as Ruskin put it, "Every fool in Buxton can be in Bakewell in half an hour." What ironies there are in human progress. A hundred years afterwards, when the line was closed and the viaduct threatened with demolition, the very people who would have sided noisily with Ruskin in wishing to preserve the landscape now raised their voices to preserve the blessed viaduct.

Near Litton, a couple of miles north-west, are some more curious stone structures – the dry-stone walls round the village farmland. There is nothing very unusual about the walls themselves, but the

fields they enclose are extraordinarily long and narrow. The explanation is that yeoman farmers bought or exchanged several adjacent
strips from the medieval open fields and fenced them off to form
economical private fields, before the Enclosure Acts came into force in
the eighteenth century. These fields are often of reverse S shape,
because the enclosure followed the pattern of ridge-and-furrow
ploughing caused by manoeuvring teams of oxen at each end of the
strips.

Although every village had its open field before the enclosures,
however, arable farming has always been relatively rare in this region,
as Cobbett noted:

> I have not seen, except at Harewood and Ripley, a stack of wheat since I
> came into Yorkshire; and even there, the whole I saw; and all that I have seen
> since I came into Yorkshire; and all that I saw during a ride of six miles into
> Derbyshire the day before yesterday; all put together would not make the
> one-half of what I have many times seen in one single rick-yard of the vales
> of Wiltshire. But this is all very proper: these coal-diggers, and iron-melters,
> and knife-makers, compel us to send the food to them, which, indeed, we do
> very cheerfully, in exchange for the product of their rocks, and the won-
> drous works of their hands.

If Tissington is Derbyshire's prettiest village, it shares its fame with
Eyam, standing high on the exposed moorland, which is certainly its
most tragic. It is a fascinating place to look at apart from its history, for
it has some nice architecture in the better houses, and its roofs are of
graded stone tiles above the walls of grey/buff stone. The place
bespeaks its antiquity in the ancient headstones of its melancholy
churchyard, and I was not altogether surprised to see the ghost of a
monk near it once and was even disappointed when it turned out to be
a bearded old man walking along with the hood of his dark blue
dufflecoat over his head.

The people of Eyam must themselves have been made of Millstone
Grit in the seventeenth century, when bubonic plague was brought to
the community in a box of clothes delivered to the village tailor in
September 1665. Forty-five people soon died. But instead of being
hastily deserted, the stricken village became voluntarily isolated. The
leaders of this memorable self-sacrifice were the village rector, William
Mompesson, and a Nonconformist minister, Thomas Stanley, who
had been deprived of his living for his dissent. The two men persuaded
the parishioners that their Christian duty was to avoid spreading the
disease to neighbouring towns and villages and, whatever their suffering, to cut themselves off completely from the rest of the world. Food
supplies were brought to the village by outsiders but left at a safe

The plague cottages at Eyam, where disaster struck in 1665.

distance and paid for with coins left in jars of vinegar – thought then to act as a disinfectant.

The classic sign of the plague was the formation of the bubo, an inflamed swelling, usually in the groin or the armpit, accompanied by fever and delirium. After four or five days of agonizing pain, the victim was sure to die. How great the temptation must have been to put as much distance as possible between Eyam and one's self, we can perhaps imagine, but everyone remained. The father and six children of a family named Hancock all died within eight days, and it is said that the mother buried them all herself, one by one, in the open field. By the end of 1666 two-thirds of the village population had been wiped out. Among the dead was Katherine, wife of the village rector, and here she lies near the Saxon cross in the churchyard, representing the other heroic villagers who lost their lives to save others. Most of them had to be buried hurriedly, in unmarked graves, wherever a convenient patch of earth could be found, but the graves of the Hancock family have been brought together and preserved by the National Trust, just outside the village, and near the church is a row of surviving cottages where the plague first struck the community. A commemorative open-air service is held every year, on the last Sunday in August.

Other things in and around this village – the birthplace of Anna Seward, 'the Swan of Lichfield' – would deserve discussion if they were found anywhere else: the Saxon cross, the survival of village stocks and bull-ring, the elaborate sundial over the church porch, the ancient stone circle on the moor, the view of Kinder Scout. But all these fade into insignificance beside a story of collective heroism comparable with that of the Burghers of Calais or the citizens of Leiden.

The Hancock burials, known as the Riley Graves from the place-name, are outside the village towards Grindleford, and beyond that, close to the Yorkshire border, is Nether Padley. Between these two villages is another building associated with martyrdom. It stands in a disused farmyard and is the former private chapel of Padley Hall, since reduced to a cowshed and a shelter for railway navvies before it was rescued and restored. Two Catholic priests, Nicholas Garlick and Robert Ludlum, were arrested here in Elizabeth's reign and dragged off to Derby, where they were hanged, drawn and quartered and their dismembered remains impaled on stakes.

Across the moors is Sparrowpit, which would be a nice moorland hamlet among fields criss-crossed with white stone walls if it were not for the industry of local quarries which spread limestone dust all over it. But the hamlet lies below Eldon Hill and thus claims one of the so-called 'wonders of the Peak' – Eldon Hole. "A frightful chasm", Defoe called it. The gaping mouth of this awesome pit, fenced off for safety in a sloping field, measures about thirty-six yards by seven, and its black depths were naturally enough the source of ancient superstitions, not least of which was that the hole had no bottom. Defoe, not usually susceptible to idle tales, was clearly impressed by Eldon Hole. "What Nature meant", he wrote, "in leaving this window open into the infernal world, if the place lies that way, we cannot tell. But it must be said, there is something of horror upon the very imagination, when one does but look into it."

Since the hole has been descended by pot-holers, one may smile at the old superstitions and the story that Izaak Walton's friend, Squire Cotton, had let down a mile of rope without touching bottom, but the variety of depths attested to by the hole's explorers may give one cause to wonder if there *is* a bottom, for one account says 76 feet, another 180 feet, another 245 feet, and so on . . .

The large village of Castleton, beyond the Eldon Hill Quarries where stone has been scooped from the rock face as if it were ice-cream, also has a 'Bottomless Pit' in its extensive cave systems, as well as the vast Peak Cavern and its connected rock chambers. The black entrance (or, more appropriately, exit) has been known for centuries locally as the Devil's Arse, as Celia Fiennes did not hesitate to tell us, though Defoe, the author of *Moll Flanders*, showed his better manners in putting a dash in place of the offensive orifice. Standing on top of these great underground spaces is the Norman Peveril Castle, which gave Sir

Walter Scott the cue for one of his medieval romances. Lead mining and rope making have been among the profitable trades of Castleton in the past, but more exclusively Treak Cliff Hill is the unique source of the semi-precious mineral called Blue John, a translucent fluorspar prized for ornamental use since Roman times.

Hope, along the main road, is quite attractive at its northern end, but this place looks like a sort of geological rendezvous, for its buildings display stones in a curious range of colours.

Edale, below the Peak (which Defoe reckoned the "most desolate, wild and abandoned country in all England" until he got to Westmorland), is the last of Derbyshire's stone villages we shall notice but by no means the least, as it is, among other things, the starting-point of one of those long-distance walks which have become so popular in recent years. The Pennine Way stretches from here to the Scottish border. The village itself is in the narrow valley of the River Noe, hemmed in by Mam Tor, the 'shivering mountain', on one side and Kinder Scout and its neighbours on the other. Surprisingly, the village is not as bleak and rugged as one might expect from its position, for this is softer, more rolling country than that to the south, but it *is* rather nondescript with buildings of brick among its stonework. The pagan associations of upland country surround it. Mam Tor's name is Celtic for 'mother mountain', and an Iron Age hill-fort stood on top of it, whilst below is the Odin lead mine, so named from the belief that it was worked by the Vikings.

As we cross the border into South Yorkshire near Sheffield, it may come as a surprise to find a fairly secluded village with grey stone cottages, graced by mullion windows, hardly six miles from the centre of the stainless-steel city. But Bradfield is situated on the hillside of a narrow valley, and there are superb views from the top end. It is somewhat ill-famed, however, for there are several reservoirs around it, and in 1864 the dam of one of them burst, flooding a huge area in which over two hundred people were drowned.

South Yorkshire has little else to offer in the way of characteristic stone villages, but West Yorkshire, perhaps even more surprisingly, has several which cannot possibly be missed out. Even that dreary industrial country near Wakefield and Pontefract is not totally devoid of interest, for Ackworth has some fine houses, and a foundling hospital built here in 1758 was converted into a co-educational Quaker school some years later by Dr John Fothergill, an advocate of vaccination, prison reform and the abolition of slavery, among other causes.

On the north-east side of Leeds, now mercifully standing aside from the Great North Road, rather than sitting in the middle of it, is Bramham, with its large towny neighbour Boston Spa not far away. The creamy stone which makes these worthy villages is quarried near

Tadcaster and is from a narrow belt of Magnesian or Dolomitic lime-stone which runs north along the eastern edge of the Carboniferous rock from Nottingham to South Shields. It is a fine building stone, worked by the Romans, and second only to Portland in Wren's opinion; its greatest monument is York Minster. It goes without saying, then, that its fine grain lends itself to intricate carving that we shall not see much of in the northern villages.

At Harewood, scarcely outside Leeds nowadays, we are at once back in the Carboniferous country, standing on a ridge overlooking the River Wharfe. Its stone, creamy grey when quarried, is blackened now by weathering and industrial pollution, but this is another estate village, very different in character from the Pennine settlements to the west. It was built by Edward Lascelles, the first Earl of Harewood, whose fortune was in West Indian sugar-cane, and he engaged John Carr as architect for the cottages here as well as for the great house, though the latter had the additional advantages, which the villagers did not, of 'Capability' Brown to lay out the gardens and Thomas Chippendale to provide the furniture. The village is gaunt, but elegant by West Yorkshire standards, and suffers only from being in a very busy main-road position.

Stately homes and church monuments are the only usual sources of the fine arts in villages, and though it is not there now, there is one significant piece of stone carving which I always associate with Hare-wood. Jacob Epstein often used stone from the northern quarries for his larger works, but it was from a piece of Seravazza marble that he made his controversial statue 'Genesis', just fifty years ago as I write. When the work was first unveiled, the Press leapt upon it with that hysterical abuse it reserves for the original and intellectually honest, such as the works of Darwin and Ibsen, and Epstein's noble and awe-inspiring figure has ever since been absurdly derided by the easily shockable as a vulgar monstrosity and an insult to womanhood. At one stage it was consigned to a side-show on Blackpool's 'Golden Mile', where it stood to be gawped at briefly, and merely, as an incredibly ugly and stupendously pregnant woman, before being rescued and taken to sanctuary by Lord Harewood. It has changed hands a few times in its tempestuous career, but it is a pleasure to note that the north of England, generally more puritanical than the south, has extended its customary hospitality to this refugee from southern hypocrisy. She is the primeval mother-goddess to whom all of us owe our existence, and so far from being an insult to womanhood, she is a tribute to the very nature of woman. After immense labour, a great human progeny will issue from her womb. Her wide nostrils and thick lips foretell the African; her narrow, slanting eyes are Oriental; her long face with its high, receding forehead belongs to the American

Indian. She may be primitive and mindless, but her care for all her children is instinctive, and she will defend them to the last ounce of her strength. She is paradoxically, at one and the same time, the parent and the offspring of such as the Cerne Abbas Giant and the sheela-na-gig. She is the foundation of humanity, and her proper place is in the Tate Gallery, the national showplace of modern British art.

Right at the edge of modern Bradford is another estate, built by Sir Titus Salt, which qualified as a stone village when it was put up a century ago, deliberately sited away from the city's smoke and grime. Bradford's tentacles have reached out and encircled Saltaire now, so that it is a suburb, but it is worth seeing as the first example of a model *industrial* village, built with the best intentions, for the workers in Salt's palatial mohair and alpaca mill. The place cannot be called attractive in the usual sense. Its close terraces stand in rows with military precision in the poorer quarters, and much of its stone has become grimy, but the more opulent parts are still good, and Salt's bearded statue stands in the park, contemplating his handiwork and looking very like Karl Marx.

At the edge of Halifax, by contrast, is Luddenden, a place of steep and narrow cobbled streets and four-storey gritstone houses of yellowy black, which was a centre of the cottage weaving industry and has the more traditional atmosphere one expects in West Yorkshire. The village is in a cleft with a stream flowing down to the river at Hebden.

Up the road at Hebden Bridge and Heptonstall, industrial contrasts in stone building can still be seen within a mile of each other. Hebden Bridge in the valley is a sizeable industrial town and has the woollen mills and the railway line, whilst Heptonstall up the hill retains its old weavers' cottages and some of its ancient customs. It is not only the weather that Heptonstall's moorland population has been exposed to, although the old church was so severely damaged by storm in 1847 that they built a new one. Plague and civil war took their toll of villagers in the seventeenth century, and the graveyard is so heavily populated that some headstones are engraved on the backs of old ones which lie face down, paving the floor of the ruined church as well as the graveyard. The dead of Heptonstall constituted a health hazard to Hebden Bridge below, at one time, through pollution of the water supply. The spookiness of this dark, death-packed but fascinating village was enhanced when the rebuilding of some cottages near the church in 1960 uncovered evidence of a charnel house on the site. Rumour has it that the cottage stairs were made from coffin lids. But the place is an irresistible museum piece of northern industrial village building, with its vernacular sign still heralding one's arrival at 'Top oth town'.

Decomposing bodies in the crowded churchyard at Haworth much

Heptonstall, West Yorkshire, on the Millstone Grit.

concerned health inspectors investigating the village's alarming death-rate in the nineteenth century. Here the Millstone Grit lends its brooding solidity most, in West Yorkshire, to an atmosphere already charged with a gloomy foreboding in most visitors' minds even before they arrive. The place is a rugged moorland village as characteristic of the region as Heptonstall, but auto-suggestion plays its part in what people see at Haworth. A vision of Patrick Brontë presiding over his ill-fated family at the gaunt and spartan parsonage preconditions reaction. It is this that relic-worshipping coach-parties have come across the moors to see, and this is what they *do* see. One can hardly blame the village for cashing in on tourist curiosity, but one would think the place had no existence apart from the Brontës. Yet the villagers who listened to the Reverend Mr Brontë preaching against "bad passions and practices" in church on Sunday, and watched his son Branwell drinking himself to death in the 'Black Bull' during the week, were hard-working weavers or quarrymen employed at Penistone Quarry on the moor. The weavers' houses with their long rows of upper-storey windows can still be seen along the steep cobbled streets, and to be strictly truthful, Haworth not only is not a village but is far from being remote or lonely, since it stretches out its long arm to within a stone's throw of Bradford and shares the blackened yellow stone of industry. Civilization's one concession to the old image seems to be the lack of helpful road signs in the place.

The desolate moors form the bleakest scene we have encountered since leaving Dartmoor, and the sturdy stone is entirely in character with the surroundings. There is no need for rendering or paint on these walls: the rock of which they are built will stand up to everything the elements can throw at them. Emily Brontë described the situation of *Wuthering Heights* by mentioning the stunted fir trees blown to an excessive slant by the north wind. "Happily, the architect had foresight to build it strong: the narrow windows are deeply set in the wall, and the corners defended with large jutting stones." Part of the romantic yearning of the three bewitching sisters was conceived far away in Cornwall, where their mother and devoted aunt came from. Emily was closer to nature than her sisters. She used the imagery of stone several times in that novel which is the greatest product of the Brontë family's melancholy imagination. She knew the moor's crags and quarries and guidestones and has Catherine exclaiming that her love for Heathcliff "resembles the eternal rocks beneath – a source of little visible delight, but necessary".

It is necessary for us to pass into North Yorkshire now, and Lothersdale is the first stop, where Charlotte Brontë was a governess for a while, using the house, Stonegappe, as a model in *Jane Eyre* later. It is a long village with a stream running down to Airedale, and an old woollen mill houses what is claimed to be the largest waterwheel on the English mainland.

Beyond Skipton, we are back in the Carboniferous limestone country, and a string of grey villages in middle Wharfedale is worthy of attention, the first of them being the charmingly named Appletreewick, hemmed in by Simon Seat rising on one side and Rylstone Fell on the other, and guarding the eastern approach to Burnsall, which is one contender among rather widely scattered claimants to the title of Yorkshire's prettiest village. The local Olympics in August include a traditional race up Burnsall Fell, whilst a maypole on the green unashamedly proclaims the survival of paganism, and the ancient stones in the church and graveyard keep company with a modern tomb designed by Eric Gill.

Thorpe is next upstream, tucked away quietly off the main roads, beneath the fells, with one or two stylish seventeenth-century houses mixing with old barns and farmhouses; and then there is Linton, which was proclaimed 'loveliest village of the North' once, with bridges and stepping-stones crossing its beck, and a dignified building at each side of the green like the host and hostess lording it over their guests at dinner with the grey stone cottages around it, and the Fountaine Inn pouring the drinks. One of this pair of buildings is the eighteenth-century Linton Hall, the other Fountaine's Hospital, founded by Richard Fountaine for six poor women. Sex discrimination is not exercised here these days, for men have an equal right to be poor and infirm, and they are allowed in too. The almshouse is a grand building to find in such a wild and woolly place, and it is attributed to Vanbrugh, no less, for Richard Fountaine was his timber merchant. Both Linton and Burnsall, incidentally, could boast free grammar schools in the seventeenth century, founded by local philanthropists, and there was nowt to stop a Wharfedale lad going to Cambridge if he had a mind to. Both schools eventually became public primary schools, and Burnsall's children learned their alphabets in a lonely stone building with mullioned and latticed windows.

Grassington is across the river, and a cobbled market square proclaims its authority in this district, its prosperity having come from the lead mines on Grassington Moor. It is a place full of interest, not least in its street names – Jacob's Fold, Salt Pie Hill, The Woggins, Chamber End Fold, Hungry Laugh Hill. Cattle-drovers and coaches came this way, providing work for the village blacksmiths, one of whom murdered the village apothecary long ago, and commuters from Bradford who bought up miners' cottages also brought the railway up the dale from Skipton, though it has now gone again. They say that Edmund Kean acted here once, and the Iron Age Brigantes had a settlement at Lea Green, just north of the village. It is another place where the old open fields were divided up by seventeenth-century landowners and enclosed to form long narrow fields like those we noticed in Derbyshire.

Kettlewell in upper Wharfedale and Arncliffe in nearby Littondale also had lead-mining interests, and the rock that provided the hard-won mineral ore also provided the grey walls of the cottages, which are occasionally whitewashed here. Kettlewell shelters from the north-east below Great Whernside, among the highest of the Pennine peaks. Arncliffe is one of those northern villages which retain their ancient Easter Monday custom of 'Pace egging', when the local children roll hard-boiled and brightly decorated eggs down a hillside until the shells break, at which point they are allowed to eat them. This is a travesty of the former, more intricate ceremony in which adults used to take part, but it certainly has some link with Leicestershire's hare-pie scrambling which takes place on the same day, its real origins lost in the mists of old ritual and magic. Near Halton Gill, a hamlet higher up-river, a neolithic passage tomb called Giant's Grave stands as evidence of the early habitation of this remote area.

Along the fringe of North Yorkshire to the west, where Ribblesdale runs into Lancashire, villages such as Clapham, Stainforth and Long Preston display the grey limestone well. Long Preston, in taking

Arncliffe, North Yorkshire.

advantage of its main-road trading position, laid itself open to Victorian development, and much of its housing is rendered and painted, but it has attractive corners, whilst Stainforth is well known for Catrigg Force tumbling down the limestone rocks, and its old packhorse bridge over the bubbling stream.

Clapham, however, is the most priceless of these villages, to my mind. It lies below Ingleborough, the second of Yorkshire's famous Three Peaks, in a wooded valley where rustling trees shade the houses in mutual comradeship with Clapham Beck chattering through the middle. The botanist Reginald Farrer lived in Ingleborough Hall and planted rare trees and flowers he had sought in the uttermost corners of the world, so that his name is remembered in nurserymen's catalogues as 'farreri' after one species name or another which he discovered in China or Burma or Tibet.

Clapham has a tranquil indifference, it would seem, to the cavernous and often cloud-capped mountain rising menacingly above it. And this is surprising, for here, up the slopes from the village, is the yawning mouth of Gaping Gill, whose vast limestone throat could swallow York Minster and wash it down with Fell Beck, which comes down the mountain side and disappears into the awesome pothole, passing through Ingleborough's eerie show caves lower down before being spewed out into Clapham over a small waterfall.

The occurrence of slate in the Craven area has given rise to some strange quarrying activity around these villages, but the Carboniferous limestone dominates the region, and the village of Malham lies at the heart of one of its most dramatic landscapes. The village itself stands amid stone-walled slopes with three clapper bridges crossing its stream and would be a peaceful place if it were not that its roofless neighbours draw thousands here for the hospitality it offers in true northern style. For Malham Cove and Gordale Scar, north of the village, are among the great tourist attractions of the Yorkshire Pennines.

The geological fault that formed the vast, high, curving cliff of Malham Cove and the collapsed cave of Gordale brought visitors of the romantic age to wonder and shudder at the sights which frightened Thomas Gray, gave Kingsley the germ of the idea for *The Water Babies* and moved Wordsworth to pen one of his less memorable sonnets to

> Gordale chasm, terrific as the lair
> Where the young lions crouch.

But it was the painters, not the writers, who got most out of Gordale Scar. Turner and Girtin, of course, found it to their taste, but no one who has seen James Ward's huge canvas in the Tate Gallery can doubt that the honours go to him. He painted the picture in 1815 for Lord Ribblesdale – Mr Lister as was (the pub on Malham's village green is the 'Listers Arms'). Ward exaggerated the scale and grandeur of the scene somewhat, but his work is a masterpiece of romantic landscape painting, and it was standing spellbound before it that first drew me to the place itself, years ago.

Right over to the east of the Pennines, near Masham, are Grewelthorpe, with honey-coloured houses round a green, and West Tanfield, another village on the narrow belt of Magnesian limestone. It barely qualifies for inclusion here, for brick and other materials interrupt the walls of creamy stone, but we may let it pass. It stands at the centre of several neolithic and Bronze Age remains, and more recent graves include the famous Marmion tombs in the church. John Marmion was given licence to castellate his mansion here in return for his services in the wars with Scotland, and Walter Scott made him a fictitious hero of Flodden Field. Only the gatehouse of the castle is still standing, but the family's ancient alabaster tombs fill the church with an atmosphere of medieval pomp.

Ilton, up on the moor above Masham, is another place of fiction.

The 'Druids' Temple' at Ilton, North Yorkshire.

Standing near this isolated hamlet, suitably well hidden among lanes and surrounded by woodland, is a little-known megalithic monument which looks for all the world like a superior if diminutive Stonehenge. A grotto built into the hillside looks out on a remarkable circular structure before it, with several dolmens and trilithons surrounding an unmistakable phallic symbol at the centre, as well as a sacrificial table and several monoliths scattered round the site. It is known as the Druids' Temple, and what barbarous rituals were performed here by the Celtic priests of long ago we may only too readily imagine as we stand and look at the ancient stones. But alas, the whole thing is an elaborate fake. The 'temple' was built no farther back into prehistory than the 1820s, when unemployed local men were paid a shilling a day by William Danby of Swinton Hall to erect this splendid folly. If all the records had been lost, we should be mesmerized by this tantalizing 'ruin' of grey stone, as we are by some other supposedly prehistoric remains, not least among which are some of those chalk carvings in the south. Have the visitors who carved their tourist graffiti on the stones been hoodwinked, one wonders? If they feel able to claim their little share of immortality on a monument that was not here long before their great-grandfathers, they might as well initial a derelict mill or a tumbledown bus shelter.

The road through East Witton and Middleham brings us to lovely Wensley, up and down hillsides and once an important market town, as can be seen from the style of its church, which takes us back into the dim past of the settlement here with two grave slabs inscribed 'Donfrid' and 'Eadberehct'. Westward along the valley, West Witton and Swinithwaite show off their warm, mellow stone to passers-by.

Wensleydale's river, the Ure, tumbles along between wild, sweeping moors and cascades down its rocky Pennine route over several waterfalls, among which is the well-known Aysgarth Force, staggered along half a turbulent mile of the river's course. Grey stone cottages give every village in the dale a sturdy attraction now, but in the Middle Ages the lonely moorland farms were practically outnumbered by monks and men-at-arms. Jervaulx Abbey cast its powerful influence widely and owned the church at Aysgarth, whilst up the slopes to the north stood Bolton Castle, called a "climax of English military architecture" by Pevsner, with its village, now called Castle Bolton, along a sloping green. Richard II's Lord Chancellor Scrope built the castle where Mary, Queen of Scots, spent six months in custody. West Burton, south of Aysgarth, has one of the largest of Yorkshire's village greens and its own little waterfall.

Askrigg and Bainbridge occupy opposite banks of the river a little way upstream. Both are attractive places, but one exhibits its old bull-ring, and the other its village stocks of stone, to remind us that savages lived here once, however peaceful and innocent the places may look now. Askrigg also has a rather tatty stone pump near the church cross. Bainbridge, on the other hand, became a centre of the Society of Friends and does not even have a church, although it is a finer village than Askrigg, but the houses clustering round its green meant welcome refuge for travellers lost on the lonely moors in wild weather, for they sounded a hunting horn here every winter evening in the days when other villages were busy building their steeple-houses, and kept this more practical custom up for seven hundred years. The stocky houses here have stone-tiled roofs, and grey, fawn and honey tones enhance their walls.

Gayle is another attractive settlement of stone houses and a one-time cotton mill beside the little market town of Hawes. The Gayle Beck tumbles over limestone terraces right beside the house walls. From here one can take the scenic road north over Buttertubs Pass, between Great Shunner Fell and Lovely Seat, to Swaledale, where Muker demands our attention. The village is the 'capital' of upper Swaledale and runs along the northern bank of the river, with the church tower rising above the dour grey Millstone Grit houses and the moors with their jigsaw pattern of walls behind. If Wensleydale's most famous product is cheese, Swaledale's is knitted goods. Knitting woollen

Dry-stone walls in the upper reaches of Swaledale.

stockings and other garments was a cottage industry in which all the women and some of the men were engaged whilst the majority of the menfolk farmed the land or mined lead. They are not such fanatical knitters nowadays, but wool still figures largely in the life of Muker, where an annual sale of Swaledale tups (rams) is still held. The familiar Swaledale sheep of this region are black-faced animals of medium size with long, hanging wool, and their agility dictates the height of the Pennine dry-stone walls, which follow the weft and warp of the local landscape and are rather higher than those of the Cotswolds.

Muker's brass band, called the Old Roy, was one of those which grew up in the mining villages, where exercise of the lungs was supposed to be good for men who spent their working lives breathing black dust which hastened their passage to the grave. Men who died in Muker or Keld, upstream, had to be conveyed to Grinton for burial, ten miles or so away, until Elizabethan times, when Muker's church was built as a chapel of ease, for Grinton had the only consecrated ground in upper Swaledale. The need for human ties was dictated by the rock here. Funeral parties carried the coffins on a two days' journey, resting at traditional places on the 'corpse road', one of which was Ivelet

Muker, North Yorkshire.

Bridge, where a rough-hewn slab was known as 'the corpse stone'. The place is said to be haunted by a headless hound.

Grinton, though later dwarfed by the industrial growth of Reeth nearby, was the centre of a large parish stretching to the Westmorland border, and its church of St Andrew was known as 'the Cathedral of the Dales'. Keld, meanwhile, was the home of Richard Alderson, well remembered in local tradition and nicknamed Neddy Dick, who played the harmonium enhanced by bells. One day, whilst climbing among the local rocks, he made the discovery that stones of varying shapes and sizes sounded different notes when struck, so he began to collect suitable stones and created a one-man limestone band. Thus the beginnings of rock music!

Downholme is a scattered farming hamlet beside the main road, with its church a little distanced from the centre of population, whilst Gilling, north-east, is a pleasant street village of warm stone with a bridge over the stream separating the best part (north) from the worst.

Nearer the Durham border is Ravensworth, a spacious village in gently undulating countryside, with the ruins of a Norman castle which has provided much stone for the village buildings in the centuries since its demise. Kirby Hill is a delightful little place just south of it, with almshouses and a former grammar school in a group with the church dedicated to St Peter and, if you please, St Felix. And on a little tributary of the Tees, near Darlington, Aldbrough St John also has space enough, with its green extending to the river bank and beyond, the two parts joined by a bridge with pointed arches.

Passing into Durham (only briefly, for this is coalfield country, given to building in brick), we reach the Tees-side village of Gainford. It used to be described as a pretty place, but although it has a large green back from the main road, too much brick has crept into its buildings now to merit more than passing mention. Even its Millstone Grit is colour-washed. Winston, nearby, is a little shy of exposure too, for here is the Dunhouse quarry which produces dark browny-grey Carboniferous sandstone for repair work at Durham Cathedral. It is a pleasant village, with little cottages and bungalows and bright gardens of flowers, but council houses of brick spoil it, like a beautiful face flawed by smallpox. The Durham villages are too overwhelmed by industry nowadays to invite any real flirtation with tourists. The best one can say of them is that they have hearts of stone. Too often an *apparently* charming hamlet suddenly reveals round the corner the huge untidy yard of a scrap-metal merchant or used-car dealer.

Staindrop is no better than most, though its assets include some nice houses facing one another across one of those long Durham greens, and the Neville stronghold, Raby Castle, with its deer park, its stone minstrels' gallery and that crazy hilltop folly whose windows are not only pointed but painted!

Painting of a higher order, not to say genius, is associated with Rokeby, a tiny place near Barnard Castle, not itself of more than passing interest but having at Rokeby Hall (the Howards' place) a stone-fronted mansion whose roof once protected the bare flesh of one of England's most seductive women, the immigrant from Spain (or perhaps Italy) known as the Rokeby Venus. Let us leave Pevsner alone, for once, to admire the "expanding curves" of the house front while we dwell on those of the Señorita's alluring backside. She resides at the National Gallery now, looking at her reflection in a mirror and indifferent to the gaze of her admirers, like Molly Bloom with her secret thoughts, but this intriguing masterpiece hung at Rokeby for ninety years before she became a national star in 1906. What has this to do with stone villages? Nothing whatever! I digress willingly at the risk of offending the inquisition, as Diego Velasquez did when he painted those soft pink buttocks. Besides, an odyssey without Aphrodite is unthinkable.

Let us hasten north-west to Romaldkirk, where my reputation may be rescued by Durham's prettiest acquisition from Yorkshire's North

Blanchland, Northumberland.

Riding in 1974. The unity of stone and style in the houses scattered about several greens shows commendable restraint on the part of villagers and local council, for the place is so far unspoiled by lapses in taste that Pevsner's own restraint gave way and he wrote of "perfection" here, though he found little to praise among individual buildings.

Although the stone has not entirely expired when we reach Cleveland, there is too much brick in that industrial county to detain us in the present context, but Hutton Rudby, just inside North Yorkshire, is worth a pause. It is a village of golden stone much favoured by the commuters of Middlesbrough and Stockton-on-Tees. The river running through it separates the Hutton bit, round its green on the hill, from the Rudby part, which has the church and is properly called Rudby-in-Cleveland, despite the fact that the absurd legislation of 1974 which created Cleveland county left this place in Yorkshire. Hutton-le-Hole and Hutton Rudby are far from being the only Yorkshire villages with that distinguished prefix deriving from a powerful northern family.

Now what are we to make of Blanchland, just inside Northumberland? This is a planned village of the sort I have been rather less than enthusiastic about, on the whole – the work of an all-powerful creator rather than of evolution. God in this case was the Earl of Crewe, Bishop of Durham, who needed to house the workers in his lead mines and so built the village from – and indeed upon – the stone of a ruined abbey by the Derwent. One has to say that it is a place of great dignity and character. Built of brown gritstone round a gravelled square, its houses all roofed with graded stone tiles, small at the ridges and increasingly large towards the eaves, it has some of the atmosphere of a medieval cloister offering welcoming hospitality from the wild and lonely moors surrounding it. It is as if the stone keeps its old purpose about it and refuses to resign itself to its new function. One almost feels that it would be a mortal sin to shout to a friend across the street. Perhaps the spirits of the White Canons still whisper in its secluded corners. The coffin lids of two abbots are in the parish church which was rebuilt from the chancel of the old abbey. But it is an eighteenth-century creation, one of those exercises in superimposing a community on the land-scape, and though here it may be regarded as successful eccentricity, the culmination of this practice is the dread city of Milton Keynes.

Northumberland has a fair number of model villages, some more appealing than others, but in this large county of vast open spaces and the scent of wild roses, the problems of over-population do not intrude much into one's appreciation of the countryside.

The River Tyne might seem an unpromising source of English village building to those who think of it only in terms of Newcastle and the coalfield, but Bywell might serve to dispel that illusion. It is scarcely more than a hamlet now, but it was a large village once, with a castle and two churches, and Pevsner calls it "the most picturesque and architecturally rewarding of all Tyneside villages". Ironworkers inha-bited it in the sixteenth century and worshipped on the Sabbath either in St Andrew's, known as 'the white church' because it had belonged to Blanchland's Premonstratensian canons, or in St Peter's, known as 'the black church' because it belonged to the dark-habited Benedictine monks of Durham. St Andrew's has a fine Saxon tower, and the village's market cross and the remnants of its castle stand with the cottages and manor house dispersed among the trees of this shrunken but highly attractive place of ancient stones and venerable beeches.

Over to the west, on the southern branch of the Tyne, Haydon Bridge straddles the river below the site where the medieval village stood, and what is left of the old church still stands, built of stone quarried from Roman ruins. Its font was a pagan altar centuries before Christian Englishmen were named over it, and many a stone in the modern village, if only its surfaces could be made to render up their secrets like the grooves of a gramophone record, could resound with the tramping feet of imperial legions.

The Millstone Grit stretches north-east beyond the Roman wall in a narrowing band to the coast, and one or two more villages on it are worth our attention. Belsay is an extraordinary place in this county whose wide northern landscapes and relatively sparse population do not prepare one for the surprises of architectural sophistication frequently to be found here. Sir Charles Monck-Middleton built Belsay Hall of the local warm sandstone in a style befitting a Mediterranean resort, with the front façade rising from a podium and divided by Doric columns. The old village would have blocked the view from the drawing-room windows, so he shifted the whole thing and rebuilt it out of sight but introduced the same neo-classical style in some of the houses and shops. How different from the old bare castle, which has been described as "an aggressive muscle-bound thug". The stone for the nineteenth-century improvements was quarried on the site, where the hall's gardens now flourish beneath overhanging rock.

Small local quarries on the sandstone can be seen like red scars, gouged out of the hillsides to provide sufficient stone for particular purposes, then abandoned to the elements.

Whalton, on the other side of the River Blyth, is a tidy and attractive street village with brown stone houses flanking the broad green, where pagan ritual survives in the form of a great fire in the village centre, not on 5th November but on 4th July. They say the fire has burnt in the same place on that day for two hundred years, but it has nothing to do with stars and stripes. The date was Midsummer Eve before the Gregorian calendar was adopted in Britain in 1752, lopping eleven days off people's lives, as they thought. In Whalton they ignored science and stuck to tradition, continuing to light their fire on 4th July in memory of the ancient Midsummer fire-festivals by which cattle and crops were purified and made fertile.

Capheaton, Cambo and Kirkwhelpington stand on higher ground at the edge of the Mountain limestone. The first is a model village, with terraces of one-storey stone houses of creamy grey, built by the Swinburne family whose baroque mansion evolved here late in the eighteenth century out of the earlier house and was well known to Sir John Swinburne's grandson, Algernon Charles – he of the intoxicated verse.

Cambo is yet another model village, built partly by the Trevelyan family of Wallington Hall, where Swinburne was among the literary and artistic guests of Pauline, Lady Trevelyan, and possibly reinforced Sir Walter in his temperance resolve to empty his superb wine-cellar into the Wansbeck! This eventful house also emptied Ruskin, Effie and Millais on to the road for their fateful journey to Scotland. It was

Apparitions at Wallington Hall, Cambo. Carved heads brought here from London's Old Aldersgate.

another Sir Walter – Blackett – who owned Wallington before the Trevelyans and laid out Cambo village, which was a successful operation carried on by the Trevelyans into this century. 'Capability' Brown was educated at the village school, now a village hall, and may have worked for Blackett on the Wallington grounds, though there is some doubt about it.

The village is sited a little way from the medieval settlement on the ridge of a hill and is a peaceful place with fine views and a drinking-fountain on the green, where red-haired Caledonian warriors seem even more improbable than long-haired Pre-Raphaelite poets, but the village post office was once a pele tower, one of those northern fortresses, small, square and solid, where the English hid from marauding Celts before the Act of Union relegated such skirmishes to Wembley Stadium.

Kirkwhelpington, it is a relief to note, is a natural village that just growed alongside the River Wansbeck. One of its vicars, John Hodgson, wrote a seven-volume history of Northumberland. It had a village green once, which the landlord Duke of Somerset, in a sort of personal enclosure act, split up into allotments for the villagers. Now 'tusky' grows out of all control outside garden walls. The stone church and cottages form a compact village surrounded by rolling farmland, and it is satisfying to note that new houses have been built of stone too. Though there is some brick at the fringes, what lets down the village centre is the police house, which makes it clear that the police are above the aesthetic law, if no other.

Colwell and Great Bavington are grey farming villages typical of the Pennine country which they hug at its edge. The stone westward from here is the cold grey of the rough, hard limestone; that eastward, the warmer colour of the hell-bent sandstone.

The Millstone Grit rushes out to sea at Alnmouth Bay, and our village hunting is resumed on the Carboniferous limestone some way up the coast at Bamburgh. The village is completely overshadowed by the huge mass of the great castle, perched on its rocky pedestal like an eagle in one of the most spectacular castle sites in Britain. It was the seat of Northumbrian kings and was rebuilt in Norman days of red sandstone, in contrast to the village of mellow greyer stone which sits quietly in subjection at its feet. The dominance of the castle is emphasized by the fact that Bamburgh remains very much an unspoiled English village. If it had grown to town size, with all the accompanying appendages implied by town status, as Warkworth has farther south, the castle's overwhelming massiveness would be less apparent, but Bamburgh has not only resisted the temptation to turn itself into a seaside resort but has kept its village character around its triangular green in spite of the tourists who pour into it and who would undoubtedly empty their pockets into it if the temptation were there. It must be said that credit for this is due to the owners of the castle who rescued it from nineteenth-century dereliction and took the village under their wings. If Bamburgh might in any sense be called an estate village, we should be thankful for it in this instance.

One of England's best-loved heroines was a native of Bamburgh and is buried here. Grace Darling was the twenty-three-year-old daughter of the Longstone Lighthouse keeper, who persuaded her father to row out with her in a fierce storm in 1838 to rescue nine survivors from the wrecked ship *Forfarshire*, whom she had seen clinging to the rocks at dawn.

Right up at the Scottish border, on the southern banks of the Tweed, the villages of Horncliffe and Norham have a secure place in our present theme. Horncliffe stands on a cliff above the river, south of the crossing where Sir Samuel Brown's Union Bridge links Northumberland with Scotland. The village houses are built of red sandstone, for this is an area where the Carboniferous rock produces a crop of what is called Fell Sandstone. Its hard and stubborn nature gives added emphasis to the rough northern character of many of the local villages.

Norham is one of the larger villages in this county of scattered hamlets. Its twelfth-century castle is planted in seemingly impregnable dominance, like Bamburgh's, on high rocks above the Tweed, but this did not prevent its destruction by King David of Scotland, nor later again by James IV. The last Scot to conquer it, however, was Sir Walter, whose poem 'Marmion' is a medieval romance featuring the siege of the castle by his countrymen before Flodden. Norham acquired a reputation as the most dangerous place in England at the time of the border warfare. An Englishman of last century, however, transformed its image into one of rare beauty. Turner came here on several occasions and made sketches of the castle on its precipitous pedestal. His watercolours and drawings of the scene, covering a period of forty years in which he kept returning to the theme, culminated in the magical oil painting 'Norham Castle, Sunrise' now in the Tate Gallery. The gaunt stone structure and its supporting rock alike, seen from the river, melt in hazy sunlight. All the landscape painters through four centuries had been striving to make their stone appear as hard and solid as it is in reality, when along came this eccentric English genius and dissolved the stuff in light and colour. Turner floated his evanescent vision on to the canvas with a vaporous delicacy which is almost hair-raising and gave us a picture which has nothing to do with a massive solid sandstone ruin but rises to the stature of poetry and heightens our capacity for imagination. If we could stand at Norham and see the castle as Turner saw it, the village at its foot would seem the more real and solid structure, with its church of Saxon origin, its market cross, stone houses and the local, aptly known, for once, as 'The Mason's Arms'.

Flodden Field, where the famous battle of 1513 took place, is just outside the well-kept village of Branxton, a few miles south of Norham. The Bishop of Durham fought with true Christian ferocity on one side and the Bishop of St Andrews on the other, in that bloody massacre of ten thousand Scotsmen and five thousand Englishmen of which the building of all those border castles was a portent, as clearly as the building of the Fylingdales early-warning station is a portent of nuclear war. The cross of granite standing on the spot where James IV is supposed to have fallen, head and hand practically severed by the slashes of English axes and hatchets, is a monument not, as it pretends, to the "brave of both nations" but to the folly of mankind. The fifteen thousand corpses strewn over this battleground died for nothing, unless to fertilize the cornfields with their blood, and five hundred years afterwards we are still unable to divert our trapped and feeble minds from the ingenious instruments and strategy of war and turn them instead to the potential triumph of human evolution, the conquest of poverty and suffering. We should look back in anger at the events which put this ground into the history books, not sanctify it as a place of Christian heroes.

Overleaf: Bamburgh, Northumberland.

Etal, across the River Till from Branxton, was taken by the Scots, like Norham, in their successes before Flodden, and the ruins of its pink castle define one end of the village street with the manor house at the other, and in between stone houses untypical of Northumberland, some being stone-tiled and some thatched, and all painted cream. But then this is another of those neat estate villages which sprang up everywhere in the eighteenth and nineteenth centuries, picturesque and distinctive in its way, but in no way characteristic of the area in which one suddenly comes upon it.

Ford, though famous, is perhaps even less so. This village was built by Louisa, Marchioness of Waterford, whose husband was a hard-living Irish hunting fanatic, known with some justification as 'the Mad Marquis'. He was killed in a hunting accident, and Lady Waterford came to live at Ford Castle, which she inherited. Instead of turning to God in her grief, she turned to Ruskin (which amounted to much the same thing in those days) and devoted her life to art and good works, both of which reached their culmination in her rebuilding of Ford and the painting of religious murals in the school, in which the villagers are portrayed. I have read somewhere that Ford is built of brick, but this is certainly a libellous insult to Lady Waterford's good taste, and possibly to that of God and Ruskin also, neither of whom would have recommended brick if asked. There is a little rendering here and there, but Ford, slightly suburban though it might be, is a stylish and attractive place of pinky-grey stone in walls of ashlar or rubble, with some of that northern maroon paint glaring from the woodwork.

Doddington gives its name to one of Northumberland's sandstones, which we see in this locality, quarried near the village. It is a fine-grained stone of pink colour with grey and purple flecks. The village itself is much reduced from its former prosperous state and looks a little dilapidated, but the ruin of a pele tower remains in a farmyard, and a watchtower was built in the churchyard to protect the graves against resurrection men. Body-snatchers here would have had to take their conspicuous loot fifty miles to Edinburgh, where much of the local stone went, for there was no school of anatomy closer at hand. I doubt that the price they would have got could have justified the labour cost, but the alarm generated by Dr Knox's most efficient suppliers, Messrs Burke and Hare, no doubt gave panic some precedence over logic, although it must be added that there was also a lively export trade in corpses between towns and cities linked by regular roads or sea transport.

Akeld is a farming hamlet down the road with random rubble walls of pink and fawn stone, whilst a little farther south a signpost points to South Middleton, one of Northumberland's deserted medieval villages, where a road and a stream once bounded a community whose stone foundations and strip fields can still be detected centuries after it became a place of mere ghosts.

The Cheviot Hills support no significant settlements on their higher ground, and we move to their south-eastern flanks for our next stone villages, which include Whittingham and Glanton. The first is attractive and well kept, with several greens among its grey houses, mostly roofed with grey slate, although some have red pantiles. Glanton is more nondescript.

Three hamlets along the course of the River Coquet are worth pausing over – Alwinton, Harbottle and Holystone. Alwinton is the highest of this trio. The winding salmon river cuts through a sandstone gorge just before reaching the village, after coming down from moorlands where sheep graze untroubled by much human activity, and its tributary the Alwin meets it here, giving the creamy-grey village its name. The place looks a trifle uncared for, with mixed building and the army much in evidence, but its lovely setting saves it from total disaster. The 'Rose and Thistle' played host to Scott during the writing of *Rob Roy*. The church is half a mile away from the present village, at Low Alwinton, where the original settlement stood, and it has its own stable, with a stone-tiled roof, in this wild country where travelling could only be done on horseback. An old drovers' road, known as Clennell Street, leads from the 'last village in England' to the Scottish border at Windy Gyle, over the hills and not so far away.

Tidier Harbottle's stone houses have a huge earthwork rising above them which was the site of a Norman castle and was probably built by early settlers here as a meeting-place of local chieftains long before the place became a market town. A dramatic rock formation nearby, called the Drake Stone, is believed to take its name from the Celtic 'draag' or dragon and is, perhaps fancifully, supposed to be associated with the rites of druids. Superstition possessed the locals up to the last century, for they used to pass sick infants over the top of the thirty-foot stone as a cure.

Holystone, downstream, is an attractive hamlet near the junction of two Roman roads, where legend has it that Paulinus baptized three thousand local people in AD 627. Whatever the holy stone was, it is the holy well that gives the place its distinction now. It is a clear spring-fed pool across a field behind the Salmon Inn, surrounded by trees, with a modern cross standing in it, and an older statue of Paulinus which was brought here from Alnwick in the eighteenth century. There is nothing very holy about this place now. The moors rising to the west of these hamlets have been turned into an artillery range, and the sounds of war still rumble around this long-troubled border country, not only in the form of gunfire but with armoured vehicles roaring along unclassified roads which are often like roller coasters.

To the south is Elsdon, once isolated in wild moorland country, and a settlement of great antiquity, which has even been called a city in its time. It was the capital of Redesdale in ancient days, and the heavy air of paganism hangs about its earthworks and its church, for three horses' heads were found to have been deposited in a box in the church spire, possibly sacrificial victims in some primitive ceremony. The bones of more than a thousand men found in a mass grave were the more recent victims of human sacrifice – soldiers who died in battle in 1388 at Otterburn, known in border ballad as 'Chevy Chase'. The victims whose bodies hung on the gibbet which still stands outside the village have unknown resting-places, but the dry corpses of trapped moles hanging on farm fences serve to remind us that this is a place where death *en masse* is a familiar sight.

The fortified former parson's house at Elsdon is well known, and on the wide green, with its stone pinfold for stray cattle, is a house that was once an inn and has a sculpture of Bacchus above the doorway – a reminder of another common expression derived from the rock beneath – being 'stoned' was a state not unfamiliar to the hard-living and unruly men of the northern marches.

Bellingham lies in the valley of the North Tyne as it descends from the northernmost reaches of the Pennines in the Cheviot Hills to flow eastward to the coalfield. Bellingham's stone houses, grey among the green moors, are the successors of Anglo-Saxon homes where church and well, as with so many holy places in the northern extremity of England, were dedicated to St Cuthbert. The church has a barrel-vaulted stone roof, built after the original timber roof had twice been destroyed by fire, and the outward thrust of its weight caused the walls to be buttressed in the eighteenth century. A curious legend has grown up around a grave in the churchyard. It is said that a pedlar with a heavy pack asked for lodging at Lee Hall and was refused by the maid because the master was away, but she allowed him to leave his pack. Later on, the pack was seen to move by itself, and another servant fired a shot at it. Blood poured out, and the body of a young man was found, with a horn slung round the shoulders, evidently to signal his companions when the coast was clear. The servants got help from the village, then blew the horn, and a band of robbers expecting an easy job were greeted by such a spirited defence that they fled empty-handed. The body of their unidentified crony was buried in the churchyard. Suddenly we seem not quite so far away from Swinbrook in the Oxfordshire Cotswolds.

A dozen miles down river, at the edge of the Millstone Grit once more, is Chesters, on the Roman wall, known to its builders as Cilurno. It was among the largest of the forts along Hadrian's northern frontier. Though the wall is nearly two thousand years old, it is still by far the

Elsdon – the former parsonage built on to a pele tower.

most immense stone structure in Britain. Its purpose was, as Romans themselves put it, to separate Romans from barbarians. Some say that Hadrian was inspired to build it by travellers' accounts of the Great Wall of China. The influence of stone is far-reaching. Along the middle of its seventy miles length from coast to coast, where it crosses the Pennines, the wall was built along the craggy north-facing crest of a volcanic outcrop known as Whin Sill. This is the most spectacular stretch of the serpent-like rampart, with Chesters as its eastern terminus. A little way to the west, at the wall's most northerly point, is Limestone Corner, where the Millstone Grit and the Mountain limestone meet. The stone for the wall was quarried at various points along the route, and the method of construction was basically similar to the building of dry-stone walls. Two outer faces of dressed stones were laid in courses, and the space between was filled with rubble, bonded with clay or mortar. Drains were laid through the foundations to run off any water which collected in the walls. It is probable that ten thousand Roman soldiers were occupied in building the wall, using native labour for quarrying and carting the stone.

At Chesters the wall was carried over the North Tyne on a stone bridge. The garrison here was provided with barracks, officers' quarters, commandant's house, stables, bath-house and strong-room, some of their stones inscribed with phallic symbols to reinforce the elementary superstitions of the imperial troops. A civilian village grew up near the site under the fort's protection, peopled perhaps by the native labourers, but when the legions departed, the village was deserted as too dangerous a place to remain in, and it gradually disappeared. There was little Roman activity on the wall, it would seem, after Magnus Maximus masterminded a campaign against Picts and Scots in AD 382, and in the following centuries the wall itself became an inexhaustible quarry for the builders of abbeys, castles, farms and houses in its vicinity. Some of it found its way into the present village nearby, not unreasonably named Wall, where there are also some seventeenth-century yeomen's houses with various inscriptions on the stones, including the owners' initials on lintels over the doorways.

A few miles to the west is Housesteads, called Borcovicium by the Romans. The remains of this fort are the best along the wall. Here, too, are the foundations of a British settlement, once thriving with shops, taverns and market place, which lost its *raison d'être* when the imperial army returned to Rome. It seems that Housesteads was a trade route for imports from the north, for a gap in the wall was constructed with double gates like a frontier Customs post, and no doubt innocent commercial travellers bringing wool or hides to the south were just as irritated as modern airline passengers at being frisked by border guards. The civil settlement was of a kind called by the Romans a *vicus*, having a degree of self-government. It had a temple dedicated to the pagan gods which was evidently destroyed by Caledonian barbarians when the Romans had gone.

Hadrian's Wall continues westward, beyond the inn called 'Twice Brewed' – a favourite viewpoint for this northern boundary of empire, where the wall can be seen snaking dramatically along the ridge of Whin Sill – to the final area of our quest for stone villages.

CHAPTER 7

The North West

The Roman wall brings us into Cumbria near Gilsland, where the stone barrier crosses the River Irthing as it flows down from the Cheviots towards Carlisle, passing between the remains of the Augustinians' Lanercost Priory and the Howards' Naworth Castle. Birdoswald, the Roman Banna, is a five-acre fort guarding the river crossing, and it is an important place in the wall's history, for originally the wall westward from here was built of turf. Some experts have suggested that the reason for this was simply that the wall had run beyond the easily available limestone at this point, but this is an insult to the ingenuity of Roman engineers, and indeed the turf wall was rebuilt later with the local sandstone. Some of it was taken from a quarry at Coombe Crag, near Nether Denton. Imperial troops working the quarry left their names inscribed on the rock faces.

From this fort, a road ran north-west to the outpost fort at Bewcastle, which was probably built to protect Brigantian territory where the wall, for good strategic reasons, crossed it instead of defining its northern limit. This fort, on an exposed site, was finally abandoned during the reign of Theodosius. The church, rectory and farm buildings of the modern village (otherwise known as Shopford) lie within the Roman fortifications, and needless to say much village building has been done with Roman stone. Indeed, some of the stone in the place may well have been used several times over, for the Danes built a castle here, also within the Roman fortifications, which was destroyed during the Civil War.

The enduring fame of Bewcastle, however, rests in its churchyard cross, one of those works of art that make 'Dark Ages' seem a misnomer in one sense, yet paradoxically in another sense reinforce the feeling of pagan forces in which Christianity is but the polythene wrapping on a ripe cheese. This elegant Saxon monolith, skilfully carved from top to bottom on all sides with birds and beasts, runic inscriptions and Coptic devices, lost its head early in the seventeenth century, when it was sent to the antiquary William Camden for research purposes and was never replaced. Not the least of the mysteries about what remains is how a column of carved sandstone

Langdale, beneath the famous Pikes.

can have stood up so well to the weathering of a thousand years in this bleak and windswept place, when Carlisle Cathedral, only half its age, was said thirty years ago to be in danger of becoming "a shapeless mass of crumbling stone".

The explanation lies partly, but not wholly, in the inferior stone used for the cathedral, which came from quarries at Wetheral in the Eden valley east of the city. The New Red Sandstone here was more friable – a fact that accounts for the worn appearance of many of the villages in this area. Wetheral itself, though it has sandstone buildings round the village green, has acquired such a dose of jaundice with rendered and yellow brick buildings that it is no longer a stone village in any real sense at all.

Cumbria's red sandstone villages are spread out along the Eden valley and the lower western slopes of the Pennines like tulips at the edge of a rock garden, and following the river upstream we come to Kirkoswald. The name derives, obviously enough, from the church dedicated to St Oswald, the Christian King of Northumbria. The bell tower of the church stands on a hill separate from the main building, no doubt so that the bells calling the faithful to worship could be heard in the remotest corners of the parish, for the church itself is in a hollow, where pagans once worshipped a well. The spring still rises beneath the nave, with an outflow by the west wall, and the original church was built on oak piles to support it on the soft ground. Alas, much of the village is built of brick, and the Victorian building occupied by the Midland Bank is a monument to brick's hideousness in this stone region.

Further up the valley is Great Salkeld, a street village of the ubiquitous Penrith Red Sandstone, and a very tidy one, too, but the sandstone is dressed to small square blocks which can easily be mistaken for brick at a cursory glance – and *has* been so mistaken by writers of guidebooks. In contrast, the church tower, with its high, narrow window slits, was once a pele tower, built for defensive purposes against Scotch marauders, and it has huge blocks of rough sandstone in its walls. The river can only be crossed by road at Lazonby, to the north, or Langwathby, to the south, but on the opposite bank, near Little Salkeld, is the stone circle known as Long Meg and Her Daughters.

William Wordsworth came upon this monument and – as befits a poet – described it as a druid temple, following Aubrey, Stukeley and others:

> A weight of awe not easy to be borne
> Fell suddenly upon my spirit, cast
> From the dread bosom of the unknown past,
> When first I saw that sisterhood forlorn.

Opinion now holds that this is a Bronze Age circle, roughly contemporary with Stonehenge and predating the Celtic settlement. It was probably used for some ceremonial purpose, but what is certain is that these venerable stones have captured the imaginations of local people for many centuries. Like the Merry Maidens far away in Cornwall, Long Meg and Her Daughters are supposed to have been turned to stone for dancing on the Sabbath. I have already mentioned in a previous chapter that the stones cannot be counted accurately, and the descriptions of various visiting authors seem to support this belief, not to mention the height of the stones and the shape of the formation. Wordsworth referred to "a perfect circle, eighty yards in diameter, and seventy-two in number . . .". Pevsner described "an oval setting of fifty-nine stones". Another account says that it is "a prehistoric circle . . . composed of 65 stones", and another: "Of a former total of 59 stones, 27 are still standing, and perhaps a dozen more have disappeared." Long Meg herself, a monolith standing apart from the circle, is variously put at twelve, fifteen and eighteen feet high. Anyone who counts the stones correctly will break the spell, and they will turn to dancing girls before his very eyes.

Whatever the truth about the size, shape and origin of this arrangement of stones, it is undeniably impressive, being of such extent that a farm lane lined with trees runs right through the circle. They were dedicated men who hauled these huge blocks of sandstone here and set them up for good or evil purposes 3½ thousand years ago, and men less imaginative than Wordsworth have been emotionally affected by them. When Colonel Lacy, who owned the land on which they stood, tried to reclaim it by employing labourers to remove the stones by blasting, a frightful thunderstorm blew up, and the gang of strong men fled in terror. The job remains undone to this day.

Further east, below heights with names like Fiends Fell, Low Scar and Meikle Awfell, are Gamblesby, Melmerby and Ousby, with name-endings that remind us of the Viking hold over this territory, whose abrasive language of fells and screes, gills and becks, also reflects the Norse influence. No one of this trio is a pure stone village. Indeed stone is little in evidence in Melmerby and Ousby, though Gamblesby has plenty round the village green. The red sandstone is frequently whitewashed, and much brick building has intruded, but these villages, in spite of having little to show for it, belong firmly in the local culture and tradition – farming communities among the fields and dry-stone walls which have influenced all their lives.

Out of the valley, across the fells and the Roman road known as Maiden Way, are the villages of Garrigill and Nenthead, near Cumbria's junction with Northumberland and Durham, on the bleak and barren Alston Moor, made of the Carboniferous limestone again.

These villages were built early in the nineteenth century for the employees of the London Lead Company, a Quaker organization which exploited the moor's mineral deposits. Nenthead is a derelict and depressing place on the high and treeless moorland road. What was once the Mining Men's Reading Room, born of the usual Quaker concern for the welfare of their employees, is now the over-sixties' rest room, and many of the stone houses have been painted over in an apparently desperate attempt to brighten village life. But whereas Nenthead is exposed to all the ravages of time and moorland weather, Garrigill is sheltered in a valley and looks tidy and well cared for, with its dark grey stone in tune with the bleak landscape.

Just across the Northumberland border from Nenthead is the derelict mining hamlet of Coalclough, whose cottages of massive stone formed the highest settlement in England. The Quaker mine-owners had previously developed Dufton, farther south on the Pennine Way and back in the sandstone Eden valley, along a wide rectangular village green which sports a Georgian stone pump rivalling many a more primitive monolith in its suggestion of phallic symbolism and unaccountably painted in maroon. The stone is not much in evidence here, many of the houses round the green being painted or rendered.

Milburn is a little way north-west – a village of old enough foundation but largely rebuilt in modern times. Although most of its houses are rendered or limewashed, it deserves mention in this book by virtue of its interesting formation, for it did not grow haphazardly round a green or along a street but was planned at some early stage as a nucleated village. The houses, cottages and barns of assorted construction – some ashlared, some of snecked or roughly coursed rubble, and many displaying the maroon paint so characteristic of the Pennine region – form a rectangle all round a large green, with road access at the four corners. The two roads at the eastern end lead nowhere, and there is no through traffic, so that Milburn enjoys an unusual quietness at its centre. The village green, where cattle could be enclosed when raids threatened, was sporting a veritable village menagerie when I was last there. The former village school also stands on the green, and a maypole rises from the stone base of a former market cross. The church is some distance away to the west, as if to keep religion out of everyday affairs.

The road west leads to Newbiggin, a red sandstone village about a minor crossroads, where martins nest in derelict buildings, and farther on, to Temple Sowerby, along the main road and near the River Eden. Knights Templars and Knights Hospitallers owned this manor in turn before the Dissolution, and a large stone fireplace in the entrance hall of Acorn Bank, formerly the manor house, has masons' marks like some at Aigues Mortes in France, from where Louis IX set forth on his

Sandstone walls and graded slates at Askham, Cumbria.

second crusade in 1270. Dorothy Una Ratcliffe, the Yorkshire dialect authoress, owned this Tudor house of sandstone and cultivated the gardens which the National Trust now opens to the public, the house itself being leased to the Sue Ryder foundation. The village with large greens has a most respectable look, and many of the house walls have granite cobbles set into them for decorative effect.

Across the Eden and its tributary the Leith, beyond Whinfell Forest, are Askham and Lowther, just at the edge of the Lake District National Park. Askham is a traditional and attractive place, with sandstone houses sometimes rendered, sometimes whitewashed, sometimes naked. Lowther, however, separated from Askham by the River Lowther, is one of the most incongruous of those villages which have been imposed on the landscape by sometimes well-meaning but usually tasteless landowners and, in this case, empire-building capitalists. The Lowther family had grown in power and influence in this district over a long period, with coal mining and other interests, until a seventeenth-century head of the family, Sir John Lowther, who represented Westmorland in Parliament, was made Viscount Lonsdale, in recognition of his active support for William of Orange. As First Lord of the Treasury, he was badly wounded in a duel with a Customs officer, who challenged him after being dismissed from his post, and a propensity for fighting seems to have remained in the family, the sixth Earl having given to boxing the Lonsdale Belt.

The ancient village of Lowther stood between the family mansion and the church, and Sir John wanted to extend his park in that direction, so he built a new village of grey limestone out of sight to the east, screened it with conifers and rhododendron and moved his workers from the old village into it, lock, stock and barrel. Then he completely demolished the old village, except for the church, which he rebuilt. The stone foundations of the vanished homes can still be detected, as can the medieval origins of the church, though not from the outside. The churchyard contains a family mausoleum, built in 1857. Meanwhile, Lord Lowther extended his mansion with the stone of the ruined Shap Abbey, which he also owned. This house, however, was largely destroyed by a fire in 1720. In 1765 Sir James Lowther began to build another new village, restoring the lost name Lowther to the map a little to the south-east of Newtown and quarrying the stone nearby. The idea of this was evidently to stop Newtown from growing bigger and to move the population even farther away from milord's sight. The plan is attributed to the Adam brothers and would be quite at home in Bath or Edinburgh, with its formal closes of terraced one-up, one-down cottages, originally intended to end in crescents forming a circus. Here among the Cumbrian fells it looks as unbeliev-ably artificial as the ruins of the sham medieval castle that crowned the Lowther megalomania, built by Robert Smirke for the Earl of Lonsdale in the early years of the nineteenth century and soon abandoned as being beyond upkeep in the twentieth. Where once Westmorland women shrieked in labour to bring laughing children to their village streets and fields, this spectacular ruin still stands – a roofless and redundant Xanadu, with Emperor's Drive leaving towards the uncer-tain site of another lost village, Thrimby, which may also have been a victim of Lonsdale private enterprise.

Not all those villages which have been lost were destroyed by land-grabbing capitalists, nor deserted after the Black Death or for more hospitable sites. One lies under Haweswater. Mardale was a farming hamlet at the southern end of the lake, of which Harriet Martineau wrote: "The inn at Mardale Green is full a mile from the water; and sweet is the passage to it. . . . The path winds through the levels, round the bases of the knolls, past the ruins of the old church, and among snug little farms." Of the lake itself, Wordsworth said: "Haweswater is a lesser Ullswater, with this advantage, that it remains undefiled by the intrusion of bad taste."

That was all before Manchester turned Haweswater into a reservoir and built a concrete dam among these dry-stone walls, barns of rough granite, and fells where golden eagles soared. The gilt weathercock on the square tower of Mardale's Holy Trinity church was blown up in 1935, and nearly a hundred corpses were exhumed from the church-yard and reburied at Shap. The farmhouses and cottages, the barns, the school house and the 'Dun Bull' inn were all bulldozed to the ground, and the water level rose until nothing of Mardale could be seen except the dry-stone walls on slopes where the village farmers had kept their sheep and cattle. In dry summers, when the water level is very low, the ruined walls of Mardale can sometimes be seen, and legend has speedily grown in these supposedly materialistic times to tell us that the bells of the old church can be heard ringing under the water.

On the other side of Shap, whose quarries still produce the famous porphyritic granite sometimes known as 'heathen' by the quarrymen, are Maulds Meaburn, Crosby Ravensworth and – away to the south-east – Crosby Garrett. Though the modern names of the Crosbys indi-cate Danish origin, there were settlements on the limestone hills of east Cumbria before the Romans came – hamlets surrounded by walls and ditches, where neolithic men perhaps involved in the axe trade lived, for it is known that stone axes were made and exported from the Lake District to all parts of the country and to the Continent of Europe, via trackways which the Romans converted into their military roads. One such is the famous High Street, along the ridge of the fells between Haweswater and Ullswater, which the Romans later used to link their forts at Penrith and Ambleside. What deprivations the imperial sol-diers – many of them young men from southern Italy – must have suffered in protecting their empire here in bleak and frozen winters.

The remains of a fairly extensive British settlement have been found near Crosby Ravensworth, which lies around a cluster of streams and bridges. The village's grey stone buildings are generally nondescript, but there are exceptions, where ashlared walls and mullioned win-dows appear in large and older houses. The field walls are sometimes most attractive, with blocks of pale grey/brown sandstone flecked with pink, salmon and orange.

Maulds Meaburn is a pleasant village set in a valley with a stone bridge over the stream and sheep on the village green. From Tebay, where the concrete serpent M6 weaves past like a snake in the grass announcing its presence by its rattle, a road leads east through pleasant grey stone hamlets, Kelleth and Newbiggin on Lune, to Raven-stonedale, watered by the rippling Scandal Beck. Here are names to conjure with. Ravens which inhabited the lonely limestone crags menaced the livelihoods of sheep farmers, and right up to the eight-eenth century anyone who produced a raven's head was rewarded with a bounty of two pence. There are still ravens in Lakeland, and their great black bearded shapes still occasionally swoop down from the mountains to feed on the carcass of a lamb which has failed to survive the winter.

Ravenstonedale is a stylish grey village. The 'Black Swan' at its centre is attractive with mullioned windows, and a bell-cote surmounts the stone village school. The church is mainly a modern rebuilding job, but the old church used to have a refuge bell. Any criminal who could reach the bell tower and ring the bell before his pursuers caught up with him was allowed to go free. It was a more demanding way to sanctuary than reaching the frid stool in Chewton Mendip, but more happily decisive in its result. One local woman who failed to make it is commemorated in a window. Elizabeth Gaunt was brought before Judge Jeffreys, fresh from the Bloody Assize in the West Country, in 1685, and she was sentenced to be burned at Tyburn. Her crime was that she had sheltered one of the Duke of Monmouth's supporters. She was an elderly Baptist, well known for her good works, and no one thought the sentence would be carried out, but there was no mercy or conscience in those days of terror. The man whose life she had saved gave evidence against her, and she was consumed by flames amid a great storm which Protestants optimistically took to be a sign of Almighty anger.

Most of the women of these villages in later days were preoccupied with woollen knitting, and famous among local places was Dent, at the head of Dentdale. It is in Cumbria now but was formerly a Yorkshire town – it is still within the Yorkshire Dales National Park. It is a tight village of narrow lanes and alleys, and many of its stone houses are painted or rendered. Although the village street was being dug up when I was there, Dent has a slightly untouched look about it, as if it has been forgotten since Dickens's time, and this is not surprising, for it is fairly isolated, in country dotted with grey stone barns and farm houses, sometimes forming attractive groups miles from the nearest village. Stone walls go hand in hand with natural outcrops up hill and down dale of these fringes of North Yorkshire.

One of the pioneer geologists was born at Dent – Adam Sedgwick – and a rough monument of Shap granite stands as a memorial to him in the street near the church. The men who were not farmers here were usually quarrymen. The local stone was favoured for millstones in gunpowder factories, because it was free from iron pyrites which caused sparks. But it was the women who won Dent its dubious reputation, for sparks flew in the clatter of their knitting needles rivalling the sound of their clogs on the cobbled village streets. It was a Lakeland woman, Betty Yewdale, who told Robert Southey's representatives about her childhood days when she and her younger sister had been sent by their father to Dent to learn hand knitting. Betty was seven, and her sister Sally five or six. The pace at which the local women knitted coarse worsted stockings overawed the children, whose only thought was to return home. All sorts of devices were invented by the masters to make children knit faster, like making three or four of them knit off several balls of yarn wound together, so that she "'at knit slawest raffled t'udder's yarn, an' than she gat weel thumpt". One winter's night, Betty related, "we teuk off." They wore only their bedgowns and aprons, clogs and hats, and they survived a twenty-five-mile trek home over the fells during two days and nights of rain and snow. "They er terrible knitters e' Dent," Betty said.

We can move conveniently west into the Lake District with Betty Yewdale, for Wordsworth got to know her before Southey, when she lived at a tiny place called Hacket near Little Langdale. Her husband Jonathan was a quarryman, and Wordsworth says he came upon her one dark night holding up a lantern to light Jonathan's way home. The poet found this image irresistible and used it to drown his poem 'The Excursion' with floods of the lofty sentiment he bestowed on the peasantry:

> I never see
> Save when the Sabbath brings it kind release,
> My helpmate's face by light of day. He quits
> His door in darkness, nor till dusk returns.
> And through Heaven's blessing, thus we gain the bread
> For which we pray.

Southey's account of Betty was a little less romantic. In reality, she smoked a pipe of strong tobacco and was not beyond driving her drunken husband home from the pub with a stick. He, it turned out, was a bit simple-minded, or 'short o' leet' as they say in these parts, and Betty would switch him as he crawled through the 'hog-hooals' left in dry-stone walls for lambs to pass through.

It was common then for quarry workers to spend the week at their places of work. The journey on foot to and from home was often too hard to undertake every day, but the men would go home on Saturday night and leave again early on Monday morning. Sometimes carrier pigeons were used to send important messages between quarries, the companies' offices and the quarrymen's homes. The quarrymen's working lives were hard and dangerous, and they tended to live hard and drink hard as one would expect, much to the consternation of moralists who supposed that they were responsible for the debauchery and ignorance of the local people, many of whom could not say the Lord's Prayer. But illiteracy and 'heathenism' arose largely from the sheer physical isolation of the area. If only God had taken a crash-course in logistics before creating the world! As it was, cock-fighting became the passion of these men's brief week-ends of respite from hard labour, and the sport continued long after it had been officially banned in 1835. Some say it continues still.

The Herdwick and Swaledale sheep of the Lake District are agile animals, so the dry-stone walls here are different from those of the Cotswolds in size and from those of the Pennines in materials, sometimes being built of huge slabs of slate standing on end. This type of wall is generally confined to the valleys of the Silurian slate region, for this fissile rock can be split into flat 'flags' which are set up and interlocked at the edges. The walls on the fells were made with the more conventional cobbles, often with a 'through' here and there; that is a long stone placed crossways in the wall and projecting at either side, giving the structure extra stability. The walls are usually built like the walls of a cottage, with rubble or 'hearting' in the cavity between the facing stones. Thinner slabs placed upright in rows along the tops of the walls discourage sheep from trying to jump them.

Although the general principles of dry-stone walling are the same, however, variations in appearance are as numerous as the types of stone used. Thus you may see one wall built of huge boulders and another built of thin slabs, whilst the arrangement of the 'cam' or coping stones can show nonconformist originality. The stone for most of these walls was obtained from the beds of the becks or by clearing the land of the rough stone lying on the surface, and occasionally one sees a pile of stones in a field where supply exceeded demand. In other parts, stone was not so easily come by and had to be quarried specially for the purpose.

The quarries from which the seventeenth- and eighteenth-century enclosers took their stone are dotted about all over the Lake District, usually quite small pits abandoned after extraction of sufficient material for the job in hand, and now overgrown or rain-filled, sometimes giving shelter to sheep in gale-force winds and hosting stunted trees with exposed roots gripping rocks as if to squeeze moisture from them.

Many old quarries, large and small, are still being worked in the Lake District, however, producing both slate for roofing and the slate-stone which has been used for building in this region in more recent times. Some of them are situated high on the fells, in seemingly inaccessible places, such as the craggy mountain called Coniston Old Man, Honister Pass between Buttermere and Borrowdale, and Kirkstone Pass, all these at well over a thousand feet up. E. Lynn Linton described the working conditions of the quarrymen on Honister in the nineteenth century, when much of the slate was mined:

This slate quarrying is awful to look at; both in the giddy height at which men

Sledging slate on Honister. The man between the 'stangs' had to control the forward momentum of a quarter-ton load.

work, and in the terrible journeys which they make when bringing down the slate in their 'sleds'. It is simply appalling to see that small moving speck on the high crag, passing noiselessly along a narrow grey line that looks like a mere thread, and to know that it is a man with the chances of his life dangling in his hand. As we look the speck moves; he first crosses the straight gallery leading out from the dark cavern where he emerged, and then he sets himself against the perpendicular descent, and comes down the face of the crag, carrying something behind him – at first slowly, and, as it were, cautiously; then with a swifter step, but still evidently holding back; but at the last with a wild haste that seems as if he must be overtaken, and crushed to pieces by the heavy sled grinding behind him. The long swift steps seem almost to fly; the noise of the crashing slate comes nearer; now we see the man's eager face; and now we hear his panting breath; and now he draws up by the road-side – every muscle strained, every nerve alive, and every pulse throbbing with frightful force. It is a terrible trade – and the men employed in it look wan and worn, as if they were all consumptive or had heart disease. The average daily task is seven or eight of these journeys, carrying about a quarter of a ton of slate each time; the downward run occupying only a few minutes, the return climb – by another path not quite so perpendicular, where they crawl with their empty sleds on their backs, like some strange sort of beetle or fly – half an hour. Great things used to be done in former times, and the quarrymen still talk of Samuel Trimmer, who once made fifteen journeys in one day, for the reward of a small percentage on the hurdle and a bottle of rum; and of Joseph Clark, a Stonethwaite man, who brought down forty-two and a half loads, or ten thousand eight hundred and eighty pounds of slate, in seventeen journeys; travelling seventeen miles – eight and a half up the face of the crag, and the same number down, at this murderous pace. . . .

Later the mountains echoed with the thunder of explosions as great slabs of slate were detached from their host rock by blasting, and tramways saved the backs of the men to some extent in hauling slate from the working faces, now done by lorries weaving about on precipitous tracks.

The ring of limestone and sandstone that encircles the Lake District encloses three distinct rock formations in east-west belts. The rock of the mountainous central region is known as the Borrowdale Volcanic series. That to the south of it, surrounding Windermere and Coniston Water, is a younger belt of Silurian grits and shale, and to the north, beyond Derwentwater and Buttermere, are the so-called Skiddaw Slates, formed by the compression and crumpling of the earth's crust. Ironically, it is the Borrowdale Volcanics and the Silurian beds that contain workable building stone – the Skiddaw Slates do not. The production of slate is a thriving business today, and among other buildings which have incorporated 'Westmorland slate' is the new Coventry Cathedral.

The differences between the landscapes produced by the Borrowdale Volcanics and the Skiddaw Slates can be seen most clearly at the lower end of Borrowdale, where the soft and wooded slopes of Cat Bells flank Derwentwater on one side and the sheer rock of the volcanic Falcon Crags on the other. The slate-stone used for building walls as well as making roofs in the old cottages seems often to have been laid dry by skilful masons, although subsequently cottages were built with stone bedded in mortar which was set back from the face of the wall so that it had the appearance of dry-stone construction. Chimneys are often a distinctive feature of the old Lakeland cottages and farmhouses, ending in circular tapering stacks, to avoid the necessity of forming corners from stone that could not be shaped accurately. Lakeland village churches are simple and low – slate does not lend itself to elaborate carving or to building steeples.

There are relatively few 'pure' stone villages in the Lake District. All of them are practical and unassuming, well aware that the natural scenery is what people come here to see. The vernacular tradition is strongly in favour of rendered or lime-washed walls so that the rough stone is often unseen. As Penrith is a red town, for instance, and Kendal a grey one, so Hawkshead, one of the most charming of Cumbrian villages, is almost entirely white.

One village where the grey-green slate is to be seen in both old and modern buildings, however, is Coniston. It stands on the western shore of Coniston Water facing heavily wooded hills on the other side, but behind it rise wild, craggy fells culminating in the so-called Old Man of Coniston, rising to over 2,600 feet. The name of the mountain may be a corruption of the Celtic *'alt maen'* meaning 'high crag'. Mining and quarrying since at least as long ago as Roman times have pock-marked the mountain with holes and craters like a lunar landscape, and many of the residents of Coniston village are still quarry workers today. The village grew up as a mining community when copper was extracted from the fells, and when the copper ran out, early in this century, slate quarrying took over as the chief industry. The copper miners had to get their ore to smelters at Keswick, a twenty-mile journey by packhorse over what was in earlier days very rough terrain, travelling over Dunmail Raise. One of the early exploiters of Coniston's copper deposits on an industrial scale was the German mining en-gineer Höchstetter, in the reign of Elizabeth I, and men came from Germany to work here as well as from Cornwall. But the profitable business did not please everyone. Flooding and pollution were caused by the mining operations, and the modern problem of industrial waste was a heated topic here as far back as the seventeenth century.

The real Old Man of Coniston was Ruskin, who bought Brantwood, on the east bank of the lake, in 1871 and lived there for the last twenty-nine years of his life, famous, weary and at times mentally unbalanced, the stormy state of his mind reflected in his customary keen observation of nature: "Three times light and three times dark since last I wrote, and the darkness seeming each time as it settles more loathsome, at last stopping my reading in mere blindness. One lurid gleam of white cumulus in upper lead-blue sky, seen for half a minute

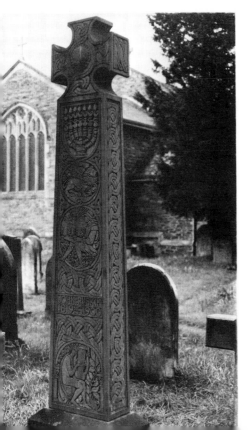

Ruskin's gravestone in Coniston churchyard.

through the sulphurous chimney-pot vomit of blackguardly cloud beneath, where its rags were thinnest."

Ruskin may have become 'short o' leet', but his influence spread across the world and is still with us. His own mind, before he lost his faith in Nature, had been profoundly affected by rock and stone. He filled the fourth volume of *Modern Painters* with descriptions of rock formations and made collections of rocks and minerals, some of which can be seen in Coniston's Ruskin Museum, along with assorted trivia and, not to be missed, Ruskin's exquisite drawings of the stones of Venice. When he could only see the "cruelty and ghastliness" of the nature he had once thought "so divine", he still found comfort in studying his geological specimens.

When he died in 1900, he was buried in Coniston churchyard beneath a tall cross carved with elaborate decoration by H. T. Miles to a design by W. G. Collingwood. A single block of green stone was used for the shaft and head, obtained from Mossrigg Quarry at Tilber-thwaite, above Yewdale. Mr Miles made a little extra income from the commission by selling pieces of the remaining stone and apparently also some miniature models of the cross: such was the awe in which Ruskin was held.

Ruskin had written of the "dependence of architecture on the inspiration of Nature", likening cathedrals to mountainous landscapes and always deploring the mean and ugly dwellings of the urban areas of Britain. "An architect should live in cities as little as a painter. Send him to our hills, and let him study there what nature understands by a buttress, and what by a dome." The imaginations of the local men who saw a medieval fortress in the Castle Rock of Triermain would presum-ably have appealed to him. This rock, called Green Crag before Sir Walter Scott wove an elaborate tapestry of Arthurian romance round it, is in the Vale of St John and was described by the Cumberland historian Hutchinson as having "various towers, making an awful, rude, and Gothic appearance with its lofty turrets and ruined battlements". You need a vivid imagination to see any resemblance to a castle in the rock, in these materialistic days, but the legend contains the spirit of Rus-kin's view of architecture. "What sort of chisels, and in what work-man's hands," he wondered, "were used to produce the large piece of precious chasing or embossed work, which we call Cumberland and Westmorland?"

The rivers and valleys, lakes and waterfalls of Cumbria, and the shapes of the mountains as we know them today, were formed during a million years of glaciation. It is probable that the once-volcanic mountains were enclosed in a massive dome of ice, with Scafell at the centre, and that when the ice began to retreat, the glaciers carved out the valleys and formed the lakes as they descended outwards from the centre. This would explain the cartwheel pattern to which the Lake District is often likened, and the fact that the lakes are generally long, narrow and straight. Those mighty chisels that Ruskin wondered at were made of ice.

What resulted from this immense and prolonged upheaval – the crushing and shattering of rocks by ice and frost, the gouging-out of valleys and the eroding of river beds and formation of waterfalls – was a landscape of perfect scale. It is one of the Lake District's greatest attributes that everything is in manageable proportions and within clearly defined limits. It is like an exotic island in the middle of a great ocean.

The Greeks – more poetic and imaginative than the Romans, Scots, Danes and English who subsequently colonized the area – would have invested the misty mountain tops and bubbling streams with elaborate religious significance. They would have visualized Aphrodite casting aside her silver-edged mantle of clouds at dawn to gaze vainly at her reflections in a score of jewelled mirrors. In fact, however, most of the mythology of the Lake District derives from the Norsemen who gave Cumbria so much of its language, and the local folklore is peopled by fairies, elves and goblins at one end of the scale and by giants at the other.

No doubt the northern taste for exaggeration, so clearly seen in the Cumbrian mania for tall stories, derives from the same sources. What is certain is that, wherever it came from, the folklore has lasted a long time in this remote part of England. As late as 1885 a Newcastle man was reported by a clergyman, of all people, as having been dragged from his horse by fairies, and only saved from being carried off through a fairies' door in a hillside by having a page of the Bible in his pocket! Fairies were generally regarded as malevolent creatures in medieval England, far removed from the miniature playmates of modern children's fiction, not to mention the effeminate male adult with whom they have lately become mistakenly synonymous. Elf-shot humans and domestic animals were quite beyond the physician's healing talents, and it was common in Celtic regions until quite modern times for farmers whose animals died unaccountably to blame elves, who were supposed to shoot them using tiny arrows with heads of flint.

Troutbeck, near the northern end of Windermere, was once renowned for breeding giants. A good deal of bare slate-stone can be seen in this long street village beside the road up to Kirkstone Pass, and the houses are roofed with Lake District slate. Troutbeck is actually a series of ancient hamlets on what must once have been inhospitable farming land, with groups of buildings situated near the precious springs which provided the only water. Not surprisingly, perhaps, the springs are dedicated to saints – St Margaret's Well, St John's Well, St

Farm buildings of slate rubble at Troutbeck.

Slate used in a dry-stone barn
wall at Troutbeck.

James's Well. The village church is rather isolated in the valley below, beside the main road. The common style of chimney referred to previously can be seen clearly at Townhead, the National Trust's statesman's house at the southern end of the village.

Slate quarrying brought some prosperity to Troutbeck in the middle of the eighteenth century, and many of its houses and farms were rebuilt using the readily available quarry waste. There are numerous disused quarries on the fells rising from the valley on the east side, where the Roman road called High Street runs along the ridge. The dry-stone walls of farmyards and barns show what could be done with rough slate-stone, and opposite Robin Lane is an interesting bank barn with a spinning gallery at first-floor level, where the wool of the local Herdwick sheep would have been spun by the farmer's wife before being taken to the town for weaving and fulling. Several such spinning galleries, open to the light and air, survive in the Lake District as testimony to the importance of the cottage industry of spinning and weaving when the menfolk – 'statesmen' farmers – eked out a bare living from the small areas of land they owned by hereditary tenure.

No better description of the older Lake District cottages can be given than that in which Wordsworth anticipated Ruskin's joining together of nature and architecture in an ideal marrage:

> It is a favourable circumstance, that the strong winds, which sweep down the valleys, induced the inhabitants, at a time when the materials for building were easily procured, to furnish many of these dwellings with substantial porches; and such as have not this defence, are seldom unprovided with a projection of two large slates over their thresholds. Nor will the singular beauty of the chimneys escape the eye of the attentive traveller. . . . These dwellings, mostly built, as has been said, of rough unhewn stone, are roofed with slates, which were rudely taken from the quarry before the present art of splitting them was understood, and are, therefore, rough and uneven in their surface, so that both the coverings and sides of the houses have furnished places of rest for the seeds of lichens, mosses, ferns and flowers. Hence buildings, which in their very form call to mind the processes of Nature, do thus, clothed in part with a vegetable garb, appear to be received into the bosom of the living principle of things. . . .

To resume with Troutbeck, its tradition of giant-breeding seems to have evolved in times of raids by marauding Scots, since such men as Hugh Heard, Tom Hickathrift and Great Will of the Tarns are credited with feats of great strength in repelling the red-haired barbarians from the north, to whose kingdom of Strathclyde Cumbria had once belonged. Great Will reputedly stood nine feet six inches high and was known as a fine labourer until he took it into his head to carry off the maid of Lady Eva le Fleming of Coniston Hall, whereupon a posse of local men hunted him down and killed him in the course of rescuing the maiden in distress.

Hugh Heard, or Hird, is supposed to have been the son of a nun who was expelled from Furness Abbey when she became pregnant. The accounts of him are vague and often contradictory, but they say that he could lift a thirty-foot oak beam without difficulty, was an outstanding archer and wrestler and slaughtered the Caledonian hordes who came down Scots Rake from High Street. A man of "prodigious strength and stature", he was once asked by the king about his diet and replied that he normally ate thick pottage and cream for breakfast and a whole sheep for dinner but sometimes would go for days without eating at all. He may have died around 1682, some say through pulling up trees by the roots. The name Hird still occurs in the Troutbeck valley, where the giant owned a tenement called Lowick How, granted him by the king.

If you take the Windermere ferry from Bowness to Hawkshead, the road from the west bank passes through Far and Near Sawrey. Both villages have much rendering, but Near Sawrey rather less than its neighbour, and among the houses here is Beatrix Potter's home, Hill Top, well known to children throughout the world as the place where Jemima Puddle-Duck found a secret nesting place under the rhubarb leaves.

Beatrix Potter, like Ruskin, fled from an unnatural and repressed childhood in London to the space and air of the Lake District, where she took to breeding Herdwicks and acquiring land, which she left to the National Trust. And as the sage of Coniston, a quarter of a century before her, had sat for hours on a throne of slate slabs in the grounds of Brantwood, the story-teller of Near Sawrey sat in stone shelters used by shepherds and watched the sheep she waxed lyrical about: "Wild and free as when the stonemen told our puzzled early numbers; untamed as when the Norsemen named our grassings in their stride . . . we have held the stony waste."

To the west of Ambleside, at the foot of Langdale, are the quarrying villages of Chapel Stile and Elterwater, beyond Skelwith Bridge, where stone barns and houses are clenched round the river crossing. Great Langdale was once the site of a huge lake, but now the fells sweep up from the fields beside the beck to the familiar Langdale Pikes, where the local stone industry has been proved to have very ancient origins. One of the mysteries of Lakeland prehistory is that the presence of stone circles, such as the Castlerigg circle near Keswick and Long Meg and Her Daughters, has clearly contradicted the notion that this inhospitable area was shunned by early man in these islands. Discoveries during the last few decades have shown that in fact men of the late Stone Age and the Bronze Age were not only familiar with the territory but were carrying on a thriving trade in stone tools. Neolithic axes found all over the British Isles, in Scotland and Wales, the Isle of Man and Dorset, Gloucestershire and the Yorkshire dales, have been traced to factories around Scafell and Langdale Pikes. The fine-grained volcanic rock around Pike of Stickle and Harrison Stickle provided the material from which sharp-edged tools could be fashioned and exported via mountain tracks over four thousand years ago. The axes were evidently roughed out on the site and then sent to the coast via Styhead Pass for polishing and trading. Styhead Pass, the crossroads of the central fells, was still used to transport quarry products before the advent of motor traffic and surfaced roadways.

The grey slate-stone houses of Chapel Stile were mostly built for

Houses in Elterwater, Cumbria.

Thrang Quarry, Chapel Stile.

quarrymen and the gunpowder workers of a mill near Elterwater village. Gunpowder was made from ash charcoal in the Lake District for about a hundred years before the invention of dynamite, mainly for blasting purposes in the local quarries. The gunpowder mill at Elterwater was owned by ICI until its operations ceased early in the present century. The gunpowder and slate-quarrying industries brought some prosperity to these poor farming communities where the curate was obliged to sell ale to support his family in the eighteenth century.

Nowadays both villages are much visited by tourists, and Elterwater is like a living museum of local architecture, with huge, shapeless lintels and dressings of quarry waste contrasting sharply with the thin courses of green slate in the walls. A footpath from Chapel Stile's church leads up to the dramatic Thrang Quarry hanging over the village, with colossal boulders of slate threatening to topple on it if it should put a foot wrong. Behind this village, off the main road, Walthwaite sits like a grey egg in its nest below Raven Crag.

"Champion," said a Grasmere bookseller to whom I gave the right change for a book I wanted. And the village is champion among local tourist centres – the Lake District's Bourton-on-the-Water, so bursting with coach parties and gift shops that one could easily dismiss it impatiently as a place trading on Wordsworth and pass on. But Grasmere has more than Dove Cottage and the poet's grave. (Wordsworth lies beneath an upright slab of plain slate in stark contrast to

'Some corner of a foreign field' –
a climber's grave at Wasdale Head.

Ruskin's ostentatious monument.) Although the church is pebble-dashed into inconsequence, many of the village buildings are stylish and attractive, with their stone taking on purplish tints which give Grasmere a Victorian distinction not to be scoffed at.

The Styhead Pass route, passing westward between Great Gable and the Scafell massif, leads to Wasdale, via the wettest place in Britain – a fact conspicuously absent from the records proudly claimed here. They say they have England's highest mountain, its deepest lake, its smallest church and its biggest liar, but they tend to keep quiet about its heaviest rainfall. Nothing could be more extreme, in the subject of this book, than comparison of the refined Grasmere and its lovely tree-fringed lake with the remote Wasdale Head and its great black pit below the Scafell screes.

The church at Wasdale Head is not actually the smallest in England, but it is the smallest in Cumbria, and its little walled churchyard contains the graves of climbers who lost their lives on Scafell and Great Gable, for this little village is a popular starting-point for those tackling the highest Lakeland peaks. The dry-stone walls here, creating a complicated pattern of fields, led Wordsworth to characterize Wasdale as "a large piece of lawless patchwork".

The telling of tall stories was a Cumbrian pastime for centuries in the long dark nights before radio and television made it the national sport of politicians, and the undisputed champion in the region was Will

Ritson, who kept the Wasdale Head Inn, now the Wastwater Hotel, standing out in its whitewashed rendering as you approach the village from the west bank of Wastwater. Throughout the nineteenth century visitors came to hear the famous raconteur holding court in his back kitchen seated on a wooden bench, solemnly telling the gullible among them his most far-fetched tales in broad Cumberland dialect. Stories that would pass as short jokes with other people attained the stature of epics on Will Ritson's lips, as he told about the pony race down Styhead or stories of his friendship with Professor John Wilson, who wrote under the pseudonym 'Christopher North'. But Ritson's most triumphant tale was a magnificent one-liner. He was taking part in a competition to see who could tell the unlikeliest story. When it came to Will's turn, he said he wanted to withdraw from the competition. The audience was dumbfounded. Was the local champion throwing in the towel without a fight? The chairman asked him why. "Because," said Will solemnly, "I cannot tell a lie." They gave him the prize on the spot.

He was no more a respecter of persons than Dolly Pentreath of Cornwall. He once took a clerical gentleman up Scafell and told him: "Tha'll nivver be nighter t'heaven than noo." And he explained the fat trout in the local stream as feeding off "what's weshed off fwoak frae Lunnon", who came here "lousy as sheep afore soavin' an' dook in t'beck". That was perhaps a bit rich, even for Auld Will, for Harriet Martineau, noting that the children here were especially dirty, discovered a local superstition that if a child's arms were washed before it was six months old, it would grow up to be a thief. Or was that one of Will's tales too?

Will Ritson's father featured in a local enclosure award in the year of his son's birth, three years after the Battle of Trafalgar, when he was ordered to make and repair two-fifths of a wall up to Black Crag, and his neighbour John Benson was to make the remaining three-fifths. Black Crag is above Mosedale, and Black Beck runs down from it to join forces with Mosedale Beck in an attractive waterfall called Ritson Force in honour of the local hero.

The alternative route across the mountains to the west coast is via the Wrynose and Hardknott passes. The top of Wrynose sports another of those marker stones made redundant in recent years, the so-called Three Shire Stone having formerly been the meeting-point of Lancashire, Cumberland and Westmorland. If Wrynose Pass is a notoriously difficult road, Hardknott Pass is worse – a switchback road of hair-raising bends on one-in-three gradients make it the most difficult road in England, but just below the summit on the Eskdale side are the remains of a Roman military post called Mediobogdum. It would hardly win a prize for northern exaggeration if I called the place a lost stone village.

The fort occupies an awesome site on the high fells, with dramatic drops on two sides, and was built to guard the route from the fort at Ambleside to the Roman port at Ravenglass. With typical thoroughness, the imperial army (or their British slaves) not only built the fort with foundations, walls and main buildings of stone, for their living quarters, but went to the lengths of levelling out a large area of rocky terrain nearby to create a parade ground. The fort had granaries, baths and centrally heated quarters, and a gate in each of its four stone walls, and five hundred men may have occupied it once – this desolate stronghold dedicated by an inscription on local slate to "the Emperor Caesar Trajan Hadrian Augustus, son of the divine Trajan, Conqueror of Parthia, grandson of the divine Nerva, Pontifex Maximus, thrice Consul . . .". The bronzed Mediterranean soldiers who spent whole winters in this wild and wind-lashed outpost of empire must have yearned for their homeland as their modern counterparts on foreign tours of duty in the national service can hardly contemplate.

Hardknott Castle, as it is often called, has been plundered for its building stone for hundreds of years, and farmers are said to have carried stone away by the cartload in the last century. How many barns and dry-stone walls in Eskdale, one wonders, have stones in them on which Roman soldiers pissed?

The road from Windermere over the Kirkstone Pass (where a rock "whose Church-like frame, Gives to the savage pass its name") bring one to Patterdale at the head of Ullswater. It is a village with much modern building and walls of neatly dressed slate. Nowhere in Cumbria is the omnipresent rock more closely tied to the life of the people, however, than over to the west in Borrowdale. The name means 'valley of the fortress' in Old Norse, but as the tale of the stone wall built to keep the cuckoo in was borrowed from the Wise Men of Gotham, so the equally unbelievable Bowder Stone, perhaps the most famous single stone in England, was borrowed, as it were, from Scotland, whence it came with the movement of ice. The name of the stone is said by some to come from 'Balder', one of the sons of Odin, but it makes no appearance in literature before the middle of the eighteenth century. 'Bowder' is simply a dialect word for boulder, so 'Bowder Stone' is really tautological, like 'Lake Windermere', but nevertheless (as BBC men insist on saying) we are stuck with it. If the ancient Greeks had known this rock, it would have featured in the twelve labours of Hercules, for it weighs nearly two thousand tons and stands like a fat ballerina on tiptoe with a ladder at its side for the benefit of tourists, whom it does a lot to attract to Borrowdale.

Robert Southey satirized early nineteenth-century exploitation of the Bowder Stone, saying that the landowner, Mr Pocklington, had built "a little mock hermitage, set up a new druidical stone, erected an

The Bowder Stone, Borrowdale – a permanent resident from north of the border.

ugly house for an old woman to live in who is to show the rock, for fear travellers should pass under it without seeing it, cleared away all the fragments round it, and as it rests upon a narrow base, like a ship upon its keel, dug a hole underneath through which the curious may gratify themselves by shaking hands with the old woman". But Thomas Gray, that earlier poet from the other side of the Jurassic Boundary, did not find Borrowdale quite so amusing:

> . . . the rocks a-top, deep-cloven, perpendicularly, by the rains, hanging loose and nodding forwards, seem just starting from their base in shivers; the whole way down, and the road on both sides, is strewed with piles of the fragments, strangely thrown across each other, and of a dreadful bulk. The place reminds one of those passes in the Alps, where the guides tell you to move on with speed and say nothing, lest the agitation of the air should loosen the snows above, and bring down a mass that would overwhelm a caravan. I took their counsel here and hastened on in silence.

The Bowder Stone, provided with a National Trust car-park, stands near a small slate quarry half a mile south of Borrowdale's chief village, Grange, where an arched slate bridge crosses the River Derwent as it emerges from the Jaws of Borrowdale and travels to its marshy delta at the head of the lake. The monks of Furness Abbey referred to "*grangia nostra de Boroudale*" in the fourteenth century, to indicate their own-

The church at Grange-in-Borrowdale.

ership of farmland in the valley, but the present village church dates only from 1860. Pevsner notes that the voussoirs, or wedge-shaped stones used to make the arches of the windows, project inwards in spikes and remarks that the architect "must have been an aggressive man". Compared with the architects of Dorset and Somerset, who had easy limestone to shape to smooth sides, perhaps he was, but here the Viking successors are all relatively rude men, even when they are poets. David Verey does not make the same judgement about the perpetrator of the south porch arch at Little Barrington in Gloucester-shire, but it strikes an even more jarring note in the context of a lovely Cotswold village than this jagged slate in what are, after all, slightly aggressive surroundings. If the mason at Grange was aggressive, the one at Little Barrington was hysterical. Wordsworth himself had a face which Benjamin Haydon described as being "carved out of a mossy rock, created before the flood". Men are everywhere like the stones which surround them, and draw into themselves the spirit of the rocks, so that even Wordsworth was intimidated by the Lake District moun-tains on occasion, referring in 'The Prelude' to a huge cliff which

> Rose up between me and the stars, and still,
> With measured motion, like a living thing,
> Strode after me.

The church at St John's-in-the-Vale, restored by the dialect poet John Richardson.

It was a local mason, oddly enough, writing a bit of poetry in his spare time, who expressed the gritty native speech in his writing as well as he expressed the character of the stone in his walls. John Richardson was a builder for twenty-five years, then became a schoolmaster in the village school he had built himself. His poem 'It's nobbut me!', about his courtship of Grace Birkett of Wythburn, is one of the masterpieces of dialect poetry:

> Ya winter neet, I mind it weel,
>> Oor lads 'ed been at t'fell,
> An', bein' tir't, went seun to bed,
>> An' I sat be mesel.
> I hard a jike on t'window pane,
>> An' deftly went to see:
> Bit when I ax't, "Who's jiken theer?"
>> Says t'chap, "It's nobbut me."
>
> "Who's *me*?" says I. "What want ye here?
>> Oor fwok ur aw i'bed" –
> "I dunnet want your fwok at aw,
>> It's *thee* I want," he sed.
> "What cant'e want wi' me," says I;
>> "An' who the deuce cann't be?
> Just tell me who it is," an' then –
>> Says he, "It's nobbut me."

"I want a sweetheart, an' I thowt
    Thoo mebby wad an' aw;
I'd been a bit down t'deal to-neet,
    An' thowt 'at I wad caw;
What, cant'e like me, dus t'e think?
    I think I wad like thee" –
"I dunnet know who 'tis," says I,
    Says he, "It's nobbut me."

We pestit on a canny while,
    I thowt his voice I kent;
An' than I steal quite whisht away,
    An' oot at t'dooer I went.
I creapp, an' gat 'im be t'cwoat laps,
    'Twas dark, he cuddent see;
He startit roond, an' said, "Who's that?"
    Says I, "It's nobbut me."

An' menny a time he com agean,
    An' menny a time I went,
An' sed, "Who's that 'at's jiken theer?"
    When gaily weel I kent:
An' mainly what t'seamm answer com,
    Fra back o't'laylick tree;
He sed, "I think thoo know who't is:
    Thoo knows it's nobbut me."

It's twenty year an' mair sen than,
    An' ups an' doons we've hed;
An' six fine bairns hev blest us beath,
    Sen Jim an' me war wed.
An' menny a time I've known 'im steal,
    When I'd yan on me knee,
To mak me start, an' than wad laugh –
    Ha! Ha! "It's nobbut me."

Further up Borrowdale above Seathwaite, where the road ends, are the diminutive waste heaps of the graphite, or black lead, mines which gave Keswick its pencil industry. The deposits were the purest in the world, and the 'wadd', as the locals called it, was so valuable that illicit mining and smuggling had to be curbed by Act of Parliament and the posting of armed guards. But the local people had known about the stuff for ages, and they did not want it for pencil lead, as most of them could not write. Farmers used it to brand their sheep; cloth-dyers used it to make their colours fast; metal-workers used it as a protection against rust; old wives ground it into a paste and took a teaspoonful in a glass of white wine, as an infallible cure for all sorts of distemper. Some said the wadd was soot from the fires of hell, but when the capitalist

Watendlath, Cumbria.

landowners caught on, the resulting exploitation was like the Klondike gold rush, with which it coincided.

Another minor road, branching off the single road through Borrowdale, peters out at Stonethwaite, true to its name but slightly careless of its appearance, its stone walls half obscured by coats of whitewash.

A tortuous narrow road leaving the east bank of Derwentwater leads up between woods, jutting rocks and dry-stone walls above the famous Lodore Falls to Watendlath, crossing the photogenic Ashness Bridge and passing the breathtaking 'Surprise View' of Borrowdale and the lake. Watendlath itself is a charming stone-built hamlet consisting of a few cottages beside a tarn in a secluded and rare upland valley largely owned by the National Trust. It was the home of Hugh Walpole's unlikely heroine Judith Paris in the 'Rogue Herries' novels and is consequently much visited by tourists who have apparently not heard of its reputation for 'inaccessibility'.

At the southern extremity of Cumbria, a village on the grey limestone worthy of mention is Beetham. Although it sits virtually on the A6 trunk road, it is an attractive place, with two watermills on the River Bela. One is a working paper-mill; the other a restored corn-mill open to the public. Local tradition has it that Cromwell's troops did a great deal of damage to the village church and kept their horses in it, spurred on by the sacrilegious scholars of the local school.

As you travel south from Kendal on the A6, the stone field walls change from the cold grey to take on warmer hues as you pass through Lancashire, and it remains only for us to look at the handful of stone villages which that county has not lost to Cumbria in recent local government reorganization. They occur mainly in the valleys of the Rivers Lune and Ribble, although Yealand Redmayne and Yealand Conyers catch your eye as soon as you cross the border. People in southern England still often think of Lancashire as a place of little black Lowry-figures scurrying along cobbled streets to t'mills in Bolton and Rochdale. Lancashire has lost industry to Merseyside and Greater Manchester, as well as scenic beauty to Cumbria, but it still has plenty of both and specializes in extremes, producing as it has comedians and hangmen as well as Blackburn and a few quiet villages of warm stone (one or two of which it has gained from Yorkshire). The walls are sometimes of rubble, sometimes of stone dressed to gaunt squarish blocks, giving a solid appearance that suits the north, and the taste for extremes is seen again in the painted architectural details and bright mortar which are deliberately contrasted with their surroundings when in other places they would be discreetly subdued. Lancashire folk, indeed, are noted for lavishing all the care on the outsides of their houses which other people reserve for the insides.

Hornby is a dignified village of Millstone Grit with several good inns on the main road between Lancaster and Kirkby Lonsdale. Sir Edward Stanley built the original castle, though it was mostly rebuilt in the nineteenth century. A fragment of an Anglo-Saxon cross in the church-yard was rescued from a barn, in the walls of which it was found embedded. A good view of Hornby Castle is from the road towards Caton, downstream, where Turner painted the well-known beauty spot Crook o' Lune.

Caton itself consists mostly of rendered modern housing, but there are scattered groups of buildings of a warm buff-grey colour. Some miles to the south-east, Whitewell is a village of grey limestone houses nestling in the Hodder Valley below the ancient royal hunting preserve the Forest of Bowland.

In Ribblesdale, Bolton-by-Bowland is a grey stone village with two greens, one of which still bears the old village stocks – an ominous note as we move south to Downham and Pendleton, both villages in the shadows of the whale-backed mass of Pendle Hill, the A59 linking the two passes through a cutting which shows dramatically the layered formation of the rock. Grindleton, to the west of Downham, is a long village with some nice cottages along the side of the river, but its name is supposed to have come from the fires kindled locally in devil-worship.

Tributary streams of the Ribble run through Downham's green – also with stocks – and through Pendleton's village street, where white iron

A corner of Downham, Lancashire.

railings line it between cottages of brownish stone. Downham is often called Lancashire's prettiest village. Ducks and children vie for paddling space in the stream crossed by a stone road bridge, and old walls of warm stone define winding lanes and little fields. It is certainly the jewel of the villages around Pendle. These are ancient settlements. Bronze Age men knew this valley, the course of a Roman road runs nearby, and sinister associations cling to the Carboniferous limestone bulk of Pendle Hill, helped along by the Manchester novelist Harrison Ainsworth and other embroiderers of the tale of the notorious Lancashire Witches.

On the hill from which, only forty years afterwards, George Fox saw "the sea bordering upon Lancashire" and set off north-westwards to the places where the Lord "had a great people to be gathered", the women accused in the first trial of the Witches of Pendle were said to hold their covens. All except one of the twenty-one people brought before Mr Justice Bromley at Lancaster in 1612 were sentenced to death and hanged for bewitching sixteen local people "by devilish practices and hellish means". One of the supposed victims was Richard Assheton of Downham, whose family were lords of various manors in the area for centuries. Witnesses swore that the accused women dug up corpses from local graveyards and took their teeth and scalps. Among those executed was a well-to-do woman, Alice Nutter, who lived in a house at Roughlee, built of stone in 1536 and since converted into three separate cottages. It seems that she was a victim of a conspiracy by those, including her relations, who had a grudge against her.

In 1634 a second trial of Lancashire witches took place, and although seventeen women were found guilty of witchcraft by the jury, all of them were eventually acquitted after testimony from Dr William Harvey and the Bishop of Chester, much to the consternation of the gullible as far away as London and Kent. The accuser of these women was a boy, Edmund Robinson, who exploited the passions of the time by inventing fantastic tales to save himself from punishment for playing truant.

We could call any English witch the Circe of this odyssey – a sorceress changing men into swine not by some magic potion but by arousing their hysterical superstitions to such a pitch that they could commit deeds of the most appalling cruelty. The Jews in Hitler's Germany died in vastly greater numbers, but they hardly suffered more hideous barbarism than the witches of Christian England and other 'civilized' European countries.

The witches of Pendle were popularly believed to fly to their evil sabbats on the hilltop from their homes in the surrounding villages, and one of the more uncommon uses of the local slate was to provide seats for them on the roofs of houses. Projecting slates built into the chimneys formed ledges where the midnight hags could rest in comfort and perhaps take a more kindly view of the house and its thoughtful occupants. One such seat survives on a cottage at Feizor, just over the Yorkshire border near Settle. I believe there is such a Hag's Seat on a house on the Isle of Portland, too.

Fear and superstition were particularly strong in Lancashire. No county in England persecuted witches more zealously. In the sixteenth century the ecclesiastical court of the powerful Whalley Abbey had shown comparable zeal in censuring those who were brought before it for sexual offences. The Cronkshay family seem to have caused the court particular trouble. A certain Hugh Whitacre was brought before it at Pendle in 1531 for begetting a child on Margery Cronkshay, and though warned to keep away from her on pain of excommunication, he repeated the offence five years later. Meanwhile, in 1532, John Cronkshay was charged with incest and adultery with his cousin's wife, Emma, and made to do public penance at Padiham chapel, wearing only rags and holding a candle in each hand, reciting to his cousin Richard: ". . . where I yll dyssposed and contrary to the lawes of Good, haith intysed your wyff to yllnesse and haith commytted adultery wyth hir and had carnall knawledge of hir bodie, I beseke Good and you to forgyffe me here knellying on my knesse and doyng my peananse for that synfull dydde".

Perhaps the Abbot should have heeded the Biblical injunction

The gateway and courtyard of Whalley Abbey, Lancashire.

"Judge not, that ye be not judged", for he was himself hanged five years later outside the abbey gatehouse for supporting the Pilgrimage of Grace, whose heralding beacons he had seen from the top of Pendle Hill. One of the local gentry active in suppressing the holy protest against the Dissolution was Richard Assheton. His family later acquired the abbey and converted part of it into a house.

Such remains as there are of the large and prosperous Cistercian abbey of Whalley are superb, beginning with its impressive gateway and garden courtyard, but the stones of its former buildings, quarried and dressed by its white-habited monks, are dispersed throughout the large village, in the buff and orange-grey walls of cottages and farms and in the adjacent Elizabethan building called the Conference House.

The ancient stones of these villages around the Forest of Pendle cannot speak, but they proclaim their direct link with the human trials and tragedies of the locality, by an eloquence which is beyond words.

CHAPTER 8

Precious Stone

I said in the opening chapter that the number of stone villages left will continue to decrease. It will do so without the aid of fire, flood or earthquake, for stone does not last for ever.

Thomas Hardy expressed his concern for the future of the Dorset countryside a century ago in his essay 'The Dorsetshire Labourer', in which he regretted the disturbance, through agricultural change and industrial growth, of what he called the natives' "instinct of associa- tion" with the spot on which they had been born, as they were forced to move to urban areas by the policies of landowners who pulled down cottages that were no longer needed by their farmworkers. "This process," Hardy wrote, "which is designated by statisticians as 'the tendency of the rural population towards the large towns', is really the tendency of water to flow uphill when forced."

Today we are seeing this process in reverse, when the pressure and stress of urban life are forcing many people back into the rural areas their forefathers deserted. They do not go back to work on the land, because there is not the money in it, but they desperately want to live in the country. For the stone villages of England, this is a mixed blessing. To a limited extent, it contributes to the preservation of stone build- ings, for estate agents cannot get enough of the 'olde worlde cottage of charm and character' which city workers snap up so eagerly. The new owners of these stone cottages are usually prepared to do them up, frequently with good taste, and so extend the lives of buildings and preserve the character of the villages.

Unfortunately, where councils are not strict, the opposite is also true. New houses are put up without regard for local materials or character, cost being the only consideration, and a village that was once a fine example of vernacular architecture in local stone deterio- rates into a tasteless mess, villafied and bungaloid, with brick walls, concrete garages, double-glazed aluminium french windows and a hideously designed village petrol station for the benefit of young executives whose company cars stand everywhere, hiding from view what little bits of stone building remain.

There is immense irony in some of these changes. Well-to-do city

Doulting limestone, defaced by the elements. Statues at Wells Cathedral.

workers with flashy cars and large mortgages are now clamouring to purchase those insanitary hovels which *Punch* held up to ridicule a century ago in a well-known parody of Felicia Dorothea Hemans:

> The cottage homes of England,
> Alas! How strong they smell;
> There's fever in the cesspool
> And sewage in the well.

Meanwhile, farm labourers who once inhabited these squalid dwellings in the country now live on smart modern council estates in the towns.

In the long run, despite the present revival of interest in stone building, stone villages will deteriorate and gradually disappear, for they will not be the places to benefit from all the work and research which has gone into natural stone in recent years. Several pictures in this book – especially in the chapters on limestone – show the effects of decay on stonework.

Stone deteriorates in buildings in several ways. Excessive blasting in the quarry can cause minute and undetected fractures in stone before it is even transported to the building site, and the mason must know how to lay the stone properly to avoid further excessive damage. Stone laid against its natural bedding plane will tend to weather and exfoliate sooner than that which is correctly bedded. And if it is not bedded evenly, stress may result and cause fracturing. Laying horizontally, or 'edge-bedding', is essential for limestones and sandstones, but granite can usually be laid with its natural bed parallel to the wall, or 'face-bedded'. In stones where the natural bed is not obvious, the quarry usually marks them for the mason's benefit.

Iron dowels, much used in stonework over the centuries, have long been known to cause decay or corrosion, and damage to buildings caused by wrong choice of material for the particular purpose is widespread. The use of incompatible materials in the same building has led to severe decay. The Magnesian limestone of the north, used in conjunction with other limestone or sandstone, causes the latter to absorb magnesium sulphate and eventually crumble.

Far more important than errors in craftsmanship, however, as far as our stone villages are concerned, is the simple fact of deterioration through exposure to the atmosphere. Exfoliation and efflorescence are two long words for doom. The natural weathering of stone is due to such atmospheric pollutants as acids, smoke and soot, or to physical and organic agents of decay such as frost, lichens and fungus, to say nothing of those well-fed friends of city tourists and implacable enemies of city stonework, the pigeons. Climbing plants such as ivy, for all their temporary enhancement of many a building, also help to accelerate its decay.

Among the worst enemies of stone buildings are soluble salts. Sometimes these are present in small quantities in the freshly quarried stone, which is not surprising, particularly in limestones, because the rock was once beneath the sea. More often, salts are absorbed from the atmosphere – from sea spray in coastal areas, in rising damp from the soil, from sulphur acids in the air. Salts crystallizing on the surface of stone cause ugly stains and efflorescence, eventually result in decay. Salts crystallizing in the pores of the stone are often unsuspected until they make their presence known with dramatic force.

If stone could be totally protected from moisture – that is, from rain, moisture in the atmosphere, rising damp, evaporation from mortar and cement, and so on – many of the enemies of our buildings would be eliminated. As Hamlet's gravedigger acquaintance remarks, ". . . your water is a sore decayer of your whoreson dead body". And of its house too, for it is only true in a metaphorical sense that the houses the gravedigger makes 'last till domesday'. Those the mason makes last a good deal longer if they are well built.

Some of the most harmful attackers of stonework are town and city curses that do not much affect our country villages, otherwise the situation would be far worse than it is. They have been recognized for a very long time as health hazards. The burning of 'sea coal' was prohibited in London as long ago as 1273, for instance, and a man was executed for disregarding the law. One reason for the popularity of Portland stone in city buildings is that it stands up far better than most to atmospheric pollution and is more amenable to cleaning treatment. We have noted in earlier chapters the previous sad state of Carlisle Cathedral's sandstone walls, and the crumbling walls of Oxford's colleges. These are but two well-known examples of what might be called a national crisis in the urgent preservation of some of our finest buildings. Some interesting work has been done in recent years in the Tower of London by the Building Research Establishment. The thirteenth-century Salt Tower, at the south-east corner, was used in medieval times to store culinary salt, and the damp rubble walls of Kentish Rag with Reigate stone dressings had absorbed a great deal of the chemical, resulting in serious decay. Elaborate experiments have been carried out, with some success, to apply poultices to the walls which draw out the salt over a long period.

Experimentation has also been carried out, with only marginal success, in coating stonework with silicone water repellents, to prevent damp getting into it in the first place, and impregnating stone with protective liquid which solidifies after deep penetration of the stonework.

Needless to say, however, treatment, cleaning and restoration processes for natural stone are not only largely experimental but also
vastly expensive, and like deep fall-out shelters, they are not intended
for the likes of ordinary folk living in country villages. Appeals for
funds to save village churches are only temporary and marginal
attempts to arrest the inevitable process of decay in our oldest country
buildings.

Some stones, in some situations, seem to hold out hope of long life
yet. It will be a long time before the granite of Cornwall gives in to
lashing winds and salty sea spray, and the Millstone Grit of the
Pennines is not about to disintegrate, though it may be disfigured, by
attack from the soot and grime of the industrial north. Even granite
disintegrates in time, however.

Even granite wears away eventually. The priest's doorway of the church at
Throwleigh, Devon.

The first casualties of the slow and almost imperceptible decay of stone will be along the Jurassic Boundary, and the frontier of the stone country will gradually be pushed back. The villages of the limestone belt, where the stone is softest, will be the first to go, and that, of course, is precisely where most of our best stone villages stand. The granite walls of Cornwall and Devon will still be standing when the villages of Dorset and the Cotswolds have crumbled into dust, and Chysauster, one of the oldest stone villages in England, may well outlive them all. Those glorious golden villages of Somerset and Dorset built of Ham Hill limestone already have the writing on their walls, in the form of serious exfoliation and the lichens which are so often praised as adding aesthetic value to the appearance of cottage walls. The efflorescence on stonework has in the past been called 'wall cancer', and though it is an unscientific term, it expresses well enough the fatal growth which eats away at the surface of stone and could just as well apply to 'spalling' and exfoliation – the blistering and flaking of walls which can be seen so clearly in many Cotswold villages and on many East Midland churches, for example. We might see the enemies of village buildings as the Scylla and Charybdis of the present odyssey – one a six-headed monster consuming the very marrow of our stone structures, and the other a fearful presence regurgitating sea water in the form of efflorescence.

In the long term, there is little we can do to prevent our stone villages from crumbling. Buildings which disappear will not be rebuilt in natural stone. It is far too expensive and is likely to remain so. The revival of interest in stone building, which one hears being murmured about hopefully now and then, will be to the advantage of towns and cities, not country villages. The decline of the quarrying industry and the disappearance of skilled masons in the face of cheaper building materials only accelerate the disproportionate cost of putting up new buildings in stone. The skills of the old builders are being lost along with so many other traditional crafts. Once a busy quarry would have four or five apprentices to every skilled man. Now such craftsmen as there are are mainly occupied with repair and restoration of public buildings in urban areas.

Even in the Cotswolds, where – more than anywhere else – careful control has been exercised over the situation of new building and the materials used, economy is winning the day. Reconstituted stone has made its appearance, and its apologists say that, provided it has the right colour and texture, you can hardly tell the difference. But they say that about the stuff wrapped in polythene which passes for cheese in supermarkets.

Death from old age is not the only cause of disappearance. We have come across instances of villages, once built of stone, which have

'The Stone-breaker' by Henry Wallis.

vanished from the landscape through various physical causes, and this is a continuing hazard. One can only guess, at the time of writing, what will become of the villages on the Liassic limestone in the vicinity of mining operations beneath the Vale of Belvoir, but it is a safe bet that when new houses are built for miners, they will be built of brick. Northamptonshire has not emerged unscathed from exploitation of its iron deposits, and although the Cotswolds and east Leicestershire may have escaped the fate West Yorkshire suffered in the Industrial Revolution, their future as unspoilt rural areas is far from guaranteed.

This is a gloomy outlook for those of us who regard stone villages as being among the finest human adornments of our green and pleasant land, but I think we can only console ourselves with the thought that the change will be a slow and gradual one. By the time the last village of mellow stone sinks from sight in a red sea of brick (if it has not been blasted out of existence by nuclear warfare), people who have not known a land of stone cottages will not miss them and will probably look back on the old custom of building with natural materials as 'quaint' or primitive.

In the meantime we must make the best of them, and for this traveller in the late twentieth century it has been a privilege and a pleasure to see so many monuments to the departing country craftsmen whose hands moulded the rock beneath their feet into beautiful repositories of so much tradition and folklore and, above all, peacefulness.

When all the villages of stone have finally disappeared from the English scene, however, the old influence of the rock will remain, still uniting the people of the stone country whose lives have been so moulded by it over thousands of years, for their ancestors lived by turning its unpromising coldness and solidity to their advantage, learning its silent nature, until sometimes they could make it give up its secrets.

Quarrying as a rural industry has attracted very little attention from writers and artists, but the so-called 'stone-breaker' has been a figure of some symbolic significance for artists such as Courbet and Millet in France, Wallis and Landseer in England. Spending his life smashing rocks into small fragments for use as roadstone, he has been at the bottom of the social scale, representing the hard, lonely struggle for existence in the minds of many artists, the epitome of meaningless physical exertion, often carried out by convicts, as on Portland and Dartmoor. But only Courbet and Henry Wallis have realized the full implications on canvas. It was all very well for Ruskin to say that Brett's 'The Stone-Breaker' (Walker Art Gallery, Liverpool) could be "examined inch by inch with delight", but the beautifully painted landscape does nothing to ram home the hard life of a boy who rather casually smashes stones whilst his pet dog plays happily at his side. Landseer's sentimentality made him include the stone-breaker's daughter. The version by Wallis is in stark and dramatic contrast to these romantic images, like the painting by Courbet which was destroyed during the bombing of Dresden in the Second World War.

Wallis's 'The Stone-breaker', now at Birmingham, was exhibited at the Royal Academy in 1858, the same year as Brett's, and Ruskin called it "the picture of the year". It shows the man not merely alone in unromantic surroundings but lying dead in them, having expired from his exertions, and the painting was exhibited with a rhetorical quotation from Thomas Carlyle: "Hardly entreated brother! For us was thy back so bent, for us were thy straight limbs and fingers so deformed; thou wert our conscript on whom the lot fell, and fighting our battles wert so marred. For in thee too lay a God-created form, but it was not to be unfolded. . . ." This painting was a socialist statement – a claim for the dignity of rural labour, depicting the stone-breaker's almost subhuman working conditions.

At the other end of the scale, though, stonemasons have reached the

The grave of Eric Gill at Speen, Buckinghamshire.

status of great artists. Michelangelo himself spent some time in his early life working in the quarries at Carrara.

> The best of artists hath no thought to show
> Which the rough stone in its superfluous shell
> Doth not include: to break the marble spell
> Is all the hand that serves the brain can do.

To see the figure in a block of stone so clearly, one must have grown up with the material from an early age. Michelangelo's wet-nurse was the daughter and the wife of stonemasons; he quipped that he had drunk in hammer and chisel with her milk.

More recently, in England, Eric Gill was one of the leaders of a revival in stone carving following the long European degeneration after Michelangelo which only ceased with the coming of Rodin. When Gill was sent to study under Maillol in Paris, he returned to London in the middle of his first night there. Maillol was a modeller, making his images in clay and then having them carved to scale in stone. Gill wanted to learn about the use of hammer and chisels, and Maillol could not teach him that. It would be better, Gill said, to apprentice himself to a monumental mason and "learn to hack idiotic angels out of white marble". He was proud to call himself simply a stone carver.

Britain's most eminent modern sculptor, Henry Moore, is also a

Gargoyle and friends carved in limestone on the church at Tilton-on-the-Hill, Leicestershire.

stone carver. He, a Yorkshireman familiar with stone from an early age, reached an almost unique empathy with the material he worked on, considering – as Herbert Read expressed it – "the structure of the stone, its degree of hardness, the way it reacts to his chisel . . . how this stone has reacted to natural forces like wind and water, for these in the course of time have revealed the inherent qualities of the stone".

Modern sculptors such as Gill, Moore and Epstein have a direct link with our stone villages, particularly where the local material is free-stone. They have evolved from the medieval craftsmanship which we have noticed here and there. The village churches of medieval days were the books of art and philosophy, and the graveyards the books of history and biography, and all these books were written, as it were, on stone, like the Mosaic Law, that men might recognize their permanent values. They were repositories of the collective unconscious. The architectural adornment of window tracery and crocketed spires might be seen as works of craftsmanship designed to proclaim the greater glory of God, but there was something more down to earth in the creative explosion of medieval stone-carvers, freed from all the restraints of the Dark Ages, who conceived in blocks of stone those marvels of exuberant, delirious, psychotic figure carvings which are so staggering in their imaginative variety. Kings and queens, saints and angels, keep company on these ancient walls with devils and monsters, spewing gargoyles and pagan sheela-na-gigs, dragons and griffons, orgasmic lechers, deformed dwarfs and fantastic creatures, slithy toves and mome raths and men whose heads do grow beneath their shoulders.

The sublime contempt with which Lord Lytton's gardener at Knebworth lately dismissed the house's gargoyles as "them bloody monkeys" would not have been so lightly uttered in olden times, when the village church was a focus of all the beliefs and fears of an unenlightened community, reminding each passer-by of something he tended to keep hidden in his unconscious mind – the village poacher of the nightmares of conscience perhaps, the village prostitute of the wages of sin, the village idiot of the dangers of temptation. Masons and sculptors, as well as parsons and schoolmasters, were among the great educators of rural England.

*

Who should be waiting for me when I got home but Penelope, clutching a pair of doves to her breasts? I never saw anything less stony. She is made of bronze. Actually, her creator, Carrier de Belleuse, Rodin's benefactor, intended her as Aphrodite, but she is so obviously French that I called her Madeleine at first. Henceforth, however, I shall not think of her as anyone but Penelope.

As for me, I have returned to my hilltop dwelling of stone from where I can look down on what passes for Ithaca in my imagination, whilst my wife watches me sitting up like the king of the country pumping the wrong end of the spoon up and down in my egg.

A Hundred Stone Villages for Visitors

This is a personal selection by county. I have no doubt that many readers will throw up their hands in horror when they realize that their own favourites are not included. But what I have tried to do here is to cover all kinds of stone and all kinds of village – not necessarily the hundred most picturesque. Not every village included here is discussed in the main text, but anyone who sees these hundred will have a fairly comprehensive idea of the variety of English village building in stone. Just for fun, I have selected my own Top Ten, and their names are printed in capital letters, but I draw the reader's attention to the remarks of E. V. Knox quoted in Chapter 3. Next week, my choice may be different; next month, different again.

Buckinghamshire
Weston Underwood   William Cowper was a sometime resident of this neat model village. The 'local' is called 'Cowper's Oak'.

Cornwall
Altarnun   One of Cornwall's best-kept villages, its church is known as the Cathedral of the Moor.

Blisland   A gaunt village on the edge of Bodmin Moor, with a fine Norman church. Captain Bligh was born not far away.

Cadgwith   Much rendering and lime-washing obscure the granite and 'Serpentine' stone of this typical Cornish fishing village, but some is still visible.

Chysauster   Remains of a prehistoric village of stone on the moors above Penzance. The beginning and end of stone villages in England, one might say.

Delabole   A slate village where vast quarry workings can be viewed by those for whom holes in the ground have an irresistible fascination.

Godolphin Cross   A granite village named after the family which owned local tin mines for centuries. Miners were once notorious for plundering ships stranded on this coast.

Port Isaac   An Atlantic coast village of steep and narrow streets with slate-hung cottages. See Squeezibelly Alley, bisecting one of the houses.

Zennor   A granite village between St Ives and St Just, with prehistoric Zennor Quoit nearby.

Cumbria

ELTERWATER   Possibly the *magnum opus* of Cumbrian stone villages, with slate in various forms built into the house walls.

Grange-in-Borrowdale   A secluded village of green slate cottages surrounded by fells in one of the loveliest parts of the Lake District. Nearby is the famous Bowder Stone.

Grasmere   Unmistakably Victorian, but very attractive and stylish in a commercialized way, with much purplish slate-stone.

Great Salkeld   A well-kept village of precisely dressed sandstone, with Long Meg and Her Daughters within easy walking distance.

Ravenstonedale   A dour but stylish village which used to have a refuge bell. If a pursued felon tolled the bell before being caught, he was allowed to go free.

Troutbeck   A most interesting street village of Lake District slate, rich in vernacular architecture. 'Townend' is a typical Lakeland 'statesman's' house (NT), and 'The Mortal Man' one of the best-known Lakeland inns.

Wasdale Head   A wild village at the head of Wastwater, popular with climbers, for Scafell, Great Gable and Lingmell tower above it.

Watendlath   Reputedly 'inaccessible', it is nevertheless crowded with tourists eager to see where Judith Paris lived in Walpole's 'Herries' tales.

Derbyshire

Edensor   The curious – not to say eccentric – estate village of Chatsworth built in local stone in a motley assortment of styles.

EYAM   A grim village of Millstone Grit high on Peak District moors. Not so much picturesque as poignant, it has much stylish building and other interest apart from its fame for self-sacrifice during the plague years.

Tissington   A lovely old village near Ashbourne, famous for the Ascension Day well-dressing custom, supposed to derive from pure water preserving the village from drought and plague.

Devon

Buckland-in-the-Moor A picturesque granite village with thatched roofs, on the southern edge of Dartmoor.

Widecombe-in-the-Moor A Dartmoor village of granite famous for its September fair, which attracts tourists in the wake of Uncle Tom Cobleigh and all.

Dorset

Abbotsbury Near the coast and the famous Chesil Bank. Well known for its Swannery and one of the finest tithe barns in England. Orange limestone and thatch.

Bradford Abbas A street village of golden Ham Hill stone. It was once owned by the Abbots of Sherborne, hence the name. Fifteenth-century church with fine tower.

Burton Bradstock A lovely village of thatched stone houses at the west end of Chesil Bank.

Corfe Much of the quaint stone-roofed village was built with material from the demolished castle above it, where King Edward the Martyr was murdered.

STOKE ABBOT A lovely village of warm, mellow Ham Hill limestone, near Beaminster.

Trent A delightfully haphazard village of golden limestone near Sherborne, with much interest in its church.

Worth Matravers A limestone village on the Isle of Purbeck, at the centre of much quarrying activity in the past, especially Tilly Whim caves not far away.

Durham

Romaldkirk Teesdale boasts no prettier village. It has a large green "eddying out", as Pevsner puts it, "in a variety of directions", with stocks and village pump. The unusual dedication of the church is to St Rumwald, son of a Northumbrian king.

Gloucestershire

Aldsworth A spacious Cotswold village west of Burford. There are fascinating carvings of grotesque heads round the outside walls of the quiet little church.

Bibury Hordes of summer visitors along its narrow streets, but not to be missed. Arlington Row is a group of cottages converted from a weaving mill.

Bisley An attractive old village of Oolitic limestone with fine Cotswold houses and winding lanes.

Bourton-on-the-Water The coach-tour Mecca of the Cotswolds, best seen in winter, when you can move freely. The River Windrush flows through the middle with picturesque stone bridges across.

Chedworth A sprawling village with limestone cottages built on hillsides. There are pockmarked gargoyles on the outer wall of the Norman church, and Roman remains.

Little Barrington A stylish village in a much quarried area of the Cotswolds, near Burford.

Lower Slaughter A highly picturesque village of Jurassic limestone – the largest and most popular of the Swells and Slaughters group.

Sheepscombe A simple Cotswold village built on hillsides, with 'The Butcher's Arms' lording it over cottages and church of golden stone.

Slad The village where Laurie Lee had cider with Rosie. Limestone cottages perch on slopes, and the modern by-pass leaves them quiet and peaceful.

SNOWSHILL A fine Cotswold village with a church on the central green, its name tells everything about its situation, but summer has compensations.

Stanton A lovely village of 'Cotswold stone' near Broadway, with fine old cottages.

UPPER SLAUGHTER Inconspicuous among reeds and willows, this tiny Cotswold village on the River Eye is a dreamy vision of rural England.

Hereford and Worcester
BROADWAY 'The Painted Lady of the Cotswolds' – a less-than-complimentary nickname for a village which has no equal for sheer stylishness, despite its busy main-road position.

Lancashire
Downham An attractive little village near Clitheroe and facing Pendle Hill, notorious in witchcraft lore. Many interesting corners.

Leicestershire
Clipsham An appealing village of local limestone, with an important quarry nearby still supplying stone to Oxford.

Exton Formerly in Rutland, a fine village on the limestone belt famous for its superb church, with monuments by Grinling Gibbons and others.

Hallaton   The prettiest village of old Leicestershire (excluding Rutland) is also its most bizarre, with curious survivals from a pagan past drawing crowds on Easter Monday.

Horninghold   A stylish model village, not as old as it might appear, and a trifle stand-offish, but showing to good effect the careful use of warm local ironstone.

Lyddington   Ironstone houses round a triangular village green. The church contains rare clay acoustic jars, and the Bede House was the palace of the Bishops of Lincoln.

Preston   A fine ironstone village formerly in Rutland, standing quietly parallel with the main road and easily missed.

Lincolnshire

Edenham   An impressive estate village near Bourne, built by the Earls of Ancaster of nearby Grimsthorpe Castle. Charles Kingsley is said to have written *Hereward the Wake* here.

Fulbeck   Perhaps the best of Lincolnshire's villages, built of the pale limestone from quarries at Ancaster.

Northamptonshire

Aldwinkle   A street village of ironstone near the River Nene, east of Kettering. John Dryden was born in the rectory.

Ashton   A modern stone village near Oundle, owing its existence largely to a rare butterfly, the Chequered Skipper.

AYNHO   On a hill on the Banbury-Bicester road. An immaculate street village with dove-grey stone cottages facing the manor house, Aynhoe Park. The village stocks survive, alas.

Collyweston   A large village famous for the roofing slates quarried here and seen on stone houses over a wide area.

Rockingham   An attractive ironstone village with a steep main street leading up to the church and Rockingham Castle, where Dickens was a frequent guest.

Northumberland

Bamburgh   An unspoilt coastal village dominated by the rocky Norman fortress of Bamburgh Castle. Birthplace of the famous heroine Grace Darling.

BLANCHLAND   A sandstone estate village, dignified and totally unspoilt, on the River Derwent, where a monastery once stood. Built by the Earls of Crewe for lead-mine workers.

Bywell A scattered and quiet stone hamlet beside the unlikely setting of the River Tyne, near Corbridge.

Cambo The estate village of Wallington Hall, tastefully rebuilt on the site of the medieval village of Camhoe by Blacketts and Trevelyans.

Elsdon An isolated village of sandstone houses round a huge village green. Once an important Norman garrison, only the earthworks of its castle remain.

Ford As neat and tidy a village as you could wish to find, but permanently wearing the Sunday-best of model villages in general.

Oxfordshire

Adderbury A lovely village of warm-coloured ironstone with many stone medieval carvings round the outside walls of the church.

Coleshill An attractive street village owned by the National Trust. Nearby at Great Coxwell, the National Trust also owns a fine tithe barn, a veritable cathedral of ecclesiastical capitalism.

Great Tew An attractive honey-coloured village of stone and thatch, undergoing much-needed restoration after neglect.

Kelmscot The village of grey limestone where William Morris lived for twenty-five years in the gabled Elizabethan manor house.

Swinbrook The peaceful village in the Oxfordshire Cotswolds where the Mitford family had their home. Nancy and Unity are buried in the churchyard.

Somerset

Brympton d'Evercy Not strictly a village, nor even a hamlet, but an exquisite private stone-built estate at the edge of Yeovil.

Combe Florey A sandstone village in the Quantocks, the home of the Reverend Sydney Smith and the irreverent Evelyn Waugh.

Cothelstone A delightfully compact village of red sandstone in the Quantock Hills.

East Coker A delightful village of local golden limestone, where T. S. Eliot's ancestors came from. Not spoiled like its sisters to north and west.

Hinton St George Narrow lanes lead to this typically attractive Somerset village near Crewkerne.

Mells A beautiful village west of Frome, with cottages of limestone and thatch scattered round several small greens.

Montacute A stylish village of mellow Ham Hill stone, famous for Montacute House, among the finest mansions in south-west England.

Nunney   Houses of Mendip limestone line the street with the inn sign of 'The George' spanning it.

Warwickshire

Priors Marston   A cosy village of rich-coloured Liassic limestone, noted for chair-making at one time.

Warmington   A village on the county's Cotswold fringe, often said to be its loveliest. Rewarding church.

Wiltshire

Castle Combe   One of England's best-known villages, it lies in a valley with the By Brook flowing under its famous three-arched bridge.

Teffont Evias   A delightful village in the Nadder valley, built of cream-coloured Chilmark stone. Little bridges lead across a stream to the houses.

Tisbury   Older houses and cottages built of locally quarried limestone in a spreading village west of Salisbury.

North Yorkshire

Clapham   A pretty tree-clad village of grey stone on the lower slopes of Ingleborough. The beck flowing through it tumbles into the village via a waterfall after passing through Gaping Gill pot-hole.

Coxwold   A street village with cobbled verges, famous as the home of Laurence Sterne, vicar and author of *Tristram Shandy*. Shandy Hall can be visited on Wednesday afternoons in summer.

Goathland   A scattered village uncomfortably close to Fylingdales 'radomes', but lovely for all that. Unexplained cairns, possibly prehistoric, on the moors around the village.

Grassington   A grey Wharfedale village with a medieval bridge over the river, and a cobbled market square.

Hawnby   On the River Rye north-west of Helmsley in a remote valley. Small Norman church half a mile away.

Hovingham   A stylish village of limestone grouped round a green. The Hall is the home of Sir William Worsley, father of the Duchess of Kent.

Howsham   The toffee-coloured little village where George Hudson, the 'Railway King' was born, near Malton.

HUTTON-LE-HOLE   A showplace village of the moors where sheep wander freely and keep the greens tidy. Ryedale Folk Museum shows local agricultural life over four centuries.

Kettlewell   A grey stone village in Wharfedale. Great Whernside and Kilnsey Crag attract climbers to the area.

Lastingham   A grey stone village set in a little valley and well known for its beautiful and interesting church whose Norman crypt is especially notable.

Lockton   A sleepy old grey limestone village on the North Yorkshire Moors above Pickering.

Malham   Set amid a rugged limestone landscape, Malham Cove is to the north and Gordale Scar to the east, both dramatic studies in rock evolution.

Rievaulx   The village itself is not such as would excite anyone unduly, but the incomparable ruins of Rievaulx Abbey give it distinction.

ROBIN HOOD'S BAY   A delightful coastal village of quaint streets and houses pouring themselves down to the sea, via endless steps.

Thornton-le-Dale   A pretty and highly popular village of tidy limestone at the southern edge of the moors near Pickering.

Wensley   A tranquil grey limestone village at the head of Wensleydale with a fine church that indicates the village's former importance.

West Yorkshire

Harewood   Dark grey stone houses built in terraces were part of John Carr's complete design for both the village and its great house, home of the Earl of Harewood.

Haworth   A large village – arguably a town – high up on the moors. It needs no introduction to Brontë enthusiasts but has much interest for others too.

Heptonstall   A fascinating industrial hill village of the gaunt Carboniferous limestone, with ruins of an old church paved with gravestones.

Sources

The huge number of general topographical books I have consulted during my travels, in addition to the more specialized works which follow, have included Robert Hale's 'County Books' and 'Portrait' series, the Shell Guides, Eyre Methuen's excellent series 'The Regions of Britain' and Hodder & Stoughton's volumes in the series 'The Making of the English Landscape'. Batsford's series 'The Folklore of the British Isles' has also proved helpful.

Ashe, Geoffrey (ed.), *The Quest for Arthur's Britain*, Pall Mall Press, 1968.

Ashurst, John, and Francis G. Dimes, *Stone in Building*, Architectural Press, 1977.

Aubrey, John, *Brief Lives*, Penguin edition, 1972.

Bede, Venerable, *Ecclesiastical History of the English Nation*, Everyman's Library edition, 1975.

Beresford, Maurice and John G. Hurst (eds.), *Deserted Medieval Villages*, Lutterworth Press, 1971.

Bettey, J. H., *The Island and Royal Manor of Portland*, University of Bristol, 1970.

Bodman, Janet, *West Country Stone Walls*, Redcliffe Press, 1979.

Bord, Janet, *Mazes and Labyrinths of the World*, Latimer New Dimensions, 1976.

Bord, Janet and Colin, *Mysterious Britain*, Garnstone Press, 1972.

—, *The Secret Country*, Elek, 1976.

Bowley, M. J., *Desalination of stone: a case study*, Department of the Environment, 1975.

Breeze, David J. and Brian Dobson, *Hadrian's Wall*, Allen Lane, 1976.

Brunskill, R. W., *Illustrated Handbook of Vernacular Architecture*, Faber & Faber, 1978.

—, *Vernacular Architecture of the Lake Counties*, Faber & Faber, 1974.

Burgess, Frederick, *English Churchyard Memorials*, Lutterworth Press, 1963.

Burnett, John (ed.), *Useful Toil*, Allen Lane, 1974.

Clark, Kenneth, *The Gothic Revival*, John Murray, 1962.

—, *Ruskin Today*, John Murray, 1964.

Clifton-Taylor, Alec, *The Pattern of English Building*, Faber & Faber, 1972.

Cobbett, William, *Rural Rides*, Everyman's Library edition, 1912.

Cole, G. D. H., and Raymond Postgate, *The Common People 1746–1938*, Methuen, 1938.

Crossley, F. H., *English Church Craftsmanship*, Batsford, 1941.

Daniel, Glyn, *Megaliths in History*, Thames & Hudson, 1972.

Darby, H. C. (ed.), *A New Historical Geography of England*, Cambridge University Press, 1973.

Darley, Gillian, *Villages of Vision*, Architectural Press, 1975.

Davey, Norman, *Building Stones of England and Wales*, Bedford Square Press, 1976.

Defoe, Daniel, *A Tour through the Whole Island of Great Britain*, Penguin edition, 1971.

Dury, G. H., *The East Midlands and the Peak*, Nelson, 1963.

Evans, George Ewart, *The Pattern Under the Plough*, Faber & Faber, 1966.

Evans, George Ewart and David Thomson, *The Leaping Hare*, Faber & Faber, 1972.

Frazer, J. G., *The Golden Bough: A Study in Magic and Religion*, Macmillan, 1957 edition.

Frere, Sheppard, *Britannia: A History of Roman Britain*, Routledge & Kegan Paul, 1967.

Gaunt, William, *The Pre-Raphaelite Tragedy*, Jonathan Cape, 1942.

Gay, John D., *The Geography of Religion in England*, Duckworth, 1971.

Graves, Robert, *The White Goddess*, Faber & Faber, 1952.

Hair, Paul (ed.), *Before the Bawdy Court*, Elek, 1972.

Hoskins, W. G., *The Heritage of Leicestershire*, Leicester Publicity Department, 1972.

Hoskins, W. G. and Dudley Stamp, *The Common Lands of England and Wales*, Collins, 1963.

Hudson, W. H., *The Land's End*, Hutchinson, 1908.

Keating, Peter (ed.), *Into Unknown England*, Fontana, 1976.

Keith, W. J., *The Rural Tradition*, Harvester Press, 1975.

Kendall, Paul Murray, *Richard III*, Allen & Unwin, 1955.

Lane, Margaret, *The Tale of Beatrix Potter*, Warne, 1968.

Lee, Laurie, *Cider with Rosie*, Hogarth Press, 1959.

Linton, E. Lynn, *The Lake Country*, (London), 1864.

Macauley, Lord, *History of England*, (London), 1848–55.

Massingham, H. J., *Cotswold Country*, Batsford, 1937.

Maurier, Daphne du, *Vanishing Cornwall*, Gollancz, 1967.

Opie, Iona and Peter, *The Lore and Language of Schoolchildren*, Oxford University Press, 1959.

Pearson, Hesketh, *The Smith of Smiths*, Hamish Hamilton, 1934.

Penny, Nicholas, *Church Monuments in Romantic England*, Yale University, 1977.

Penoyre, John and Jane, *Houses in the Landscape*, Faber & Faber, 1978.

Pevsner, Nikolaus, and others, *The Buildings of England*, Penguin Books, various dates.

Priestley, J. B., *English Journey*, Heinemann/Gollancz, 1934.

Read, Herbert, *The Meaning of Art*, Penguin edition, 1949.

Rollinson, William, *Life and Tradition in the Lake District*, Dalesman Publishing Co, 1974.

Rowley, Trevor, *Villages in the Landscape*, Dent, 1978.

Ruskin, John, *The Stones of Venice*, Faber edition, 1981.

Schaffer, R. J., *The Weathering of Natural Building Stones*, Department of the Environment, 1972.

Stone, Lawrence, *Sculpture in Britain: The Middle Ages*, Pelican History of Art, 1955.

Taylor, Christopher, *Fields in the English Landscape*, Dent, 1975.

Thomas, Keith, *Religion and the Decline of Magic*, Weidenfeld & Nicolson, 1971.

Trevor-Roper, H. R., *The European Witch-Craze of the 16th and 17th Centuries*, Penguin Books, 1969.

Trueman, A. E., *Geology and Scenery in England and Wales*, Penguin Books, 1971.

Wittkower, Rudolf, *Sculpture: Processes and Principles*, Allen Lane, 1977.

Woodforde, John, *The Truth about Cottages*, Routledge & Kegan Paul, 1969.

Wordsworth, William, *Guide to the Lakes*, Oxford University Press edition, 1970.

Ziegler, Philip, *The Black Death*, Collins, 1969.

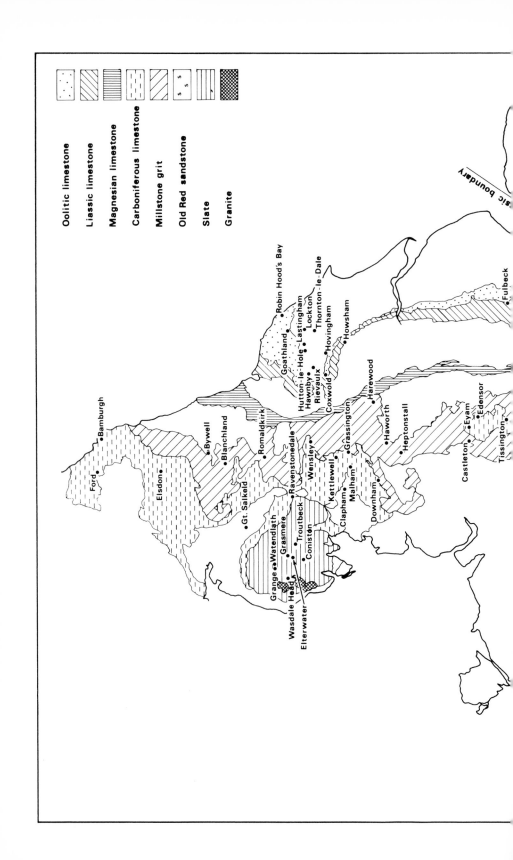

Oolitic limestone
Liassic limestone
Magnesian limestone
Carboniferous limestone
Millstone grit
Old Red sandstone
Slate
Granite

...ic boundary

Bamburgh
Ford
Elsdon
Bywell
Blanchland
Gt. Salkeld
Romaldkirk
Ravenstonedale
Wensley
Kettlewell
Clapham
Malham
Downham
Grassington
Haworth
Heptonstall
Harewood
Castleton
Eyam
Edensor
Tissington
Grange
Watendlath
Grasmere
Troutbeck
Coniston
Wasdale Head
Elterwater
Goathland
Robin Hood's Bay
Hutton-le-Hole
Lastingham
Lockton
Thornton-le-Dale
Hawnby
Rievaulx
Hovingham
Coxwold
Howsham
Fulbeck

Hallaton
Lyddington
Rockingham
Ashton
Weldon
Aldwinkle
Priors Marston
Weston Underwood
Warmington
Hornton
Adderbury
Aynho
Gt. Tew
Bourton-on-the-Water
Swinbrook
Taynton
Little Barrington
Kelmscot
Coleshill
Broadway
Stanton
Snowshill
Upper Slaughter
Farmington
Bibury
Sheepscombe
Slad
Bisley
Chedworth
Aldsworth
Monkton Farleigh
Castle Combe
Dundry
Mells
Nunney
Chilmark
Tisbury
Teffont Evias
Bradford Abbas
East Coker
Abbotsbury
Corfe
Worth Matravers
Combe
Florey
Cothelstone
Brympton d'Evercy
Montacute
Hinton St George
Stoke Abbot
Burton Bradstock
Widecombe-in-the-Moor
Buckland-in-the-Moor
Altarnun
Blisland
Luxulian
Delabole
Port Isaac
Godolphin Cross
Cadgwith
Zennor
Chysauster
Doulting
Trent

Index

All village names are indexed by their prefixes – thus Great Barrington is to be found under G. Village names are followed by their counties.